JAPAN'S ECONOMIC RECOVERY

Japan's Economic Recovery

G. C. ALLEN

Professor of Political Economy in the
University of London

Issued under the auspices of the
Royal Institute of International Affairs

OXFORD UNIVERSITY PRESS

LONDON NEW YORK TORONTO

Oxford University Press, Amen House, London E.C.4

GLASGOW NEW YORK TORONTO MELBOURNE WELLINGTON
BOMBAY CALCUTTA MADRAS KARACHI KUALA LUMPUR
CAPE TOWN IBADAN NAIROBI ACCRA

First published 1958
Reprinted 1960

PRINTED IN GREAT BRITAIN

TO

MY FORMER COLLEAGUES AND PUPILS

at the

NAGOYA KOTO SHOGYO GAKKO

(now the Department of Economics,

Nagoya University)

Contents

Preface

NEARLY twelve years have passed since the Japanese economy lay in ruins at the end of the Second World War. After a long period of confusion and hesitancy, by 1957 Japan had moved far on the path of recovery, and although a complete understanding of what was accomplished doubtless requires a longer perspective than the present can command, the task of description and explanation can now be approached with reasonable assurance. In this short book attention has been concentrated on the outstanding features of the recovery and the major causes of recent achievements. In examining and interpreting the course of events in the various sectors of the economy (agriculture, industry, finance and banking, labour and foreign trade), I have been particularly concerned with the differences in structure and organization between the present day and the middle 1930's, although every observer with an acquaintance with the pre-war economy must be conscious of the identities as well as of contrasts. No student of post-war Japan can afford to neglect the powerful influence exerted by the United States on the country's economic development and policy, both during the reformist period of the Occupation and subsequently. Among other tasks, therefore, I have tried to appraise that influence and to estimate the extent to which the initial reforms have endured or are likely to endure.

I was fortunate during the later months of 1954 in being able to revisit Japan, as this allowed me to renew connexions broken by the war, to collect printed materials, to inspect industrial establishments, and to discuss economic problems with public officials, economists, and business men. I am deeply indebted to all those who so readily provided information not only during the period of my visit but also since my return to England. As during my previous studies in Japan, I owe a special debt to Mr. Tanzan Ishibashi, recently Prime Minister of Japan and formerly editor of the *Oriental Economist*, and to members of the staff of that journal who prepared detailed answers to a long list of questions. Among the many government officials who assisted me, I am particularly grateful to

Mr. S. Okita of the Economic Planning Board, who spent much time in guiding my inquiries, and to Mr. Y. Suzuki and Mr. Kojima of the Ministry of International Trade and Industry. Mr. Y. Maruyama and his colleagues on the Fair Trade Commission were very helpful in explaining the operation of the anti-monopoly laws, and from Professor Minobe I learned much about the *Zaibatsu* dissolution and subsequent policy. Among the bankers who kindly supplied me with information about financial changes, I should like to mention Mr. T. Nakajima and Mr. S. Matsuda of the Bank of Japan's Foreign Relations Department, Mr. M. Kajiura of the Industrial Bank of Japan, Mr. S. Horie, Mr. T. Ihara, and Mr. Y. Sugihara of the Bank of Tokyo, and Mr. S. Hotta, President of the Sumitomo Bank.

I am indebted to many Japanese industrialists and company officials for allowing me to visit their plants and for informing me about industrial developments. They include Mr. N. Hirano and Mr. N. Inagaki of Nippon Toki, Mr. N. Ishiguro of the Tokyo-Shibaura Electric Company, Mr. I. Iwanaga of Toyo Rayon, Mr. T. Hodaka of Teikoku Rayon, Mr. T. Ito of the Toyoda Machine Works, Mr. Ohara of Kurashiki, Mr. H. Shimojo of the Shoei Silk Manufacturing Company, Mr. S. Takahata of the Nissho Company, and Mr. J. Yoshida of the Bando Rubber Manufacturing Company. I am indebted also to the managers of the Toyo Spinning Company, the Mitsubishi Electric Manufacturing Company, the Kawasaki Steel Corporation, the Meiji Seika Company, the Fukusuke Tabi Company, the Canon Camera Company, and many others. Mr. T. Murayama of the All-Japan Cotton Spinners' Association and Mr. M. Ito of the Institute for Economic Research, Toyo Spinning Company, have generously kept me supplied with data about Japanese textiles. I learned about the labour movement and industrial relations from Mr. S. Inaba of the Research Institute for National Economy, Mr. Kaneko of the Ministry of Labour, Mr. S. Nakayama and his colleagues of the Japan Federation of Employers' Associations, Mr. T. Horikoshi and Mr. T. Ono of the Federation of Economic Organizations, and Mr. T. Fujita of the General Council of Trade Unions. Professor Y. Wakimura of Tokyo University explained to me many features of the post-war industrial organization of Japan and threw much light on the problem of the rehabilitation of the *Zaibatsu*.

Professor S. Sakai and my former colleagues at what is now Nagoya University were most hospitable and arranged a series of instructive visits to industrial plants in Aichi Prefecture. Professor Y. Hirai and his colleagues at Kobe University guided me in my tour of industrial establishments in Kansai. Professor K. Matsui and his colleagues in Kyoto University were also most helpful. The Mitsubishi Economic Research Institute and the Tokyo Chamber of Commerce provided me with valuable data about general economic conditions. In my inquiries into agricultural changes I had the generous assistance of Professor Tobata of Tokyo University and, also, of my friend of student days, Mr. Ginji Shindo, who had personal experiences of the effect of the Land Reform. Another old friend, Mr. A. Morikawa of the Kinkai Yusen Kaisha, was deeply concerned to ensure that my visit should be fruitful. I had very useful discussions with Mr. Kano of the Hakodate Dock Company. Mr. E. G. Price of Butterfield & Swire went to much trouble in arranging meetings with foreign business men in Yokohama and Tokyo. More recently, I received generous help from officials of the British Iron and Steel Federation in interpreting data about the Japanese iron and steel industry. Finally, I must express my very great obligations to Mr. Y. Kawashima, who throughout the whole period of my stay in Japan was indefatigable in his efforts to assist my inquiries. He suggested and arranged numerous interviews, accompanied me on many visits to factories and offices, and obtained valuable documentary material.

My visit to Japan and my investigations in that country were made possible through the financial help given by the Royal Institute of International Affairs and by the Rockefeller Foundation.

My wife has helped at every stage in preparing the book for publication.

G. C. ALLEN

University College, London
July 1957

CHAPTER I

Economic Development in the 1930's

BETWEEN the World Depression of 1929–31 and the outbreak of the Sino-Japanese War in 1937 Japan passed through a period of exceptionally rapid economic growth. In manufacturing industry her progress was especially remarkable. She demonstrated her command of new skills and technologies. She made extensive additions to her capital equipment at home and she invested heavily in regions beyond her own shores. At a time when international trade as a whole was stagnating, her exports flourished. In a wide range of products and in a diversity of markets she became a formidable competitor of the older industrial countries of the West, while to the countries of Asia she made available a variety of consumption goods at prices which their impoverished inhabitants could afford to pay. These remarkable achievements were not, of course, fortuitous. The ground had been prepared for many previous decades. Those who presided over economic policy at critical moments had been bold and far-sighted, and in the middle 1930's Japan at last began to gather the harvest of her enterprise.

We are not concerned here to trace the course of the country's economic history during the modern era nor to describe in detail the work of preparation; [1] but we must at least refer briefly to the outstanding economic events of the years which immediately preceded the period of industrial expansion. These years gave little promise of the prosperity to come. From 1927, when there was a serious financial crisis, until the end of 1931 Japan passed through a period of economic stress. In the first part of that period she was engaged in a struggle to eliminate inflationary forces from her economy in preparation for her return to the gold standard at pre-war parity to the pound and dollar. In January 1930 she effected this return even though her

---

[1] For a comprehensive study of Japan's economic development see W. W. Lockwood, *The Economic Development of Japan* (Princeton University Press, 1954); for a briefer review see G. C. Allen, *A Short Economic History of Modern Japan, 1867–1937* (London, Allen & Unwin, 1951).

prices had not fallen sufficiently to justify it. The moment was
particularly ill chosen, for the World Depression had just begun.
The yen would probably have been overvalued on the ex-
changes even if world prices had not collapsed by that time. As
it was, the Japanese government felt itself obliged to resort to a
still more rigorous deflationary policy in an attempt to follow
world prices on their downward course and so make possible
continued adherence to the gold standard. Consequently the
economy suffered from an intense depression. Industrial production and exports of manufactured goods declined steeply.
In agriculture the deterioration was even more grave. The
peasants of modern Japan had come to depend increasingly for
their well-being on the export trade in raw silk, from the production of which they derived much of their cash income, and
they had been among the chief beneficiaries of 'American
prosperity'. The depression brought a sudden fall in the
American demand, with the result that silk prices collapsed.
While the cash incomes of the silk raisers were diminished, the
indirect effect on family incomes was also serious. Many members of the peasant families, having lost their employment in the
silk-reeling mills or in other textile establishments, returned to
the farms only to contribute to the mounting distress.

These domestic difficulties were accompanied by tensions in
international economic relations. The decline in the value of
raw-silk exports, which accounted for two-fifths of the total exports to foreign countries in 1929, upset the balance of payments
and led to a shrinkage in the monetary reserves. International
troubles in turn reacted on the domestic economy, for every
effort on the part of Finance Minister Inouye to restore equilibrium by the dogged pursuit of an orthodox deflationary
policy intensified the industrial depression and the social
malaise. The crisis arrived when in September 1931 the United
Kingdom and other Western countries abandoned the gold
standard. The competitive position of Japan was at once
weakened and any possibility of maintaining the yen on gold
was removed.

The period ended in a political upheaval—provoked in part
by the economic troubles—and the government which took
office towards the end of 1931 hastened to throw over the gold
standard. The yen was allowed to decline to its equilibrium

level, a considerable fall even in terms of depreciated sterling. At the same time the deflationary policy was abandoned in favour of reflation. Government expenditure, financed to a large extent by borrowing, was much increased, and easy credit conditions were instituted by the monetary authorities. The direction of the new government expenditure and the character of the additional investment encouraged by the low rates of interest were determined largely by the military clique, who were intent upon large-scale rearmament and the development of strategic industries in Manchuria. But Takahashi, the Finance Minister who succeeded Inouye, was by no means a cat's-paw of the militarists. His policy of reflation and theirs of rearmament were in general alignment up to a point; but while he aimed at increasing effective demand to the extent needed to restore 'full employment' (as we should now say), he was not prepared to allow loan-financed government expenditure to rise beyond the point at which inflation would set in. Consequently, a conflict between him and the military cliques was bound to arise sooner or later, for when the unemployed resources of Japan had been called into use (at any rate to the point at which bottle-necks were encountered), Takahashi would hold that reflation had been pressed far enough, whereas the military, who were concerned only with securing the resources necessary for their strategic designs, recognized no such limit. The crisis came in February 1936 when the military revolted against the government and assassinated Takahashi, by then the arch-opponent of their policy.

The year of Takahashi's assassination was the year of the publication of *The General Theory of Employment, Interest and Money*. For the previous four years Takahashi had successfully practised, without benefit of Keynes, a policy in full accord with what was soon to become the new economic orthodoxy. In the light of the new theory as well as of practical experience the deflationary policy of Takahashi's predecessors may seem wrong-headed and even pernicious. Yet such downright condemnation would scarcely be justified. There are reasons for thinking that no small part of the economic progress achieved during Takahashi's régime can be attributed to foundations laid in the years immediately before 1932. During the harsh conditions of that period, inefficiencies were weeded out, improved methods were widely adopted, and productivity in the manufacturing trades rose steeply. The discipline of the deflationary years was a necessary prelude to the progress achieved under the 'full-employment' policy.

A complete assessment of Takahashi's and Inouye's work cannot, of course, ignore the political and social consequences of economic policy; but neither side in this financial controversy can draw much comfort from Japan's experience. The social pressures exerted by deflation helped to produce a successful revolt against parliamentary government and to strengthen the political influence of the military cliques. The 'full-employment' policy meant lavish provision for the militarists' appetite, and this ultimately could have only one result. The Japanese term used to describe the economy of the Takahashi period, *junsenji keizai*, means literally 'quasi wartime economy'; this, says a recent writer on the period—perhaps not without irony— is the 'equivalent in modern economic terminology . . . of full employment induced by deficit financing'.[1] In other words, if deflation ended in political reaction, reflation ended in war.

There is room for controversy over the leading causes of Japan's economic expansion, but there can be no doubt about the facts. With these this chapter is mainly concerned, and it is convenient to begin with a description in outline of the industrial growth. The most striking fact of all is the rise in the quantity of output. All the estimates agree that this rise was very considerable. The index of industrial production given in the *Statistical Year Book* of the League of Nations shows a fall from 100 in 1929 to 92 in 1931 and then a rapid and uninterrupted rise to 151 in 1936 and 171 in 1937. This immense increase in output took place during a period in which production in the United States failed to regain the level of 1929; in the United Kingdom it increased, between 1929 and 1937, by less than 25 per cent.

Nearly all Japanese industries shared in this general advance, but it was the capital-goods industries that grew most rapidly. The result was a striking change in the composition of industry. Textiles, to which Japan had been very highly specialized dur-

---

[1] J. B. Cohen, *Japan's Economy in War and Reconstruction* (Minneapolis, University of Minnesota, 1949), p. 9.

ing the 1920's, diminished in importance. On the other hand, there was a marked relative growth in the metal, engineering, and chemical industries, which had previously played a minor role in Japan's economy. The *Factory Statistics*, which cover an important part, though by no means the whole, of Japan's manufacturing industry, show that in 1929 textiles accounted for over 50 per cent. of total factory employment, and metals, engineering goods, and chemicals for just over 25 per cent. In 1937 the respective proportions were 35 and 42 per cent. The various indices of industrial production point to the same conclusion. Between 1930 and 1937, while the index for consumption goods rose from 100 to 154, that for investment goods rose from 100 to 264. The increase in the output of the latter class was accompanied by a wide extension in the range of products turned out by the metal, engineering, and chemical industries. Whereas in the 1920's Japan had relied heavily upon imports of machinery to equip her manufacturing industries, by 1937 she was able herself to construct most of the plants that she required, including textile machinery, many kinds of machine tools, scientific instruments, and electrical appliances. By then she was capable of meeting her needs for complete power-station plants. She had become largely self-sufficient in the chief chemical products.[1]

This advance in the capital-goods industries was achieved without any absolute contraction in textiles. It is true that in the middle 1930's both output and employment in silk reeling were still less than in the later 1920's. But raw silk was the only large industry that suffered an absolute decline. Among other textiles there was not only a substantial rise in output but also a widening of the range of products. The cotton industry secured a steadily increasing proportion of world trade. The woollen and worsted industry, which was small before 1929, expanded and new branches of the trade, such as the manufacture of woollen cloth and worsted fabrics for Western-style dress, grew especially fast. The rayon industry was in a very early stage of development in 1929. By 1937 Japan was the leading producer of continuous filament in the world and

---

[1] For a detailed study of industrial developments during the 1930's see E. B. Schumpeter, ed., *The Industrialization of Japan and Manchukuo* (New York, Macmillan, 1941), *passim*.

she also had a large output of staple fibre. Other branches of manufacture, such as the well-established pottery trade, and a number of miscellaneous-goods industries engaged in the production of toys, rubber shoes, hosiery, and metal smallwares made a notable expansion. The fuel and power trades also grew. The output of coal rose by nearly one-third between 1930 and 1937 and electricity generating capacity by about two-thirds. By the end of 1936 there were probably about 8 million persons engaged in the mining and manufacturing industries, compared with under 6 millions in 1930.[1] In spite of the large rural population, the contribution of manufacturing industry to the national income in 1937 was more than twice that of agriculture.[2] In other words, by that time Japan could claim to be a highly industrialized State. This gave her a unique position in Asia. The industrial production of Japan in 1936–7 was probably nearly twice that of the whole of the rest of Asia (excluding the Soviet Union).

All these estimates apply to Japan Proper (that is, the four main islands of Honshu, Kyushu, Shikoku, and Hokkaido, together with the adjacent small islands and Southern Saghalien). On the continent of Asia, especially in Korea and in the newly constituted state of Manchukuo, and also in Formosa, Japan had other achievements to her credit. In Formosa the industrial development was largely limited to the food-processing industries, especially sugar refining. In Korea plants for the production of electrical goods, paper, cement, vegetable oils, iron and steel, and non-ferrous metals were operated by Japanese concerns. In that colony mineral resources were widely exploited and there was a large production of hydro-electric power. The major developments on the continent, however, occurred in Manchuria.

Before the Japanese seized control of that country in 1931 agriculture had been the predominant activity, and mining and manufacturing were mostly confined to the South Manchuria Railway zone, and to the Kwantung Leased Territory. With the foundation of Manchukuo, Japan poured capital into the

---

[1] Prime Minister's Office, *Statistical Year-Book of the Japanese Empire* (various ssues), and Oriental Economist, *Japan in 1938*, p. 19. Includes about 1 million in building.

[2] Cohen, *Japan's Economy*, p. 6.

country and set going a process of rapid industrial development.
At the outbreak of the Sino-Japanese War in 1937, a number of
heavy industries—coal- and ore-mining, iron and steel production, chemical manufacturing, and electricity generating—
were firmly established, and the foundations had been laid for
the great expansion that occurred during the next few years.
Most of the semi-products were sent to finishing factories in
Japan, and the Manchurian industries thus formed an integral
part of Japan's economy.[1]

Even outside the territories under her political administration, Japan owned and operated many important industrial
undertakings. In the development of the Chinese cotton industry, her capital and entrepreneurship took the lead after the
First World War and by 1937 nearly half the spindleage was
under her control.[2] She had interests in many other manufacturing establishments in China Proper as well as in coal- and
iron-mining. Her enterprise was also found much farther afield,
for example, in Indonesia and Malaya, where she had mining
properties.

The enlargement of Japan's economic activities both at home
and overseas was accompanied by continuous improvements in
industrial methods, a process which, as we have seen, was
stimulated by the depressed conditions between 1927 and
1931. Productivity increased both in the older industries (silk
weaving, cotton textiles, and pottery) and in the newer
trades (rayon, chemicals, metals, and engineering). This came
about partly through additions to capital equipment and
partly through the more efficient organization of plants and
processes.

The agricultural sector of Japan's economy was very dif-
ferently affected. For the farmers there was no complete recovery from the conditions of the early 1930's. The prices of
rice and of most other agricultural products remained low. The
failure of silk prices to regain their pre-depression levels meant
that cash incomes from the sale of cocoons were comparatively
small and fewer opportunities than hitherto were available for

[1] Cf. F. C. Jones, *Manchuria Since 1931* (London, Royal Institute of International
Affairs, 1941), pp. 10, 154-5, and *passim*.
[2] G. C. Allen and A. G. Donnithorne, *Western Enterprise in Far Eastern Economic
Development: China and Japan* (London, Allen & Unwin, 1954), pp. 175-7.

employment in the reeling mills. The depressed conditions in the countryside compelled members of farming families to seek employment either in large mills and factories, or in the small workshops which still accounted for a high proportion of the output of most industrial goods. This large supply of labour in search of employment enabled manufacturing industry to increase its manpower after 1932 without raising wages. Indeed, this flow of recruits from the countryside into manufacture is the key not only to the growth of industrial employment during the 1930's, but also to the movement of wages and prices during that time. Although real wages increased in the heavy industries during the period of recovery after 1932, they actually fell in the textile industry and in many other consumption-goods trades. Over industry as a whole they were probably rather lower in 1936 than they had been in 1929.[1]

Japan's experience was not, of course, unique. In all countries with large agricultural interests the catastrophic fall in the prices of primary products during the World Depression brought grave hardships, and in all of them attempts were made to divert resources to the production of those types of manufactured goods which the people could no longer afford to import. But Japan was one of the few countries that achieved an outstanding success in the pursuit of this policy. Her achievement is to be explained partly by the fact that she had already laid the foundations for extensive industrial developments and partly because she deliberately pursued a monetary policy favourable to such a redistribution of her resources. It is true that in the period now under review the policy did not succeed in relieving the farmers from their economic distress, but it certainly mitigated the effects of the rural depression.

The industrialization of the 1930's was achieved without forcing Japan into significantly greater dependence on overseas supplies of food. Her fisheries furnished most of the animal foodstuffs consumed in Japan as well as large exports. Four-fifths of the total consumption of rice was still home-produced, and most of the rest came from Korea and Formosa. These colonies, together with Manchuria which was the source of

[1] Cf. T. Uyeda, *The Small Industries of Japan* (New York, Institute of Pacific Relations, 1938), pp. 297 ff.; see also p. 11 below.

soya-bean imports, also supplied the greater part of the other foodstuffs which were not produced by Japanese farms and fisheries. The net import of food from foreign countries was very small.[1] This condition of imperial self-sufficiency in food-stuffs had not been disturbed by the immense growth in the population of Japan Proper from 60 millions in 1925 to 69 millions in 1935. But it was otherwise with the industrial raw materials which the expanding industries required in ever-growing quantities. Most of these materials had to be imported for, apart from fuel and power, timber, and materials for raw silk, Japan possessed only small domestic resources. Practically all the cotton, wool, mineral oil, iron ore, and most non-ferrous ores had to be obtained from abroad, and domestic supplies even of wood pulp, chemical raw materials, and coal were insufficient for the needs of industry.

The empire's contribution to Japan's need for minerals and textile raw materials was comparatively small. It is true that the countries which afterwards comprised the 'yen bloc' (namely China and Manchuria, together with the colonies) supplied Japan in 1936 with more than a third of her total imports, and that the relative importance of the area as a source of imports steadily increased throughout the 1930's, largely as the result of deliberate policy.[2] But the imports were mainly foodstuffs. Even at the end of the decade Japan still remained dependent on distant foreign sources of supply for the greater part of her industrial raw materials. This reliance upon areas outside her political control might have strategic dis-advantages, but it could hardly be regarded as a serious econo-mic weakness during a period in which the conditions for multi-lateral trading were still reasonably well satisfied. So long as the world remained at peace, the only danger lay in the de-liberate creation of obstacles to Japan's enterprise in the export markets. During the 1930's a number of countries tried to weaken her competition by raising tariffs or imposing quota restrictions on her imports. These obstacles no doubt worsened Japan's terms of trade, but during this decade they certainly did not arrest the expansion of her exports, for while the import trade increased in volume between 1929 and 1937 by only

[1] There was a large import of wheat but this was balanced by exports of flour.
[2] Cf. S. Okita, *Japan's Trade with Asia* (Tokyo, 1954), p. 2.

about one-third, the volume of exports grew by about three-quarters.[1] This was a remarkable expansion in a period in which international trade in general was stagnant, and it explains why Japanese competition was so greatly feared by foreign producers. Moreover, whereas before the World Depression about two-fifths of Japan's exports consisted of a commodity which did not compete with the products of her chief commercial rivals, in 1936 this commodity (raw silk) accounted for only 15 per cent. of the exports, for its place had been taken by manufactured goods. The detailed changes in the composition of the export trade and in the chief markets between 1929 and 1937 will be considered in Chapter XI.

The fact that exports during these years grew much faster than imports requires an explanation. Briefly it is as follows. Japan's balance of payments was adverse in 1929, and from then until 1932 large exports of gold were needed to meet the deficit on current trading. The fall in the yen during 1932 helped to produce an equilibrium, but it worsened the terms of trade. A similar influence was subsequently exerted by the discriminatory restrictions imposed by foreign governments on Japanese goods. By 1936 the terms of trade had deteriorated by about 30 per cent. as compared with the pre-depression period.[2] Although the fact that the Japanese were obliged to exchange more manufactures for a given quantity of raw materials does not mean that they were to that extent worse off (since productivity in manufactures had greatly increased in the interval) these circumstances nevertheless account for a considerable part of the discrepancy noted above. Further, it must be remembered that Japan was investing heavily abroad, mainly in Manchuria. Part of her export surplus on her current trading was required to implement this investment.

The worsened terms of trade and the industrial investment programme, together with the rise in population and heavy armament expenditure, explain the failure of the standard of life to improve during a period in which output substantially increased. That the standard of life of the masses in fact failed to rise is borne out both by statistical data and by the observation of contemporaries. The cost of living seems to have risen

---

[1] League of Nations, *Review of World Trade, 1937*, p. 41. Excludes colonial trade.
[2] Allen, *Short Economic History*, p. 133.

faster than money earnings during the years of recovery, with the result that the index of real earnings in the first half of 1937 was about 10 per cent. below the index for 1931 and was scarcely equal to that for 1929. Although the significance of this statistical measure is affected by the fact that there was a large increase in the number of new recruits to industry during this time, it was concluded by a Japanese economist, highly regarded for his sound judgement, that the unsatisfactory tendency disclosed by these figures must be accepted.[1]

Averages obscure divergent movements in particular trades, and they are liable to give a misleading view of economic trends unless they are supplemented by detailed figures. During this period there is no doubt that men in the engineering and shipbuilding industries, especially the skilled workers, greatly improved their real earnings. But the female textile operatives were worse off in 1936 and 1937 than they had been in 1929, except perhaps those who worked in large mills where substantial semi-annual bonuses were paid during the recovery period. The real earnings of men in the rubber, wood, pottery, and food and drink trades also declined. On the farms it is certain that standards fell. This was especially true in the northern parts of Japan. One may indeed sum up the changes in the period by stating that the increased real national income generated by higher labour productivity in particular trades, by the diversion of labour from low-productivity to high-productivity industries, and by calling into use the unemployed resources that existed in 1930–1, was applied mainly to investment (largely of a strategic kind), to providing for a greater population, and to countering the adverse movement in the terms of trade. Very little was left over to provide for increased civilian consumption per head.

The organization of Japan's economy during the 1930's was full of apparent inconsistencies. On the one hand, a considerable part of industry, trade, and finance was concentrated in the great concerns known as the *Zaibatsu*, which will be the subject of a later chapter. Each of these houses had interests in many branches of industry, commerce, and finance. They were prominent not only in large-scale highly-capitalized

[1] Uyeda, *Small Industries*, pp. 305–8.

enterprises, but also, through their banks and merchanting companies, they penetrated into that part of the economy composed of numerous small and medium-sized producers. The latter were characteristic of the trades that produced goods of a traditional type: Japanese-style clothing, footwear, furniture, pottery, prepared foodstuffs, narrow-width textiles, and papier-maché wares. Some of these trades were widely distributed; others were strongly localized. Nearly all depended heavily on manual processes and many of them, notably the *meibutsu* [1] trades at Kyoto, employed highly skilled craftsmen. Small and medium-sized firms were also numerous in industries of a modern type, including some that served the export markets. For instance, very small weaving-sheds were typical of the new worsted-weaving trade as well as of the older silk weaving. Part of the pottery exports came from small producers. In the metal and miscellaneous goods trades there were many small establishments engaged in the manufacture of castings, bicycle parts, cheap electric lamps, rubber footwear, and toys. Almost every large engineering factory was surrounded by numerous subcontracting workshops which supplied it with parts or performed processes to its orders. Some of these small-scale industries were elaborately organized. The producers often specialized on particular components and supplied them to merchants or factory owners who co-ordinated their activities. If in general their workshops were poorly constructed and their machinery inferior to that used in the factories, there were exceptions. For instance, the worsted weavers of Ichinomiya possessed well-built mills equipped with modern looms, and many of the small machine-shops used power-driven machine-tools adequate to their purposes.

The quantitative importance of the small and medium-sized units may be measured with reasonable accuracy. In 1930, 4,760,000 persons were recorded by the Census as being engaged in private manufacturing industry as their principal occupation. Of these, 58 per cent. worked in establishments with under 5 operatives, and only 21 per cent. in establishments with 100 or more operatives.[2] These figures exaggerate the importance of the small producers, since many of their employees

---

[1] 'Speciality.'

[2] Lockwood, *Economic Development*, pp. 112, 204; see also p. 75 below.

were part-time workers, and for this and other reasons labour productivity was much lower in them than in the large factories. Nevertheless, this qualification does not disturb the fact that in 1930 small producers played a most significant role in Japanese industry. Their position changed but little up to the outbreak of the Second World War.

The small unit which flourished not only in the traditional industries but also in newer branches of manufacture was to be regarded not as a survival but rather as a type of undertaking well suited to the economic conditions of modern Japan. While there were some industries in which technique prescribed that production could take place economically only in large, highly capitalized plants, there were many others where organization could be adapted to the country's factor-endowment. In that sector, the relative scarcity of capital and the relative abundance of skilled labour exerted an influence in favour of processes that could be efficiently conducted in small establishments. Since the great merchant and manufacturing firms interested themselves in the small-scale sector, providing finance, technical knowledge, and access to markets, it was often possible to combine the advantages of large-scale financial and commercial organization with those of small-scale manufacturing.

The dichotomy in Japanese industry was influenced during the 1930's by changes in the government's economic policy. The State had been active in introducing Western industrial methods during the early Meiji era, and in later times it had taken the lead in promoting the development of industries of strategic importance, often in conjunction with the *Zaibatsu*. Yet in the early 1930's the enterprises actually owned by the State were limited to special fields, such as the main-line railway system and part of the iron and steel industry. Similarly, governmental intervention in economic affairs was mainly concerned with supplying the deficiencies of private enterprise (as in the official supervision over certain processes in the raw-silk industry), or in assisting the agricultural and fishery industries to handle their price and marketing problems. In manufacturing industry there was comparatively little official supervision or regulation.

The political and economic crises of the 1930's were responsible for fundamental changes in policy. During the years when the economy was suffering from the effects of the World Depression, the government introduced schemes designed to bring about co-operation among producers and traders with the object both of raising efficiency and also of mitigating what were then regarded as the excesses of competition. Measures were devised for encouraging rationalization in the large-scale industries, and for strengthening or establishing guilds or associations (*kumiai*) of producers and traders in the small-scale industries.

After 1932 economic policy was affected not merely by the improvement in economic circumstances but also by the political and social changes of the time. The military cliques, now in the ascendant, were antagonistic to the *Zaibatsu* and were intent upon weakening their power. Both in Manchuria and in Japan Proper they turned to new capital groups (*Shinko-Zaibatsu*) to serve as the economic instruments of their strategic purposes. They also used their influence to strengthen the associations of small manufacturers and traders with the object of freeing those enterprises from the domination of the merchant companies owned by the old *Zaibatsu*. The associations received additional support for other reasons. For instance, the government tried to meet the outcry against Japan's 'social dumping' by requiring the export guilds to control sales to foreign markets in the hope of forestalling restrictions. These measures had only moderate success. Of far greater significance was the assumption by the State of control over certain basic industries for strategic reasons. An early example was the establishment of the Japan Iron and Steel Company by the amalgamation in 1934 of six private firms and the government's Yawata Works. Control was also extended over the operations of the oil-distributing companies, Japanese and foreign alike.[1]

After the outbreak of the Sino-Japanese War, State intervention was carried much further. The producers' guilds came to be used as efficient instruments for fixing prices and rationing supplies of raw materials. The electric-power industry was nationalized in 1938 and in the same year the National General Mobilization Law conferred on the government far-reaching powers of economic control. By 1940 a considerable number of

[1] The changes in economic policy are examined in detail in Schumpeter, *Industrialization*, chs. xxi, xxii, and Conclusion.

strategic industries had been brought under centralized administration, and several 'national policy companies' had been established to develop particular manufactures under official guidance. Thus, under the influence of war, economic power was increasingly concentrated in the State and in the organs of control that it created or adapted to its purposes.

CHAPTER II

The Course of Economic Recovery after 1945

AT the end of the Second World War, Japan's economy was in ruins. Her great centres of population had been laid waste. In the sixty-six cities subjected to air attack about half the dwelling-places had been burnt down; these represented about a quarter of the total housing accommodation of the country.[1] A high proportion of the industrial and commercial buildings together with the equipment they contained had been destroyed, and much plant and machinery formerly used in production for the civilian market had been scrapped to provide metal for munitions. The amount of physical destruction is estimated to have been equivalent to about twice the national income of the fiscal year 1948–9.[2] What is more, the economy had been seriously disorganized even before the surrender, for the scarcity of materials and of transport equipment together with the confusion caused by the evacuation of the larger cities had produced a breakdown of production and distribution. The once massive export trade no longer existed, and the mercantile marine, in pre-war days the third largest in the world, had been reduced to a few coasting vessels. In 1945 the people were short of food, clothing, fuel, housing, and all other necessaries of life.

In Europe it was at first confidently expected that Japan's emergence from these confusions would not be long delayed, and her former competitors, particularly those in the textile trades, awaited with anxiety her early return to world markets. These expectations proved to be erroneous, and recovery, especially in international trade, was very slow. The overestimate of Japan's recuperative capacity can be attributed in part simply to a failure to realize the extent of the physical damage sus-

---

[1] Cohen, *Japan's Economy*, pp. 406–8.
[2] Estimate of Economic Stabilization Board, see Oriental Economist, *Japan Economic Year Book, 1954*, pp. 20–21.

tained by the economy. Furthermore, foreign observers made insufficient allowance for the effects of defeat and Occupation upon the spirit of enterprise among the Japanese people. For nearly seven years, from August 1945 until March 1952 when the Peace Treaty took effect, the government's economic policy was profoundly influenced, if not entirely determined, by directives from SCAP,[1] while Japanese businessmen and officials fumbled with situations which they were powerless to control.

Some uncertainties were inevitable in the immediate post-war years when Allied policy towards Japan was being worked out. The Japanese could make some estimate of the damaging effects of the loss of their empire and of their great overseas assets upon their country's international trade and its food and raw-material supplies. But the Allied Powers at that time were actively concerned with exacting reparations and with ensuring that Japan's freedom to reconstruct industries of strategic importance should be strictly limited. Some of the reparations were in fact supplied by the distribution of the country's foreign assets. But others, so it was thought, might take the form of plant and machinery wrenched from the factories.[2] Until this question had been resolved by the victorious Powers, the Japanese moved in a penumbra of uncertainty. This was not all. In the early post-war years SCAP was indifferent to economic recovery and was committed to ambitious measures of social and political reform. Its aim was to destroy completely the material basis of Japan's imperialism and at the same time to foster institutions and forms of organization believed to be favourable to democratic modes of life. With the object of preventing the re-creation of an industrial war potential, proposals were put forward for restricting the capacity of the metal, chemical, and engineering industries and for limiting the size and speed of ships. The policy also expressed itself in various reforms calculated to diffuse wealth and economic initiative more widely. The dissolution of the *Zaibatsu*, the purging of many business leaders, the enactment of an anti-trust law, the Land Reform designed to transform tenants into peasant

[1] SCAP stands for Supreme Commander of the Allied Powers, and is used to designate both a person and also the Occupation Administration in general.

[2] Some machine tools and other types of equipment were transferred to China and other Far Eastern victims of Japan's aggression.

proprietors, the introduction of labour laws and measures for the promotion of social welfare—all these are major examples of the reformist policy in the economic sphere. An estimate of their effects will be given in some detail in later chapters. Here it is sufficient to assert that, whatever the political and social merits of these measures, they certainly made no contribution to economic recovery. Most of them actually impeded it. 'Punishment and Reform' is indeed an apt description of this first phase of American policy.[1]

Such statistical indices as are available demonstrate the deplorably low levels of economic activity in the early post-war years. In 1946 the volume of industrial production was little more than 30 per cent. of that of the pre-war period (1934-6), and in the next year it reached only 37 per cent. In the cities consumption a head was then very low, perhaps only half the pre-war consumption. An export trade scarcely existed, and the destruction of the mercantile marine and the loss of foreign assets meant that there were no earnings of foreign exchange from those sources. The value of the currency had been virtually destroyed by a violent inflation. Agriculture, which had suffered least from wartime destruction and post-war dislocation, was the only sector of the economy to show some improvement. Even there, however, output in 1946 and 1947 was still well below the pre-war level.[2]

Before the end of 1947 the catastrophic conditions in Japanese industry and the deepening financial crisis persuaded the Americans that their policies must be revised. The widespread economic distress provided an uncongenial environment for the growth of new democratic institutions and its relief imposed heavy burdens on the American taxpayer. In 1947 alone aid amounted to over $400 million. At the same time the deterioration in relations between the Western world and Russia, together with the growing recognition that Nationalist China was unlikely to serve as a stabilizing force in East Asia or an apt vehicle for American policy, caused a change in strategic plans. SCAP was, therefore, compelled to abandon its indulgence in

[1] Columbia University, American Assembly Graduate School of Business, *The United States and the Far East* (New York, 1956), p. 36.
[2] For detailed statistics and sources thereof see Statistical Appendix, pp. 192 ff. below.

reformist zeal and to concern itself increasingly with the promotion of economic recovery. Reparations were halted. Imports of raw materials and foodstuffs under the aid programme were enlarged. Private trade with the outside world was permitted under certain safeguards. The militant labour movement, which had grown up under the wing of the Occupation authorities, was sharply discouraged, and the policy of destroying the *Zaibatsu* was pursued with a more moderate enthusiasm. 'Recovery' was now the watchword, and by the end of 1948 it had been decided that an essential preliminary was the restoration of monetary stability. This policy was announced under the form of a Nine-Points Stabilization Programme which provided *inter alia* for a balanced budget, credit restrictions, and the expansion of trade and production. Early in 1949 Mr. Joseph Dodge arrived and proceeded to bend Japanese policy to this new aim.

The measures which he caused to be executed enjoyed an immediate success. The rise in prices was checked. The government and the business world were now able to grapple with the tasks of reconstruction in the consciousness that among the Occupation authorities anxiety for a rapid economic recovery had almost completely supplanted the earlier preoccupation with social and political reform. By the spring of 1950, although manufacturing production was still less than before the war, industry had already gone far towards adapting itself to the new financial situation. The crippling shortages of fuel and basic materials had been largely overcome and agricultural output had regained its pre-war level.

In June 1950 the outbreak of the Korean War swept the economy on to a new plane. Heavy 'special procurement' expenditure on account of the United Nations forces brought about a sharp increase in the output of manufactures, and orders flowed into the factories from abroad. Boom conditions prevailed throughout the economy and the short period of relative price stability came to an abrupt end. Yet since the boom was brought about by a great expansion in what were in effect foreign demands for Japanese goods and services, a rise in prices of more than 50 per cent. between June 1950 and June 1951 proved to be quite consistent with the appearance of a very favourable balance of payments. In 1951 the growth in output was such that the index of industrial production exceeded the pre-war annual average for the first time since 1944.[1]

The Korean War not merely promoted Japan's economic recovery, it also exerted a powerful influence upon Occupation policy. If Japan had not been under American control, South Korea could hardly have been defended, and it was realized that even when the war was over, Japan would remain an essential base for the deployment of American power. A strong Japan closely allied to the United States became, therefore, the key to Far Eastern strategy. The facts of the international situation left no place either for the vindictiveness or the political idealism of the early post-war years. These were the circumstances that determined the character of the Peace Treaty and the Security Treaty which were signed in September 1951 and came into effect in the spring of 1952. The treaties returned full sovereignty to Japan (although they also confirmed the loss of her empire), restored to her the right of rearming, and permitted the Allies to maintain bases and troops in the country. They were silent about the economic reforms, and while they recognized the obligation of Japan to make reparations, they also conceded her present inability to do so. One result of the Peace Treaty was that even after the conclusion of the Korean War, Japan continued to receive large dollar payments for 'special procurement' chiefly in respect of the American military establishments. Between 1952 and 1956 these payments amounted to $3,380 million, ranging between $824 million and $557 million annually. In 1955 they were equivalent to 27 per cent. of the value of the export trade.[2] It is scarcely possible to exaggerate the importance of these payments to Japan's economic recovery during the critical years after 1951. At a time when the revival of the export trade was in an early stage, they provided her with a large and fairly

[1] By 'pre-war' in this context is meant the average of 1934–6; a comparison with 1937 (when Japan's war with China began) is much less favourable. See p. 70 below.

[2] This general account of economic changes in the post-war period is based largely on Economic Counsel (Planning) Board, *Economic Survey of Japan* (various issues, later referred to as *Economic Survey of Japan*); see also S. Tsuru, 'Business Cycles in Post-War Japan', in International Economic Association, *The Business Cycle in the Post-War World* (London, Macmillan, 1955). For complete figures of procurement expenditure see Statistical Appendix, p. 203 below.

steady dollar income which greatly assisted in the re-equipment of her industries and the restoration of pre-war levels of consumption.

Even when the Korean War boom broke, Japan's industrial production continued to expand and her earnings of foreign exchange remained sufficient to enable her to build up large dollar reserves. It is true that under the influence of the continuing boom Japanese prices moved out of line with world prices and that by 1953 she was again in balance-of-payments difficulties. Nevertheless, in that year her industrial production was 55 per cent. greater than in the base period and her real national income probably 30 per cent. greater. In spite of the steep rise in the population (from 69 millions in 1935 to 87 millions in 1953) income per head had risen above pre-war level. The period 1951–3 thus saw Japan at last set on the road to economic recovery.

The industrial investments of these years, while they were largely responsible for the critical turn in the balance of payments, laid the foundations for future progress. For after the Japanese government had administered, during 1954, a sharp corrective to the inflationary movement, not only was equilibrium in the balance of payments restored, but industrial expansion was resumed at an enhanced rate. In 1955 the index of industrial production averaged 181 and in 1956 219. By this time, moreover, prosperity had become widely diffused throughout the economy. Whereas in the early 1950's the larger firms had been the chief beneficiaries both of procurement demand and of new investment, after 1955 the small and medium-sized firms began to share in the prosperity. This was a period in which the export trade, hitherto most resistant to the forces of recovery, went ahead with extraordinary speed.

By the fiscal year 1955–6 Japan could be said to have completed her economic recovery. Her gross national product (in real terms) was 44 per cent. higher than in the middle 1930's and income per head over 10 per cent. higher. For several years her international accounts had shown a favourable balance and she had accumulated substantial foreign-exchange reserves. She had carried through the re-equipment of her major industries and productivity had risen well above the pre-war level and was rapidly increasing. She had brought inflation under control, at any rate for a time, and her people had begun to save again.[1] Even if full account is taken of the American contribution to recovery, first in aid and then in procurement, these achievements were impressive for a country which had sustained such heavy physical damage during the war and had permanently lost vast overseas assets. Throughout 1956 and during the early months of 1957 the economy continued to move forward at an undiminished rate. The export trade, though still less in volume than before the war, maintained the pace of its advance, stimulated towards the end of 1956 by the Suez crisis.

The post-war economic recovery thus falls into several distinct periods and may be summarized as follows.

1. August 1945 to February 1949: the period of inflation and economic confusion, when exports were very small, imports financed mainly by American aid, industrial production far below pre-war, and substantial recovery confined to agriculture.

2. March 1949 to June 1950: the period of financial stabilization.

3. June 1950 to November 1953: the period of the Korean War boom, when investment financed by procurement payments was heavy, industrial production rose above its pre-war level, and inflation was resumed.

4. November 1953 to December 1954: the period in which inflation was checked and exports at last began to revive.

5. January 1955 to March 1957: a period of rapid growth in all sectors of the economy, including the export trade.

The process of recovery in the various sectors of industry and trade will be described in detail in subsequent chapters. We shall now briefly consider certain general factors which are of significance for the economy as a whole.

In the first place, the rise in the population deserves special attention, since this has affected and must continue to affect the demand for imports, the organization of industry and the labour market, and the capital needs of the economy. Between 1920 and 1940 the population of Japan Proper had increased from 55 millions to 72 millions. Although during the 1930's the size of

---

[1] Personal savings were estimated to amount to nearly 16 per cent. of personal incomes in 1955–6 (*Oriental Economist*, December 1956, p. 587).

the average family began to fall, a large absolute annual increase was then forecast for the next few decades because of the
high proportion of the population in the fertile age-groups.
Between 1935 and 1939 the crude birth-rate averaged 29·2 per
thousand, the crude death-rate 17·4, and the rate of natural
increase 11·8. The birth- and death-rates, though high by
Western European standards, were low by Asian standards.

Immediately after the war the population began to expand
very rapidly. The number of Japanese (soldiers and civilians)
who were repatriated from overseas territories far exceeded the
number of foreigners (chiefly Chinese and Koreans) who left
Japan. On the demobilization of the armed forces the pre-war
downward trend in the birth-rate was for a time reversed, and
between October 1946 and September 1950 the natural increase amounted to 1,630,000 a year. The Census of 1950 put
the population at 83 millions. Then a remarkable change began, and by 1956 the crude birth-rate had fallen to 18·4 and the
crude death-rate to 8. If Japan has now passed into the class
of countries with low birth-rates, her rate of increase has remained high because of the steep fall in the death-rate. The
prospect is, however, that the rate of increase will diminish,
since the death-rate is unlikely to fall much further while the
downward trend in the birth-rate will probably continue. Even
so, the population, which reached 90 millions in 1956, is likely
to rise to at least 96 millions by 1965 and to over 100 millions
by 1970. After then, it is estimated, the increase will be small
and a decline may set in before the end of the century. Long-
term forecasts of population can, however, be disregarded, for
experience shows that they are seldom fulfilled, and it is to the
changes of the recent past and of the next fifteen years that
attention can be usefully directed.

Since 1940 Japan has added over 18 millions to her numbers,
an increase of more than 25 per cent. Between 1956 and 1970
the increase will probably be of the order of 10 millions. These
figures are highly significant in any consideration of the country's economic problem. In the light of the growth in numbers
that occurred after 1940, the restoration of income a head to
the pre-war level by 1953 and its further increase during the
next four years were no slight accomplishments. The result,
however, was achieved in favourable circumstances, and it is

clear that the maintenance of even a slightly rising trend over
the next ten or fifteen years will call for considerable and continuous advances in productivity, even though the slowing
down in the rate of increase in the population may make the
problem less formidable than in the past.[1]

The net addition to the labour force has now reached over
700,000 a year, an increment which must be expected for many
years to come. Japan's difficulties cannot be surmounted unless
she can not only find employment for these additional numbers
but also absorb an increased proportion of her manpower into
work of high productivity. The magnitude of the problem may
be demonstrated by reference to the industrial distribution of
the working population. In 1956 the number of persons gain-
fully employed was 42,400,000. Of these, 17 millions found their
chief occupation in agriculture and forestry—about 3 millions
more than before the war. Productivity in agriculture is low
and although the farmers' living standards are higher than before the war, they are threatened by the pressure of numbers.
About 7 millions were in wholesale and retail trade and finance,
again a large increase on pre-war numbers, and many of these
earned very low incomes. This is true also of most of those
engaged in other service trades. Mining and manufacturing
(including building) employed over 9¾ million persons.[2] This
represents a very small increase on pre-war numbers. Yet industry is the department of economic life which, on an average,
makes by far the largest contribution a head to the national
product and which includes, along with many small and ill-
equipped firms, the great industrial establishments that rival
those of the West. In other words, manufacturing and mining,
especially large-scale manufacturing, has absorbed only a very
small part of the total increase in Japan's labour force during
the last fifteen years. In spite of the expansion in industrial
output, this sector now gives occupation to a rather smaller
proportion of the working population than it did in 1951 and
a much smaller proportion than in 1940. Most of the additional
labour has been driven into types of work where average labour

---

[1] A. Okazaki, *The Present and Future of Japan's Population* (Japan Institute of
Pacific Relations), *passim*; T. Honda, 'The Post-War Population Problem', *Oriental
Economist*, November 1954, pp. 553–5.

[2] Data from Statistics Bureau of Prime Minister's Office. See Statistical
Appendix, p. 191 below.

productivity is much lower than in manufacturing industry. If during the next ten years this trend is to be reversed, a very rapid development of manufactures and of those branches of commerce and the service trades which make high per-capita contributions to the national product will be necessary. A large provision of capital is thus required. During the early post-war years, when the national product was very low, private savings were very small, and such investment as took place was undertaken by the government or its agencies. After 1950, however, private as well as public investment rose steeply, and by the middle 1950's gross *fixed* capital formation represented about 20 per cent. of the gross domestic product.[1] This rate will have to be maintained or even increased if progress in manufactures is to continue.

Despite the urgent need for domestic investment, some foreign investment is indispensable, and it has been resumed on a modest scale. Japan started on this course in 1951 when an iron and steel firm made an investment in iron-ore mines in Goa, and by September 1956 her total foreign investment stood at about £12 million, excluding expenditure incurred in connexion with arrangements for technical assistance to South East Asia. Some of this capital has been essential merely for the re-establishment of foreign offices for her trading companies and banks; but, in addition, Japan has acquired interests, often jointly with foreigners, in mining, lumbering, and textile enterprises in Latin America and South East Asia.[2]

We have seen that dollar aid and later procurement expenditure played an important part in the re-equipment of industry by providing the means for financing imports. It might have been expected that private foreign investment would also have become substantial and that Japan would have been anxious to attract capital from abroad. As in the past, however, the amount of direct investment by foreigners has been moderate. At June 1955 outstanding foreign investment amounted to only about £50 million, of which about 65 per cent. was held by Americans. Much of this has been provided for undertakings jointly capitalized by foreigners and Japanese, or in connexion

[1] U.N., ECAFE, *Economic Survey of Asia and the Far East, 1955*, p. 210.

[2] *Oriental Economist*, December 1956, p. 590; *Fuji Bank Bulletin*, March 1957, pp. 11 ff.

with arrangements for technical collaboration, as in the oil-refining and distribution, the chemical, and the electrical industries. During the early 1950's foreigners doubted the viability of the Japanese economy. They were, therefore, reluctant to commit their resources, even though they then enjoyed tax concessions later removed because of protests from Japanese business firms to whom the incursion of foreign rivals was unwelcome. As the Japanese gain confidence in their competitive strength, and as a sustained industrial recovery makes Japan an attractive field for foreign investment, it is probable that the flow of capital from abroad will increase. Indeed the investments now seem to be rising rapidly and by July 1956 amounted to over £85 million.[1]

The heavy investment of the last few years was compatible with the recovery of consumption a head which, as already shown, attained the pre-war level in 1953. The recovery, however, was unevenly spread. At that time the rural population had done far better than the city dwellers. The latter were still consuming less than before the war, whereas the former were probably consuming over a quarter more. Since then the average level of consumption has risen further, chiefly as a result of an improvement in the standards of the city-dwellers brought about by the industrial prosperity.[2]

The recovery of exports, as we have seen, lagged behind the industrial revival. It was not until after 1954 that they began to grow rapidly, and even in 1956 their volume was a quarter less than before the war.[3] Even if procurement expenditure is added to the value of exports, the achievement remains very modest. Nevertheless, so far, Japan has been able by various means to obtain the imports needed for her industrial advance. But if the growth in production is to continue at the rate required for an improvement in the material condition of her

---

[1] This amount includes about £18 million of direct investment and £68 million of loans, including a loan of £19 million from the World Bank for an iron and steel works. No account is taken here of American aid, the status of which has still to be determined. See Industrial Bank of Japan, *Survey of Japanese Finance and Industry*, July–August 1956, pp. 10–12 (later referred to as *Survey of Japanese Finance and Industry*); data also provided by Foreign Capital Research Society, Bank of Japan. Pre-war debts are excluded.

[2] *Economic Survey of Japan, 1954–5*, pp. 176–87, 254–5; *1955–6*, pp. 195–205, Annexe Tables, pp. 72–6.

[3] See Statistical Appendix, p. 197 below.

growing population, a steadily increasing foreign trade will be essential. These questions will be considered at some length in Chapter XI. Here it is desirable to emphasize that in this field Japan is very vulnerable to changes in the outside world. The continued buoyancy of international trade as a whole is for her a lively concern. Besides this, she is closely affected by the commercial policies of her chief-customer countries. Before the war she suffered from restrictions imposed by foreign governments for the protection of their traders and manufacturers against her competition. There are ominous signs of a return to these policies. Japan was admitted into GATT in 1955, but several member countries, including Great Britain, invoked the Article which made it possible for them to discriminate against Japanese imports by means of quantitative restrictions. The United States government, which sponsored Japan's admission, has itself been under pressure from American manufacturers to restrict imports of Japanese textiles and other goods. In order to forestall measures of this sort, the Japanese have resorted, as before the war, to devices for limiting their exports to the American market, in some cases after agreements between the two governments. United States policy has also precluded Japan from essaying the doubtful prospects of trade with Communist China. On the other hand, America has encouraged Japan's participation in schemes for the development of Asia, and Japan is a member of the group of countries involved, as donors, in the Colombo Plan.

The resumption of commercial intercourse was hindered for many years by difficulties in regard to reparations. This problem has at last been solved (for all countries except Indonesia) by the introduction of arrangements which provide for the delivery of Japanese goods over a period of years. For instance, it was agreed that Japan should pay Burma $250 million in the form of machinery, of which the deliveries were to be spread over ten years. Although the payment of reparations is immediately a burden on Japan, ultimately the effect may be to open the way for a much increased Japanese trade with other Asian countries. Thus by the middle 1950's many of the obstacles to the re-emergence of Japan as a great trading nation had been removed, and new paths are now open to her, although some of them will not be easy to tread.

One of the factors that favoured Japan's economic recovery was undoubtedly the removal of the previously heavy burden of defence and armament. In the middle 1930's military and naval expenditure came to over two-fifths of the central government's expenditure, and the proportion increased after 1937.[1] The San Francisco Treaties required Japan to re-establish a limited defence force, but most of the cost was provided by the United States, and in the fiscal year 1955–6 defence expenditure amounted to only about 13 per cent. of the central government's total outlay (about 2·4 per cent. of the national income). Another saving has been effected in the servicing of the public debt, which required only 4·4 per cent. of the total public outlay in 1955–6 compared with about 17 per cent. twenty years ago. The place of armaments and the servicing of debts has been taken largely by grants to local authorities, the cost of social security measures, and subventions for industrial and agricultural development. In 1955–6 social security (social services, education, and pensions) accounted for 35 per cent. of the total expenditure and development grants for nearly 20 per cent.[2] Since part of the grants paid to local authorities were in aid of public enterprises and relief, it follows that most of Japan's public expenditure is now of a kind characteristic of a welfare state. This is symptomatic of a profound change in Japanese society.

An analysis of the composition of Japan's public expenditure is not, of course, sufficient to bring out the importance of the public sector in the Japanese economy nor the burden which that expenditure imposed on the community. In the early 1950's the ratio of the central government's annual expenditure (General Account) to the gross national income was about the same as before the war. Since then it has declined; in 1956–7 it was 14·9 per cent., compared with 16·5 per cent. before the war. If the expenditure included in the Special Accounts for railways, public corporations, Trust Fund Bureau, and food control is added, the ratio is about one-third of the national income. Although the ratio of expenditure has changed but little, since the war the revenue has been raised in very different ways. During the middle 1930's about a third of the public revenue

---

[1] *Economic Survey of Japan, 1955–6*, p. 118.
[2] Ibid. pp. 117–36, Annex Tables, pp. 45–51.

(central government) was obtained by bond issues. Since the war taxation has been relied on to a much greater extent. In 1949–50 the ratio of local and national tax revenue to the gross national income was 28·5 per cent. There has been a gradual fall since then and in 1956–7 it amounted to 19·5 per cent. Compared with pre-war years, a much higher proportion of the tax revenue has been raised by taxes on personal and cor-poration incomes.[1] This is symptomatic of another significant change in Japanese society. In the past the taxation system was very regressive and pressed lightly on the rich and the profit-earner. It was calculated to preserve a very unequal distribu-tion of incomes and to stimulate the accumulation of private capital. The reforms of the early post-war years which de-stroyed many private fortunes, together with the changes in the incidence of taxation, have produced a more equal distribution of income. In the most recent years, however, the reductions in direct taxation have gone some way towards reversing the trend. Japan's economic position is still too precarious, and her need for capital accumulation too great, to permit a whole-hearted pursuit of the ideals of the welfare state.

Trends in the general organization of the economy have been consistent with those in public finance. Some of the immense changes in organization that occurred during the period of the Occupation were imposed deliberately by the Americans. Others were the result of internal factors—the economic dis-location after the war, the long-continued inflation, and the shift in political power within the country. Some of these influences were subsequently removed or weakened. After the end of the Occupation, Japan became actively engaged in establishing, or re-creating, forms of organization considered appropriate to her economic situation. By 1955 her banking and financial system, which was in disorder for many years after the war, had been reconstructed, and displayed many of its former features. Her commercial and industrial organiza-tion, which at one time appeared to have disintegrated, had regained some of its former cohesion. Many of the institutional arrangements introduced during the reform period had been modified. Yet, in treading this 'reverse course' (*Gyaku-kosu*),

[1] *Economic Survey of Japan, 1955–6*, pp. 118–19, 121, 123–4; *Fuji Bank Bulletin*, March 1957, pp. 5, 10.

Japan was by no means returning to a type of economy and society identical with that of pre-war days. Some sections of the old ruling class had gone or had been thrust into sullen obscurity. The working people were less pliable and docile than in the past, and the peasantry, secure in the enjoyment of the fruits of the Land Reform, was in no mood to accept a return to its former inferior economic status. A redistribution of income on a considerable scale had occurred. The rural population had improved its position in relation to the city dwellers. The wealthy and the middle classes had suffered an absolute decline in their standards of life. This decline, which had been brought about initially by the post-war reforms and the inflation, was confirmed by the increased burden of taxes imposed upon them. It is clear that in this new environment the economic institutions of the past, though they may still serve as a basis for new constructions, are unlikely to be suitable in precisely their old forms for handling the issues of the present day. To trace the development of new patterns of organization and systems of economic relations in finance, trade, industry, agriculture, and labour, will be among the leading tasks undertaken in subsequent chapters.

CHAPTER III

The Reconstruction of the Monetary and Banking Systems

FINANCIAL TRENDS

JAPAN's finances during several periods of her modern history have been gravely disordered and her traditional expansionist policy has brought recurrent anxieties about the balance of payments. At the close of the Second World War her finances entered upon the most chaotic period in her modern history and a long struggle was needed before even a modest degree of stability was restored. By the middle 1950's, however, Japan's financial position, though still insecure, was at any rate no more unstable than that of most European countries, and an immeasurable improvement had occurred over the conditions of the early post-war years. In this chapter we shall trace in outline the course of financial events after 1945, and against that background examine the banking system as it emerged from the confusions of war and inflation. In this sector of the economy, as in others, reconstruction in its early stages was powerfully influenced by the ideological promptings of the Occupation authorities. It will be necessary, therefore, to pose the question: to what extent has Occupation policy exercised an enduring effect on the institutional pattern?

The collapse of the Japanese economy in the summer of 1945 was accompanied by a violent inflation which owed its initial impulse to the lavish distribution of funds by the government in settlement of war-expenditure accounts and to the withdrawal of bank deposits. At the beginning of 1946 the index of wholesale prices (1934–6 = 100) had increased to about 800, and prices in the black market had risen even more. In February and March of that year the government made its first attempt to arrest the movement. The outstanding notes of the Bank of Japan were compulsorily exchanged for a new issue, withdrawals from deposit accounts were drastically restricted, and a capital levy was carried out. These measures temporarily checked the rise of prices. But the inflation had been a symptom of a fundamental disequilibrium. Industrial production was at a very low level, and stocks of materials left over from the war were almost exhausted. Meanwhile demand was being increased by the release of purchasing power previously dammed up by wartime controls and by the heavy budgetary deficits which the government, faced by enormous claims for reconstruction finance, could not avoid. The currency reform and the capital levy wiped out past obligations but could not touch the causes of the current *malaise*. So the inflationary trend was soon resumed. By September 1946 the note issue outstanding again rose above its pre-reform peak. It continued to grow rapidly throughout the remainder of 1946 and during the next year. In the course of 1948 the expansion was at a somewhat slower rate. By this time industrial production had achieved some measure of recovery, and American aid made possible the import of large quantities of food and raw materials without taxing domestic resources. Yet the inflation was by no means under control and the note issue and prices still continued their upward course. In March 1949 the amount of bank-notes outstanding was twenty times greater than immediately after the currency reform of March 1946. The index of wholesale prices (1934–6 = 1) increased from 15 in April 1946 to 197 in March 1949, and the rise in retail prices corresponded.[1]

During this first post-war period the government and the central financial authorities supplied funds lavishly to industry both indirectly through the purchase of bank bonds and directly through subsidies. Subsidies paid to producers of basic materials came to 22,500 million yen in 1947, 62,500 million yen in 1948, and 97,900 million yen in 1949.[2] Up to the end of 1946 the Central Bank, which granted credit liberally to the other banks for financing industrial reconstruction, was the chief agent of the inflation. Thereafter the role was assumed by the Reconstruction Finance Bank. This concern was founded in February 1947 to furnish loans for the reconstruction of the 'essential' industries (such as coal, iron and steel, and chemical fertilizers), and it made an important contribution to industrial

---

[1] Tsuru, 'Business Cycles in Post-War Japan', pp. 178 ff., where an outline of these developments is given.

[2] *Fuji Bank Bulletin*, September 1956, p. 5.

recovery. Yet, since the funds it required were obtained by selling its debentures to the Bank of Japan, its operations contributed powerfully to the inflationary pressure of the time. This is not necessarily a condemnation. It may be argued that in the desperate condition of the Japanese economy after the end of the war, a transference of real resources to those who would apply them to rebuilding the country's industries was an overriding necessity and that the method used for this purpose was the only means to hand.

Throughout the period from 1945 to the beginning of 1949 the Japanese economy was insulated from the rest of the world. Foreign trade was strictly controlled, under the supervision of SCAP, and was conducted for the most part by official trade bodies. A multiple-exchange system came into being for these transactions, so that for every commodity dealt in a specific rate was constructed which represented the ratio between the Japanese price and the world price for that commodity. The rates ranged between 100 and 900 yen to the dollar. What the equilibrium rate stood at during this period is a question of only theoretical interest, for Japan's heavy debit balance on current account was met by American aid on a lavish scale. In 1947 and 1948 this aid amounted to $404 million and $461 million, equivalent to 77 per cent. and 68 per cent. respectively of the c.i.f. value of the total commodity imports. Without the aid it would have been impossible for Japan to finance sufficient imports to avoid starvation among her urban population or to restart many of her industries. The disinflationary effect of these aid imports was offset by the disbursement of counterpart funds by the government, chiefly in its subsidies to producers and traders.

The post-war inflation was brought to a sudden end by the effective intervention of the Occupation authorities, who became convinced that financial stability was a prerequisite of industrial recovery. In February 1949 Mr. Joseph Dodge came to Japan as economic adviser to SCAP and, on his advice, a rigorous deflationary policy was imposed on the Japanese government. The measures included the discontinuance of lending by the Reconstruction Finance Bank, the reduction of subsidies and of public expenditure as a whole with the object of producing a large budgetary surplus for the financial year

1949–50, and the establishment of a single exchange rate (360 yen to the dollar). This policy met with some considerable success, but it is evident that the Dodge deflation was less ruthless in practice than in original intention. The Japanese government at this time feared that the deflationary measures advocated by Mr. Dodge were likely to be so severe as to frustrate industrial recovery. So they took steps to mitigate the impact of the deflation on industry. Various means were introduced for this purpose, including the reduction of interest rates, the abolition of excess profits tax on companies, and a legal provision for the revaluation of assets which had the effect of reducing the burden of income tax on business.[1] The government also sought to alleviate the difficulties caused by the cessation of lending by the Reconstruction Finance Bank by continuing to grant loans from the United States Aid Counterpart Fund; while industry, deprived of its chief source of loans, turned increasingly to the commercial banks for accommodation, with the result that loans refused at the front door were generously provided at the back. The outcome of these inconsistent policies was that between March 1949 and June 1950 the note issue remained virtually unchanged, wholesale prices rose slightly, and retail prices actually fell.

The end of the disinflationary period was as sudden as its beginning. Although the budget for 1950–1 again provided for a surplus, the outbreak of the Korean War in June 1950 subjected the economy to the pressure of large new demands. Apart from the 'special procurement' requirements of the United Nations forces, a substantial foreign demand arose for Japanese manufactures. Since imports were strictly controlled, the result was a marked improvement in Japan's balance of payments and at the same time a renewal of the inflation. The Central Bank gave heavy advances to the Foreign Exchange Control Board for the purchase of the incoming foreign exchange and it also increased its credits to the commercial banks which were being called upon to finance the growing volume of trade and production.[2] Towards the end of 1950 the government and Bank tried to check the inflationary pressure by in-

[1] *Survey of Japanese Finance and Industry*, March–April 1955, p. 2.
[2] E. E. Ehrlich and F. M. Tamagna, 'Japan', in B. H. Beckhart, ed., *Banking Systems* (New York, 1954), p. 530.

troducing measures to encourage imports. Then, early in 1951, the Bank raised interest rates and extended its use of selective credit controls. These restraining measures, however, were insufficient to prevent a rise in prices that was very steep even by the standards of the period, and Japanese wholesale prices moved seriously out of line with world prices in the course of the Korean boom.[1] Retail prices and money-wage rates also moved upwards, while profits soared.

The collapse of the war boom in the spring of 1951 led to a decline in the foreign demand for Japanese goods, and later the restrictions imposed on imports into the sterling area brought about a further contraction in exports. 'Special procurement' expenditure, however, still remained at a high level, and for some time industrialists continued to invest heavily in new buildings and equipment. In this policy they were encouraged by the government, which made investment funds available through a number of new financial institutions set up at this time, namely the Japan Development Bank, the Japan Export-Import Bank, and the Long-Term Credit Bank. Heavy borrowing from the commercial banks continued. The result was that the disparity between Japanese and world prices which had appeared during the Korean boom persisted into the subsequent recession. These sudden changes in economic conditions were reflected in the state of Japan's financial reserves. In the period before 1949 United States' aid had been sufficient to enable Japan not only to pay for her imports but also to permit some investment in foreign exchange. The aid came to an end in 1951, but by then 'special procurement', including expenditure by United States' soldiers in Japan, had taken its place as a source of dollars.[2] By the use of these resources Japan was able not only to raise substantially her imports during 1951 and 1952, but also to make large additions to her holdings of foreign currencies. These rose from $260 million in March 1950 to $1,178 million in May 1952.

After the middle of 1952 the financial situation seriously deteriorated. Whereas abroad inflation had been brought

---

[1] Between June 1950 and April 1951 Japan's wholesale prices rose by 52 per cent., American prices by 17 per cent., and British prices by 22 per cent.

[2] For a definition of 'special procurement', see Statistical Appendix, p. 203 n. below.

under control by resort to dear-money policies, in Japan credit was still extended on easy terms. Private industry continued to invest heavily in re-equipment, and in this it was financed by the commercial banks, which in turn were provided with ample credit by the Bank of Japan. An even more important factor was the rise in government spending, especially on equipment for hydro-electric power-stations and other public utilities. Thus another boom was set going by bank-financed industrial investment and by increased government expenditure. Money wages, which had not kept pace with prices or production during 1950 and 1951, now rose faster than either, and domestic consumption expanded accordingly, to the detriment of the export trade. In 1953 these trends persisted, and the divergence between Japanese and world prices grew wider. Although procurement expenditure continued at a high level, the export trade stagnated and an enormous rise in imports led to a large deficit on current trading. A balance-of-payments crisis seemed to be approaching. Between May 1952 and May 1953 the foreign-exchange reserves fell from $1,178 million to $852 million.[1]

The crisis persuaded the government, during the later months of 1953, to introduce a retrenchment policy to correct the imbalance. Its main instrument was not fiscal (although the austerity budget of 1954–5 played its part), but rather monetary policy. Rates of interest were raised in the autumn of 1953 and again in the early months of the next year. In the execution of its lending policy the Bank of Japan henceforward made increasing use of a device that discriminated sharply against large borrowing. It allowed each of its customer banks a basic amount of credit, and varied its rates according to the extent to which the borrowings approached, attained, or exceeded that amount. Since the commercial banks depended on the Central Bank for their resources, and since industry at this time relied mainly on bank loans to finance development, these measures were extremely effective. Equipment investment diminished and stocks were liquidated. In March 1954 wholesale prices, which then stood at 60 per cent. above the level of June 1950, turned downwards. By September they had fallen by 8 per cent., and by the end of the year the disparities be-

[1] *Economic Survey of Japan, 1953–4*, pp. 1–26 and *passim*.

tween foreign and domestic prices had narrowed. As Japan was becoming more competitive at a moment when international trade as a whole was expanding, she was able to increase her exports very substantially and to end the year with a small surplus on her balance of payments. During the next two years her financial achievements were even more impressive. The enlargement of the export trade gave Japan a payments surplus in the financial year 1955–6 of $535 million, about equivalent to her revenue from procurement. For the first time since the war Japan had succeeded in balancing her accounts out of the proceeds of her current trading. Her exchange reserves now reached $1,400 million, a gain of 30 per cent. in the course of the year.

The expansion in 1955 occurred without any rise in prices; indeed, both wholesale and retail prices were lower at the end of the year than at the beginning. This contrast with the conditions of the boom in 1950–1 requires explanation, for, although the improvement started in the export trade, it might have been expected that domestic demand also would have risen as money incomes increased. Several reasons may be suggested. First, Japan entered upon this period with a surplus of industrial capacity, so that there was no immediate need for new domestic fixed investment to enable her to meet the increased foreign demand. Secondly, wage rates remained stable, largely because of the existence of many unemployed (or underemployed) who could be absorbed at the existing levels of money wages. Thirdly, there was an exceptionally good harvest. Finally, domestic demand was damped down by a large increase in savings, both by companies and by individuals, so that it was possible to finance the expansion without resort to bank credit.[1] These conditions were not seriously disturbed in 1956, although, under the impact of the continuing boom, prices moved upwards, bank credit expanded, and the balance of payments deteriorated in the later months of the year.

Thus, after a long period in which recovery in production was associated with inflation and with deficits in the balance of payments, in 1955–6 Japan seemed to have achieved, for the time being at any rate, financial stability without retarding the pace

[1] *Economic Survey of Japan, 1955–6*, pp. 1–23.

of industrial recovery. By then she had acquired substantial foreign-exchange reserves and she had escaped from extreme dependence upon special forms of foreign income, such as aid and procurement, although the latter still continued at a high level. She was beginning to attract foreign investment, and she had resumed, in a modest fashion, her career as an overseas investor. On the other hand, large financial claims were still outstanding against her. A considerable burden of reparations had been assumed. The $2,000 million in aid furnished by the Americans in the early post-war years was technically a loan, and although the amount of the debt will doubtless be scaled down, Japan is hardly likely to be entirely relieved of it. It is probable that the strong impulse of economic ambition, the persistent preoccupation with rapid economic development, will lead Japan from time to time into financial difficulties, as in the past. But, provided that international trade as a whole remains buoyant, these difficulties are not likely to be comparable with those which she has surmounted during the last decade

BANKING

An understanding of the post-war changes in Japan's banking system requires a brief reference to the evolution of that system during the modern era. As in other branches of her national life, Japan built up her financial institutions by the skilful adaptation of Western models to her own needs, an adaptation that called for experiments over many years. In the 1870's she introduced a national banking system on the American pattern, and vestiges of this were long to be found in the names of certain of the banks. Early in the next decade she abandoned the American system in favour of a central banking system of the European type. This occurred with the foundation of the Bank of Japan in 1882, an institution largely government owned and subject to strict control by the Minister of Finance. From then onwards a large number of commercial and savings banks were founded by private interests and these conducted business similar to that of their counterparts overseas. But the government's economic policy required the establishment of other banks with special functions, and before the end of the nineteenth century several banks of this type were created on government initiative.

These included the Yokohama Specie Bank, which conducted most of the foreign-exchange business of the country, the Industrial Bank of Japan formed for the purpose of making long-term loans to industry, the Hypothec Bank, which (together with numerous prefectural Agricultural and Industrial Banks) was intended to provide long-term loans to agriculture, and the Hokkaido Development Bank. Various colonial banks for operating in Korea and Formosa were also established. These Special Banks became important instruments of national policy both in Japan Proper and overseas.[1]

In the commercial banking centres the leading institutions were developed as constituents of the *Zaibatsu*, and neither those banks nor the numerous small banks that served local needs had close relations with the Central Bank. The system, therefore, presented some contradictory features. On the one hand, the existence of a group of Special Banks, over which the government exercised control, pointed to a highly centralized system. On the other hand, the commercial banks were unco-ordinated and far from responsive in their credit policy to leads given by the Central Bank.

The number of ordinary banks continued to increase until the end of the First World War and in the early months of 1920 there were nearly 2,000 of them. During the inter-war period a process of consolidation set in. A succession of financial crises, notably those of 1920 and 1927, led to the disappearance of many independent local banks by bankruptcy or absorption. The government actively encouraged amalgamations, especially during the 1930's, in the interests of financial stability and in order to secure a more highly centralized control over the creation of credit. By 1929 the number of separate banks had fallen to 874 and by 1937 to 377. Seven of these banks, with their branches, were of outstanding importance. By the end of the 1930's they were together responsible for nearly three-fifths of the deposits and for nearly two-thirds of the loans, discounts, and advances of all the ordinary banks.[2] With one exception,

---

[1] A useful account of the development and operation of the banking system in the Meiji period is given in United States Monetary Commission (1910), *Reports*, vol. xviii; see also United States Department of Commerce, *Japanese Banking*, by H. M. Bratter (Washington, 1931), and Allen, *Short Economic History*, chs. iii, vi, and ix.

[2] Ehrlich and Tamagna, in Beckhart, *Banking Systems*, p. 538.

these great banks were controlled by the *Zaibatsu*. The same
interests dominated the trust companies which held substantial
deposits, and also the chief insurance companies. In addition
to these institutions, the Japanese financial system included
many savings banks. Like the ordinary banks, these also were
reduced in number as the result of amalgamations during the
inter-war years—from 648 in 1913 to 72 in 1937. The needs of
small producers and traders were served by various types of
co-operative credit banks which were co-ordinated by a central
institution. Mutual loan companies of a type traditional to
Japan also flourished. Finally, the Deposits Bureau of the
Ministry of Finance and Post Office Insurance Authority
secured an important place in the financial system. They collected savings and premiums from the people and invested
mainly in government securities and in the debentures issued
by the Special Banks.[1]

The movement towards consolidation had created a more
stable financial structure, but it had failed to bring about fundamental changes in the character of the banking system, which
was still composed of distinct groups of banks with slender links
between them. The Bank of Japan's position remained much
weaker than that of central banks in the chief Western countries. It grew up as an institution for issuing currency, the conduct of the government's financial business, and for providing
cheap finance to the Special Banks, notably the Yokohama
Specie Bank. Yet, although it was called upon to lend lavishly
to the commercial banks in times of emergency, its control over
their credit policy remained weak. The Bank did not hold the
reserves of the ordinary banks and its rate was not a determining
one. Indeed, the leading commercial banks were members of
great economic empires and their ample resources permitted
them to maintain their independence of the Central Bank's
policy.

Throughout its history the Bank of Japan had been expected
to lend financial help to the government in times of difficulty,
and when Takahashi's reflation policy began in 1932, it was
required to issue and later to absorb large quantities of government bonds. This, as a Japanese banker declared, marked 'the
beginning of the role of the Bank of Japan as a supplier of

[1] Ehrlich and Tamagna, in Beckhart, *Banking Systems*, p. 545.

unlimited credit to the government'.[1] Nevertheless, in the Takahashi period, although the government was bent on reflation, the ordinary banks preferred to pursue a different policy and were sufficiently independent to do so. They refrained from creating private credit to match that of the government and its institutions. In fact, they reduced their loans to industry and trade. This damped down the inflationary effect of the deficit financing of the period.

Many of the peculiar features of Japan's banking system are to be explained by the absence of well developed capital and money markets. No large class of private investor in industrial securities existed in Japan. Personal savings normally went into fixed-deposit accounts in the commercial banks or into the Deposits Bureau of the Ministry of Finance. The city banks belonging to the *Zaibatsu* held a key position in the several groups and through them the *Zaibatsu* were freed from dependence upon sources of capital supply external to their own organizations. The smaller banks still financed local traders and producers, although by the middle 1930's this function was being increasingly assumed by the *Zaibatsu* trading companies.

In both classes of ordinary banks the resources provided to industry took the form of advances on promissory notes and the purchase of debentures. The *Zaibatsu* banks were accustomed to make large advances to the holding companies at the centre of each *Zaibatsu* empire to enable them to acquire shares in subsidiary or affiliated companies. All the Japanese commercial banks differed from those of England in regard to the structure both of their assets and of their liabilities. A high proportion of their deposits (normally about 60 per cent.) consisted of time deposits, and they furnished long-term as well as short-term loans to industry. The Special Banks, for their part, operated in a number of distinct fields. The Yokohama Specie Bank had the right of borrowing from the Central Bank on favourable terms, but it established only slender links with the commercial banks concerned primarily with domestic finance. The Industrial and the Hypothec Banks raised resources for long-term loans to industry, agriculture, and public utilities by issuing debentures which were largely taken up by other financial

[1] S. Horie, *Banking System and Bank Liquidity in Japan* (Tokyo, 1952), p. 5.

institutions closely connected with the government. The government itself relied to a considerable extent for long- and short-term financing on the Treasury Deposits Bureau and the savings banks as well as on the Bank of Japan.[1] In the absence of a well organized discount market to serve as a link between the operations of the various types of banks, authority over the system remained diffused.

The necessities of wartime finance caused fundamental changes in the banking structure and a more highly centralized control over the operation of the whole system was imposed. After 1937 vast quantities of government bonds were issued to cover budgetary deficits and the Central Bank itself invested heavily in them. At the same time its influence over the policy of the other banks was extended. During the first few years of the war the main instrument for industrial financing was the Industrial Bank of Japan. The government guaranteed this Bank against losses that might arise from advances to the munitions industries and raised the upper limit on its debenture issues. Then, in 1942 the government set up a new institution, the Wartime Finance Bank, with the special function of financing the worst risks in the munitions trades. Like the Industrial Bank this institution obtained its funds by issuing debentures guaranteed by the government. These were taken up mainly by the ordinary banks. Other official organs were founded for financing enterprises in territories overseas. During this period the commercial banks were subjected to strict official control, and their business was governed largely by the provision of government guarantees on their advances to the 'essential' industries. As the various *Zaibatsu* played a leading part in the expansion of war production, their banks became especially heavily committed in that field.

The government's influence was used in promoting further bank amalgamations, for it was realized that with a more highly concentrated system, central control could be the more easily exercised. The result was that by the end of the war the number of commercial banks had been reduced to sixty-one. Savings banks as distinct institutions almost disappeared. This occurred because the government, in order to increase savings, authorized the ordinary banks to establish savings departments.

---

[1] Bank of Japan, *Outline of the Financial System in Japan* (Tokyo, 1953), pp. 2-4.

Thereupon savings banks were merged with the other banks and by the end of the war only four survived. Shortly afterwards even these were turned into ordinary banks. The largest of them became the Kyowa Bank, one of the major post-war banks. In the same way and for similar reasons the various trust companies were absorbed during the war by the *Zaibatsu* banks to which they were related. What in effect had happened was that the enforcement by the government of a cheap-money policy and the overwhelming predominance of government bonds and officially guaranteed advances in the assets of the banking system as a whole destroyed the previous distinctions between the commercial banks, savings banks, and trust companies. The post-war inflation, which made the collection of savings deposits impossible for several years, confirmed the change brought about by the war.[1]

In the rest of the banking system post-war conditions were affected not only by the continuing inflation but also by the policy of the Occupation authorities. These authorities, at any rate during the early period of reform, were intent at once upon destroying the economic power concentrated in the *Zaibatsu* and also upon loosening State control over economic processes. In the pursuit of their first aim they insisted upon the separation of the *Zaibatsu* banks from other undertakings within the same group. Their determination to put an end to the former integration of finance and industry showed itself in their requirement that even the names of the banks should be changed so as to evoke no echo of the past. The Special Banks, which could be regarded as the financial instruments of Japan's imperialist policy, underwent an equally impressive transformation. Those which had operated in the colonies or overseas, including the Bank of Chosen and the Bank of Taiwan, were immediately closed, and the Yokohama Specie Bank came to an end in 1946. In their policy towards the three debenture-issuing Special Banks [2] the Occupation authorities were moved not only by a desire to democratize Japanese institutions, but also by a

---

[1] Data for post-war financial developments from Horie, *Banking System, passim*; Bank of Japan, *Outline of the Financial System*, pp. 4–23; *Survey of Japanese Finance and Industry*, March–April 1955, pp. 1–9; Ehrlich and Tamagna, in Beckhart, *Banking Systems*; and personal inquiries.

[2] Namely, the Industrial Bank of Japan, the Hypothec Bank, and the Hokkaido Development Bank.

respect for orthodox banking principles. These had been offended because, just as the ordinary banks appeared to have been all too ready to sacrifice liquidity to profitability, the banks designed for long-term lending operations attempted to increase their resources by accepting deposits on a large scale. The Special Banks, therefore, were presented with a choice which required them to confine their activities either to deposit banking, thereby surrendering their rights of issuing debentures, or to long-term financing with strict limits on the amount of deposits that they might accept. The Hypothec Bank and the Hokkaido Development Bank chose the former career, the Industrial Bank the latter.

This, however, was by no means the end of the story. The privilege of issuing debentures was of little value during the years of violent inflation when the provision of long-term loans for reconstruction was taken over by the Reconstruction Finance Bank, which obtained its resources from the Bank of Japan. With the introduction of the Dodge deflation and the abolition of the Reconstruction Finance Bank in 1949, opportunities for the operation of the debenture-issuing banks again appeared. It is true that the legal distinction between those banks and the ordinary banks was destroyed in 1950 when all banks were given the right of issuing debentures within certain limits. In practice, however, the privilege was exercised only by three of the former Special Banks, and by them only because the government subscribed to their stocks and debentures from the United States Aid Counterpart Fund and from the Treasury Deposits Bureau. Finally, by a law of 1952, the debenture-issuing privilege was withdrawn from the ordinary banks. The Industrial Bank and a new institution called the Long-term Credit Bank of Japan became specialized debenture-issuing banks for supplying industry with long-term loans, while the Hypothec Bank and the Hokkaido Development Bank remained as deposit banks. By such devious courses Japan returned to a position which had been characteristic of this sector of her finances for many decades.

The same train of events can be perceived in the field of foreign exchange. The abolition of the Yokohama Specie Bank in 1946 transferred most of the responsibility for foreign-exchange transactions to the government and the Bank of

Japan, although a number of leading commercial banks together with branches of foreign banks were authorized, as before the war, to engage in exchange business. Among these banks was the Bank of Tokyo, which had inherited the properties of the Yokohama Specie Bank and carried on business as an ordinary bank with a foreign-exchange department. As long as foreign financial transactions other than official transactions were few and were subject to close government regulation, the risks attendant upon foreign-exchange business were inconsiderable. But as Japan's international business recovered and as controls were lifted, the banking system felt the lack of the former specialized exchange institution. The ordinary commercial banks were preoccupied with domestic trade and could command neither the liquid resources nor the expertise and overseas organization adequate for the foreign-exchange business. A specialized bank, it was believed, would alone be able to operate on a sufficient scale for efficiency and to win confidence in foreign financial centres. Such a bank, as in the past, might be expected to play a part in bringing in short funds for financing foreign trade by borrowing in markets where rates of interest were low. In April 1954, therefore, the Bank of Tokyo was transformed into a specialist foreign-exchange bank by a law passed for that purpose.[1] Since then the Bank has operated under a licence granted by the Minister of Finance and has acted, like its predecessor the Yokohama Specie Bank, as an agent for the government and the Bank of Japan; in this capacity it has held part of the foreign-exchange reserves. In legal form the Bank of Tokyo is rather more independent of government control than its predecessor and it has not inherited all the privileges of the old Bank. Yet, in its actual operations, it is not likely to be significantly different. Here also policy, and the pressure of economic circumstances, have restored a feature of the pre-war banking system which the Occupation destroyed.

The exceptional circumstances of the post-war years compelled the State to undertake new financial functions beyond the diminished sphere of the Special Banks, and a number of institutions, owned and directly operated by the government, were established for this purpose. They included the Japan

[1] *Announcement* by Bank of Tokyo, 1 July, 1954, and *Semi-Annual Reports*; also *Oriental Economist*, July 1954, pp. 342–3.

Export–Import Bank for extending loans in connexion with the export trade, the Japan Development Bank for lending long term at low rates of interest to the basic industries, the Agricultural, Forestry, and Fisheries Finance Corporation for similar operations in the industries described in its title, the Small Business Finance Corporation for long-term lending to small and medium-sized firms, and several others. These banks differed from one another in practical importance. For example, while the Export–Import Bank has had a modest role, the Japan Development Bank has been active in directing government funds into large capital projects in the iron and steel and electricity industries. Thus, the old semi-official or Special Banks for long-term lending have been supplemented by a number of purely official banks with similar functions. It is evident that SCAP's policy of fostering the decentralization of financial control and of developing a securities market to promote a wide diffusion of industrial capital has foundered. The reasons are clear. The shape of Japan's pre-war financial structure was determined by her policy of accelerating industrial growth in an economy where capital was very scarce. These conditions were present in an exaggerated degree after the war, and the justification of the former structure seems to be at least as firmly established as in earlier times.

The succession of changes among the ordinary or commercial banks supports this view. Immediately after the war those banks found themselves gravely weakened. A high proportion of their assets consisted of wartime advances to industry which had been guaranteed by the government. The collapse of production in 1945 and the cancellation of the government's guarantees left them with meagre resources. The *Zaibatsu* banks which had been especially deeply committed were in an even weaker position than the provincial banks. The dissolution policy dealt them a further blow. Thus it was that in the financing of reconstruction in the early post-war years the main responsibilities were assumed by the government and its financial agencies, such as the Reconstruction Finance Bank and the Bank of Japan. After the application of the Dodge policy the commercial banks were called upon to assume the main burden of financing reconstruction. Yet since their resources were exiguous, they could meet the demand for loans only by borrowing heavily from the Central Bank. A Japanese banker himself declared that 'the commercial banks in the early 1950's became merely a channel through which the Central Bank fed industry with investment funds'.[1] The extent to which industry relied upon the banking system for new capital in this period can be illustrated by a few figures. It is estimated that before the war about 45 per cent. of new industrial investment by companies was provided by self-financing, while about 30 per cent. came from share and bond issues. In 1950–2 the proportion of investment funds provided by self-financing (retained profits and provision for depreciation) was in the neighbourhood of 20–25 per cent., while share and bond issues accounted for only 10 or 12 per cent. and direct loans from the government for 7 or 8 per cent. So the major part of the capital required (about 60 per cent.) came from bank advances. In 1953 the proportion diminished, but it was still about 50 per cent.[2]

The result was to confer a large measure of control over industrial policy upon the banking system, and ultimately upon the Bank of Japan. The Central Bank's former position of exceptional weakness had been transformed into one of power. This position was vividly demonstrated upon the introduction of the deflationary policy of 1954. Industrial companies then found themselves at the mercy of their creditor banks, to whose recommendations for retrenchment or reorganization they had perforce to conform. The creditor banks for their part found their policy dictated by the central authorities. Despite the efforts of SCAP to decentralize power in the Japanese economy, by that time financial control had become more highly concentrated than ever before.

Yet in the middle 1950's the trend changed. Deflation and austerity in 1954 removed the bad risks, promoted efficiency in industry, and prepared the way for the rapid expansion of the next two years. As industrial profits rose, dependence upon bank loans decreased, especially since the expansion in production was accomplished without much new investment. The commercial banks in turn became less dependent upon the

---

[1] Horie, *Banking System*, p. 36.

[2] Data from Industrial Bank of Japan; see also *Economic Survey of Japan, 1953–4*, p. 184; Ministry of Finance, *General Survey of the Japanese Economy* (Tokyo, 1953), Attached Tables, p. 34.

Bank of Japan. Indeed, they were able greatly to reduce their outstanding indebtedness. A result of this change was to bring down the loans of the Central Bank from nearly 300,000 million yen in December 1953 to 27,000 million yen in March 1956.[1] The Bank's note issue also fell substantially. At the same time, the old *Zaibatsu* banks drew closer to their former associates in industry and trade, and as the pattern of economic organization was restored, the practice of self-financing by each of the groups tended to return. The lessened dependence of the commercial banks upon the Bank of Japan put an end to the latter's financial ascendancy and a banking situation in many respects comparable with that before the war was re-established. As a Japanese commentator remarked: 'the redemption of Bank of Japan loans by almost all city banks resulted in the fact that the Bank of Japan lost its power of regulating finance as a central bank'.[2]

This loss of control had important consequences. The increased liquidity of the banking system during 1955 led to a fall in the interest rates of commercial banks from the high levels at which they had stood in the preceding year and, as the boom developed, the loans of those banks to trade and industry again started to rise. The Central Bank tried to check this movement by open-market operations which it began in the autumn of the same year. This evidently had some effect on the liquidity of the commercial banks since in the first half of 1956 they again began to borrow from the Bank of Japan. Later in that year the Bank raised its rates on loans in excess of the basic credit laid down for each of its customers, but this apparently failed to check the extension of credit by the commercial banks. Whether the financial situation had become dangerous by the early months of 1957 is a matter of controversy which time will resolve. From the standpoint of the present survey, this course of events in the Japanese banking world after 1955 is significant because it reveals the growing strength of the commercial banks *vis-à-vis* the central monetary authorities. The problem of how adequate control is to be exercised has thus

---

[1] Bank of Japan, *Economic Statistics Monthly*; also *Fuji Bank Bulletin*, September 1956, pp. 51–52, 63.

[2] 'Economic Conditions in Japan', *Sumitomo Bank Review*, July 1956, p. 7. Cf. also International Monetary Fund, *Annual Report, 1956*, p. 77.

come to the forefront of discussion. It has been suggested that the Bank of Japan should resort to open-market operations on a large scale whenever it is necessary to reduce the liquidity of the system and that a reserve system should be introduced by which the commercial banks would be obliged to keep their reserves with the Central Bank. A Commission has been appointed by the government to inquire into these questions.

After the violent changes of the war and Occupation periods Japan's banking system would seem by the middle 1950's to have largely regained its pre-war shape, and many of the old problems had re-emerged. Although some of the former Special Banks had disappeared, others had been reconstructed and new institutions with broadly similar functions had been founded. For example, the Special Banks concerned with long-term loans were supplemented by purely government institutions designed for the same type of business, while the Yokohama Specie Bank was reborn as the Bank of Tokyo. The private savings banks have disappeared as specialist institutions, but the Treasury Deposits Bureau [1] now plays the same role as in earlier days. The commercial banks, as formerly, fall into two groups, the city banks and the provincial banks, and a few in the former class predominate. In 1954 there were 79 commercial banks with over 5,000 branches. Of these 11 banks were outstanding. They consisted of the pre-war 'Big Seven' (reduced to six by an amalgamation), together with the Kyowa Bank (formerly a savings bank), the Bank of Tokyo (then on the point of being transformed into an exchange bank), and three of the largest provincial banks. Together this group was responsible for nearly three-fifths of the deposits of all the ordinary banks and for well over half the advances. By 1955–6 the largest of the banks had released themselves from extreme dependence on the Central Bank and had again linked themselves with the great industrial and commercial groups then being rebuilt. After a period in which the Bank of Japan was, apart from the government, almost the only source of loanable funds and had consequently acquired great influence over the whole system, the country's rapid economic recovery brought a profound change in financial circumstances and revived the old problem of how

[1] Re-named, in 1951, the Trust Fund Bureau.

the Central Bank was to maintain an adequate measure of control over the system.

Post-war reforms were accompanied by changes in the legal status of the several banks. Before the war the ordinary banks were regulated by an Act of 1927 which gave the Minister of Finance certain powers of supervision. The Special Banks, which had been established by *ad hoc* legislation, were subject to a large measure of official control and their chief officers were appointed by the government. The Bank of Japan operated under a Charter from the Crown and the majority of its shares were held by the government, which appointed its chief executives. During the war the Minister of Finance exercised a strict and detailed control over the banking system as a whole, but after 1945 this was gradually relaxed. The commercial banks largely reverted to their previous legal position in regard to government supervision. The Bank of Japan was affected by a succession of changes in the machinery by which its policy was determined. For instance, in 1949 the form of administration and control introduced during the war was replaced by a Policy Board with authority over monetary and credit policies. This body, which included among its members officials of the ordinary banks, the Cabinet Office representatives, and the Bank's own executives, operated to qualify the power of the Minister of Finance over the Bank as well as the authority of the Governor himself. In 1954, however, this Board was abolished and the former authority of the Minister of Finance was restored. These legal changes are of interest in showing the extent to which in this sphere as in others Japan is following a 'reverse course'. They also reflect the sharp conflicts of opinion that have arisen during the last few years over financial policy and over the question of where authority shall rest.

CHAPTER IV

Agriculture, Forestry, and the Fisheries

AGRICULTURE

JAPAN's economic progress in the modern era is commonly associated with the rise of industry and the appearance of a large foreign trade in manufactured and semi-manufactured products. Yet, as in other countries that have passed through an industrial revolution, the growth of the secondary industries was accompanied by far-reaching changes in agriculture. The nature of the industrial development cannot be understood without reference to these changes, since the present condition of manufacturing trades, their organization, the structure of wages, and the pattern of industrial relations, has been powerfully influenced by the circumstances of the rural economy.

We are here concerned only to depict the outstanding changes in agriculture since the Second World War, but we must permit ourselves a glance at the history of earlier times if we are fully to appreciate the most recent trends. The post-Restoration settlement, while it destroyed the feudal relationships and obligations of the Tokugawa régime, left intact the structure of agriculture and even the position of many of the peasants in relation to that of the landlord. As a result of the settlement, the ownership of the land became vested in those who had formerly paid tribute in kind (rice) to the feudal lords and were now required to pay a land tax in cash to the national government. Some of them were working farmers who now became peasant proprietors, but others were landlords who derived their income (or part of it) from rice rents received from their tenants. The inflation of the 1870's led to a redistribution of income in favour of these landlords, since their tax was fixed in terms of money at a time when the value of their rice rents rose steeply. The landlords applied this surplus income partly to investment in industry and trade and partly to the purchase of additional land and to the financing of their tenants. Throughout the modern era, and especially during periods of agricultural depression, the proportion of the arable land held on tenancies increased. By 1936 this proportion amounted to 46 per cent. of the total arable area. At that time 31 per cent. of all farm households consisted of peasant proprietors, 42 per cent. of farmers who leased some of their land from landlords and owned the rest, and 27 per cent. of tenant farmers pure and simple.[1] It is estimated that before the war the tenant paid on an average about two-fifths of the value of his products to the landlord in rent. This was a high rental, for the tenant himself provided the farmhouse, equipment, seed, livestock, and fertilizers. He enjoyed little security of tenure. He commonly rented small and scattered patches of land, sometimes from more than one landlord, and the landlord had the legal right of recovering possession without compensation, although in practice the harshness of the law was mitigated by custom or agreement.[2]

The typical Japanese landlord was a person of importance in the rural communities and up to the World Depression of the early 1930's his economic strength was growing. But he was not a large landowner in the sense in which that term is understood in Western countries. Before the war there were nearly a million landlords who were classed as 'absentee' or 'non-cultivating resident' owners. Only a quarter of these non-working landlords had more than three *chobu* of land (i.e. about 7·4 acres), and many of them owned less than 1 *chobu*. Landlords with over 50 *chobu* (120 acres) counted as large. There were only 3,000 in this class, the majority of them in Northern Japan.[3] Most landlords had interests and occupations outside agriculture. In early Meiji times they were a source of capital for new industries. In more recent times professional, military, and commercial people found land a safe and profitable investment and a considerable proportion of the small landowners were men of this type. Many of the larger landowners had extensive interests in commerce, mining, and manufacturing industry.

---

[1] S. Wakukawa, 'The Japanese Farm Tenancy System', in D. G. Haring, ed., *Japan's Prospect* (Cambridge, Mass., Harvard University Press, 1946), p. 116.

[2] Ibid. pp. 141 ff.; Y. Kondo, *The Land Reform in Japan* (Tokyo, 1952), pp. 2–9.

[3] Kondo, *Land Reform*, p. 17; N. Danno, *Japanese Agriculture Since the Post-War Agricultural Reform* (Japan Institute of Pacific Relations, 1954), pp. 4–5; also Ministry of Agriculture and Forestry, *Statistical Abstracts* (various years).

The holdings of the peasants, like the estates of the landlords, were very small. In 1936 nearly half of them were less than 0·5 *chobu* in area and 94 per cent. were under 3 *chobu*. A typical peasant with about 1 *chobu* held his arable land in about 20 small parcels. The chief crop was rice which occupied over 56 per cent. of all cultivated land. Much of this rice land carried a second crop—wheat, barley, or roots—and the upland farms bore crops of grain, vegetables, fruit, or mulberry trees. The rice yield per acre was one of the highest in the world, but this achievement required intensive manual labour, with very little help from machines or draught animals, so that the yield per person employed was very low. Japan's industrial and commercial development had not succeeded in relieving the rural over-population from which the country had long suffered.

The relation of agriculture to the growth of population must be examined further. At the time of the Restoration Japan's population was roughly about 30 millions. The number of agricultural households, it is estimated, was about 5½ million, with 14¾ million agricultural workers, nearly four-fifths of the total working population. Between then and the outbreak of the Second World War, a period in which Japan's population more than doubled, the relative importance of agriculture in the economy steadily declined. By 1930 the proportion of those engaged in agriculture to total employed manpower had fallen to 48 per cent. and by 1940 to 41 per cent.[1] Yet, in spite of this relative decline, the absolute size of the agricultural population hardly changed at all. The area of arable land also increased comparatively little. From early Meiji until the eve of the Second World War the area under rice rose by only about 20 per cent. Output, on the other hand, greatly expanded. The yield of rice per acre nearly doubled and that of other crops rose even more.[2] This increase in yields was brought about mainly by improvements in strains and by the heavy application of fertilizers. Japanese agriculture by these means succeeded to a large extent in keeping pace, in its food production,

[1] Kondo, *Land Reform*, p. 12.

[2] Statistical Section, Dept. of Agriculture and Forestry, *Statistics of Rice*, quoted in R. Ishii, *Population Pressure and Economic Life in Japan* (London, King, 1937), p. 165; Schumpeter, *Industrialization*, pp. 116–53, and Danno, *Japanese Agriculture*, p. 9.

with the growth of population; during the 1930's only about a fifth of the rice required had to be imported.

These increases in the productivity of the land were not unconnected with the modernization of Japan and the progress of her industry and commerce. Foreign trade gave her access to fertilizers, soya beans from Manchuria, phosphates from the South Seas, and ammonium sulphate from the West. After the First World War the expansion of her own chemical industry provided a local supply of ammonium sulphate. Agricultural research was fostered by the State and resulted in improvements in methods of cultivation and in strains of crops. Finally, easier communications by land and sea reduced the cost of marketing the produce and made possible the conversion of land to its most profitable uses. The progress in other branches of the economy brought new sources of income for farm households. The peasants had long engaged in many by-employments—fishing, handicrafts, and silk raising. Their opportunities were enlarged by the growth of the domestic market and by the appearance of an export demand for agricultural products. The rise in the foreign demand for raw silk was especially important. By the 1930's two-fifths of the farming families raised silk-worms. Family incomes could also be supplemented by employment in industrial establishments. The cotton mills and the silk-reeling mills were staffed by the daughters of the farmers, and male members of the families found temporary or seasonal work in numerous small firms. These non-agricultural sources of income enabled the Japanese farmers to share in some degree in the rise in the national income per head that accompanied Japan's modernization. Even so they could not completely offset the results of chronic under-employment characteristic of peasant communities in densely populated Eastern countries.

It is clear that throughout Japan's modern era agricultural and industrial developments were organically connected. In particular, the rural areas supplied a constant flow of workers not only for the factories but also for the multitude of small establishments in manufactures and commerce. The presence of this reservoir of labour had a profound effect on the form of Japan's institutions. As long as the flow continued there could be little hope of a flourishing trade union movement and the low incomes earned in agriculture exerted a drag on industrial wages. The close personal ties existing between farming families and a large part of the industrial labour force produced a social situation that was unsympathetic to the appearance of official systems of social insurance. In periods of bad trade, urban workers flocked back to their rural families, and thereby relieved both State and industry of responsibility for their maintenance. The farmers thus carried the burden of industrial depressions. But they did not carry it in silence. During the 1920's tenant farmers' associations grew in number and strength and became increasingly involved in disputes with landlords over rents and security of tenure. When Japan felt the impact of the World Depression, the causes of dissatisfaction were augmented, for not only were the farmers forced to shoulder part of the burden of maintaining the industrial unemployed but the incomes from the land also declined. Finally, the collapse of raw-silk prices brought distress to millions. Rural discontent found expression in 'fascist' political movements, and these helped to overthrow parliamentary government and to produce the revival of militant nationalism which ultimately carried Japan into the Second World War.

During the 1930's Western observers of Japan, conscious of the increasing rigidities of their own society, often commented with approval on the resilience shown by the Japanese in adapting their economy to changes in market conditions. This adaptability was, indeed, a source of strength to the country in meeting the stresses of the World Depression; but it was, in large measure, associated with the desperate search for employment on the part of the surplus rural population and the weakness of the workers' bargaining power *vis-à-vis* their employers. It may be argued that the Japanese peasant was far better off than his counterpart in the rest of Asia and that until the early 1930's his standard of life had improved. This argument, however, was unlikely to impress the countryman who had become conscious that he had been asked to bear a disproportionate share of the fiscal burden in the past, just as recently he had been required to take the strain of the industrial depression. His anger was, therefore, directed against his rulers whose policies had produced these hardships, and especially against the industrial capitalists who seemed to him to have reaped the chief rewards of economic progress. He looked to the military, also rivals of the industrialists, to rescue him from his plight.

The Occupation authorities in 1945 were right in thinking that an impoverished peasantry would be a source of revolutionary sentiment likely to retard democratic advance and to lead to a revival of militarism. The virtual destruction of the landlords and the conversion of tenancies into peasant proprietorships, perhaps the most remarkable and enduring achievement of the Occupation, depended for their justification on that premiss. Yet a change in the system of land tenure, important though it might be both politically and economically, could not of itself solve the fundamental problems of the Japanese farming communities. Those problems were rooted in the continuing abundance of the working population in relation to other resources. In the end a solution can come only by an increase in opportunities for remunerative employment in industry and commerce, an increase that depends mainly on the growth of capital and on industrial enterprise.

Even before the war the Japanese government had taken tentative steps towards reforming the system of landholding which the activities of the tenants' associations had shaken but not seriously disturbed. From 1922 there were arrangements for granting, from the Post Office Insurance Deposits Bureau, loans at low rates of interest to tenant farmers who wished to buy their land. The Agricultural Land Adjustment Act of 1938 was a more serious attempt to assist tenants by giving them a greater security of tenure, and land commissions were set up with powers to reduce rents considered exorbitant. The results of these measures were meagre and it was not until the Second World War that the structure of the rural economy was modified. Then a new era in the country's agricultural life began. An outstanding change of the war years was the redistribution of farm income between tenant and landlord. The Staple Food Administration Law of 1942 enforced the substitution of money rents for rents in kind and fixed the former at levels which, as inflation proceeded, bore little relation to the official price at which the authorities bought rice from the growers. The result was that the proportion of rent to gross farm income declined from 40 per cent. before the war to about 10 per cent. in 1945.[1]

[1] Kondo, *Land Reform*, p. 20.

Immediately the war was over the landlords sought to compensate themselves by trying to dispossess their tenants so that they might cultivate the land themselves. These attempts were soon frustrated by the land reforms introduced by the Occupation authorities. It is, however, worth observing that SCAP's policy can be regarded as having confirmed and carried further a tendency towards the elimination of the landlords which wartime policy had set in train.

Before the end of 1945 the Japanese government was ordered to introduce measures for the conversion of tenants into peasant proprietors, and ultimately the policy received expression in the Owner-Farmer Establishment Law of 1946. This provided for the complete dispossession of absentee landlords and for the retention by other owners of tenanted land of only 1 *chobu* of cultivable land in Honshu, Shikoku, and Kyushu, and only 4 *chobu* in Hokkaido, while the holdings of owner-occupiers were limited to an average of 3 *chobu* in the three main islands and 12 in Hokkaido. Farmland in excess of these limits was to be purchased by the government and resold to 'eligible' farmers at prices based on the rental value of the land as registered at the tax offices.[1] Over 11,000 local land commissions composed of tenants, owners, and owner-cultivators, in the ratio of 5, 3, and 2, were set up to administer the Law under the supervision of prefectural and national authorities. Land purchased by tenants under this scheme was not to be resold for thirty years, except with special official authorization. The programme was to be carried out within two years. In 1947 pasture land was brought within the ambit of the reform.

This vast and complicated transaction was almost completed by the end of 1949. By June 1952 the government had acquired nearly 2 million *chobu* of cultivated land and 450,000 *chobu* of pasturage and had resold most of this to the former tenants. By this process the proportion of the land farmed by tenants to the total cultivated area had been reduced from 46 per cent. to about 8 per cent.[2] Japan had become a land of peasant proprietors. This transformation, though it depended initially on

---

[1] Cohen, *Japan's Economy*, pp. 442–7; Kondo, *Land Reform*, pp. 21–25; Japan FAO Association, *Agriculture in Japan* (Tokyo, 1953), pp. 34–37. The tenants engaged in cultivating the land had priority rights of purchase.

[2] Kondo, *Land Reform*, pp. 25–27.

the determination of the Occupation authorities, could scarcely have been accomplished so speedily without the co-operation of the Japanese themselves, who, of course, were responsible for detailed administration. This suggests that the measure was gratefully received not only by the tenants but also by the nation as a whole. The reform, though proceeding from the edict of a conqueror, will be difficult to reverse, for the new peasantry is a political force of great influence.

The Law provided for what seemed at the time to be reasonable compensation for the landlords. The violent inflation which coincided with these transactions, however, meant that the landlords were expropriated. As we have seen, few of them owned large estates. Most of them, while well off compared with their tenants, enjoyed only a modest competence of which they had now been deprived. It is true that this class was conservative in temper and during the 1930's had been closely linked with those responsible for Japan's military adventures. It may be argued also that most of the landlords had become economically functionless. In early Meiji they had taken the lead in fostering new agricultural methods as well as in financing local industries, but by the Showa era these activities had been largely assumed by officially appointed bodies or by co-operative associations among the working farmers. Finally, there is no doubt that the Land Reform was politically expedient, since it helped to damp down revolutionary sentiment among the peasants and to remove a source of unrest that might have shaken the stability of the Japanese government and so weakened the American strategic position in the Far East. Yet it is ironical that the dispossession of a rural middle class should have been undertaken at the behest of the government of a country that asserts so vigorously the rights of private property. Doubtless the emotive power of the term 'feudal', as commonly applied to traditional Japanese institutions, helped to remove any uneasiness among the American authorities about the results of their own actions in this field.

The transformation of the system of land tenure was by no means the only factor that affected Japanese agriculture in the post-war period, and in describing and interpreting the contrasts between the pre-war and the post-war agricultural situation, we must have regard to other changes also. Indeed the

.causes of some developments that are commonly ascribed to the Reform are to be found elsewhere.

During the war agriculture lost manpower to the armed forces and to the munitions trades, and its output was affected by a shortage of chemical fertilizers and the diversion of arable land to non-agricultural uses. It was possible to replace chemical by natural fertilizers to a considerable extent, but only at the cost of additional effort on the part of the farmers. This intensified the shortage of workers, a shortage that could not be relieved by mechanization, as happened in England; for towards the end of the war even the simple implements normally used by Japanese farmers were hard to come by. The result was a considerable decline, especially after 1942, in agricultural efficiency and output. In 1944 the index of agricultural production (1933–5 = 100) stood at 77·6 compared with 110·6 in 1937. This steep decline was accompanied by changes in the structure of production. Policy was directed towards maintaining the output of the staple foodstuffs, and much land was accordingly diverted from industrial crops and from uses considered inessential in wartime. While the total cultivated area fell by about 3 per cent. between 1937 and 1944, the area planted with the major food crops (rice, wheat, barley, sweet and Irish potatoes) rose slightly, and the output of those crops taken together was maintained up to 1944 at about the same level as before the war.[1] On the other hand, there was a steep decline in the production of minor cereals, pulses, vegetables, fruit, meat, poultry, and eggs. Further, the area used for producing mulberry leaves, the chief non-food crop, fell by some 47 per cent. between 1937 and 1944.[2] In 1945 the collapse of the Japanese economy affected all branches of agriculture and the index of production fell to under 60.

Agriculture recovered more rapidly from the effects of the war than manufacturing industry. Its equipment had not suffered the same physical damage as that of the urban industries, and reconstruction was not impeded by questions of reparations,

---

[1] The output of these staples (in brown rice equivalents) was slightly greater on the average between 1942 and 1944 than in the period 1935–7. Potatoes, especially sweet potatoes, had increased, whereas cereals had fallen (B. F. Johnston, *Japanese Food Management in World War II* (California, Stanford University Press, 1953), pp. 93–128).

[2] Ibid. pp. 116–19, 253.

or permitted levels of production, such as bedevilled early post-war attempts to restart manufacturing industry. On the contrary, both the Occupation authorities and the Japanese government were equally anxious to increase supplies of agricultural goods so as to avert the menace of famine. Official encouragement was given to the restarting of the ammonium-sulphate factories damaged by bombing, and imports of chemical fertilizers received priority. The manpower shortage in the countryside was soon overcome, since the demobilized soldiers and the repatriates found few opportunities for employment in industry. So, whereas in manufacturing the recovery of production was hesitant until after the outbreak of the Korean War, agriculture rallied quickly after 1947. By 1952 the index of production stood at 111, and although its subsequent movements were much influenced by harvest fluctuations, in 1955 it reached 130.[1] The increase since the middle 1930's was rather less than the growth in population during the same period, but it appears to have been about the same as that achieved during the twenty years after 1914.

In estimating the significance of this increase in production, we must observe that there has been a considerable growth, for the first time in the present century, in the size of the agricultural population. In pre-war days there were $5\frac{1}{2}$ million farm households and the total (occupied) agricultural population was estimated at about 14 millions. By 1954–5 the number of households had increased to 6·1 millions and the agricultural workers to about 17 millions. Most of the increase took place immediately after the war when men were returning from overseas and opportunities for industrial employment were few. It is remarkable, however, that this enlargement should have been maintained. As a proportion of the total occupied population, agricultural employment rose from 41 per cent. in 1940 to over 50 per cent. in 1949. Subsequently the proportion declined and by 1955 had fallen to about 40 per cent.[2] Nevertheless, the reversal of the secular trend towards the diminution in the importance of agricultural employment is one of the most striking features in the economic history of the period.

[1] Ministry of Agriculture and Forestry, *Statistical Abstracts*.
[2] *Economic Survey of Japan, 1955–6*, pp. 95–97; *Oriental Economist*, July 1956, pp. 322–5; and Ministry of Agriculture and Forestry, *Statistical Abstracts*.

The additional numbers found employment in agriculture at a time when the area of arable land was declining; in 1952 it was about 7 per cent. less than in 1941. Inevitably this meant that the size of the typical holding diminished. In 1946 there were 2,232,000 households with holdings of less than 0·5 *chobu*; in 1950, after the expansion in the agricultural population, there were 2,521,000 in that size group.[1] The increase in the number of these very small farms was attributed in some quarters to the Land Reform and to post-war legislation that prescribed an equal division of farm property among male heirs in place of the former system of primogeniture. In fact, however, the increasing fragmentation of properties was to be associated primarily with the increase of the agricultural population. In these circumstances, it is not surprising to find that in 1954 labour (physical) productivity in agriculture was estimated to be only nine-tenths of pre-war.[2]

In certain other respects the changes introduced during the war and the immediate post-war period were not maintained and some former tendencies were resumed. For instance, during the years of industrial and commercial chaos just after 1945, the contribution of agriculture to the total national income rose as high as 40 per cent., but after 1950, when the pace of industrial development greatly exceeded that of agriculture, the ratio of agricultural income declined and by 1954 it was back to its pre-war percentage of under 17. Again, the pre-war trend towards the diversification of agriculture reappeared and land reverted to crops which war-time policies had displaced. There was an exceptionally large increase in the output of fruit, vegetables, and milk and a notable development of types of farming formerly of little importance, such as stockraising. On the other hand, the failure of the silk trade to regain its pre-war size meant that the production of cocoons and of mulberry trees remained very small. The output of rice, though fluctuating from year to year, showed a rising trend. In 1955 production was 9 million *koku* greater than in 1933, previously the record year, when it reached 70 million *koku*.[3] The annual average output of the period 1952–6 was about 10 per cent. greater than in 1934–8.

---

[1] Ministry of Agriculture and Forestry, *Statistical Abstracts*.
[2] *Economic Survey of Japan, 1955–6*, p. 97.   [3] *Koku* = 4·96 bushels.

Certain pre-war tendencies in farming methods were likewise resumed. The application of chemical fertilizers, which diminished during the war, was much increased after 1945, of necessity because former supplies of soya beans from Manchuria were not available. The farmers have also used insecticides more lavishly, and although Japanese agriculture is by no means highly mechanized, it now uses more power-driven machinery, such as electric hulling machines and pumps, than before the war.

The incomes and consumption levels of the working farmers have continued to compare more favourably with those of the city dwellers than was the case before the war, in spite of the more rapid advance of the latter's standards since 1952. One of the main causes of the improvement was the Land Reform which, if it made little impact on the technical organization of agriculture, exerted powerful distributional effects. Tenants who acquired the ownership of land under the reform did so at a cost which the inflation rendered negligible. Even the land still held on tenancies (now only about 8 per cent. of the total arable area) carries an annual rent of only 600 yen a *tan*,[1] a trivial burden since the gross income per *tan* is in the neighbourhood of 20,000 yen. The former tenants who have been transformed into peasant proprietors now have to pay the land tax direct, but by the 1950's this was much lighter than before the war and their burden was very small indeed compared with their former obligations for rent. For working farmers as a whole the rent–tax ratio to the total farm income fell from 22 per cent. in 1934–6 to 8 per cent. in 1953.[2] The relative increase in the price of food was another favourable influence on agricultural incomes. The farmers, it is true, were unable to take full advantage of the scarcity of rice, their chief crop, because the price was subject to official control. Under the system in operation up to 1955, the government set a delivery quota for each farm and bought the stipulated quantities at controlled prices for distribution to the consumers. However, the growers were able to compensate themselves for the relatively low prices at which they had to dispose of this part of their supply by selling the rest at much higher prices in the black market. From 1955 the government

---

[1] 10 *tan* = 1 *chobu* = 2·45 acres.
[2] *Economic Survey of Japan, 1954–5*, pp. 166–7.

ceased to require compulsory deliveries and entered into voluntary contracts with the farmers for rice supplies. The farmers were induced to enter into these agreements by the offer of advance payments at the time when the contracts were made.

The peasants' non-agricultural employments have also brought them additional income. In the middle 1930's the ratio of non-agricultural to agricultural income in the farming community was, on an average, about 20 per cent. It fell to 10 per cent. immediately after the war, but by the middle 1950's rose again to some 40 per cent.[1] This change was the result of a complex of causes not all of them favourable. For instance, it was attributable in part to the decline in silk raising, which counts as an agricultural occupation. Further, the rise in the agricultural population forced members of farming families to take up additional by-employments in the household or occasional work in industry or trade, once opportunities became available. To some extent, therefore, the increased importance of non-agricultural income occurred merely as the result of the lack of sufficient full-time jobs on the farms. But there were positive gains. Better communications, notably the spread of bus services, widened the area within which the members of peasant households could find work. Again, the dispersion of factories during the war brought industrial work into the rural areas, and after the war this tendency persisted.

The effects of the agricultural changes on the well-being of the farmers were not evenly distributed. The former peasant proprietors obviously did not secure the same advantages from the Land Reform as those who formerly rented the whole or a large part of their arable land. Even among the latter benefits differed. Rents per acre previously depended upon fertility or situation, and the purchase price of the land, payable by instalments, was related under the scheme to the rents. But in the event the cost of acquiring the land was reduced as a result of the inflation, and the land tax imposed after the war was based on area rather than on productivity.[2] Thus the peasants who formerly worked the most productive land benefited disproportionately from the abolition of rents. The effects of the reforms

[1] *Economic Survey of Japan, 1954–5*, p. 165.
[2] National Research Institute of Agriculture, Tokyo, *Summary Reports of Researches*, 1949, pp. 54–56.

on the different types of landlord also varied. Those who were able to work the land which they formerly leased to others,[1] or those who were allowed to retain farms already managed by them, at least preserved a source of agricultural livelihood. But most of the non-working landlords lost completely their source of agricultural income and many small men in this class were impoverished.[2]

We have already emphasized that one of the objects of the social and economic reforms introduced by the Americans was to reduce the intervention of the State in economic life and to diffuse economic and political power. The Land Reform was not in all respects an effective instrument to this end. For to the extent that the landlord class had preserved its traditional functions, namely, providing credit to the peasants, introducing improvements in agricultural methods, and taking part of the strain of bad harvests, its destruction compelled Japanese agriculturists to look to the State. This, however, was a continuance of a tendency that had long been present, and the effect of the change was qualified by the enlargement of the operations of co-operative societies formed among the peasantry. These societies had a long history and for many years before the war they had been engaged in the purchase of supplies, the sale of produce, and the provision of credit. During the war the agricultural co-operatives became instruments of government control, but after 1947 they reverted to their previous character and played an increasing part in the life of the countryside. In the early 1950's not only were most of the rice purchases of the government obtained through the co-operatives, but also 70 per cent. of the non-controlled crops and 60 per cent. of the chemical fertilizers were handled by them.[3]

It may be useful to summarize the main differences between the pre-war and the present situation in Japanese agriculture. The outstanding changes have been the following: (1) a 20 per cent. increase in the size of the agricultural population; (2) a conversion of tenants to peasant proprietors, without their incurring any substantial financial liability for this change in

---

[1] This new class of working farmer accounts for a considerable proportion of the increase in agricultural households since the war.

[2] Danno, *Japanese Agriculture*, pp. 4–5.

[3] Japan FAO Association, *Agriculture in Japan*, p. 46.

tenure; (3) the improvement in the economic position of the working farmer, in spite of the increase in the agricultural population, partly through the Land Reform, partly through higher agricultural prices, and partly through new opportunities for non-agricultural employment which have offset the loss of income brought about by the decline in silk raising; (4) the diversification of agriculture through the development of livestock, fruit and vegetable farming; (5) an increased application of chemical fertilizers and of materials for the control of pests and diseases; (6) a greater use of machinery, although the structure of Japanese agriculture still prevents the efficient use of many types of agricultural machines; and (7) the destruction of the landlord class and the reduction of many of its members to the status of working farmers.

These changes taken together have represented a revolution in agricultural life. Yet the identities with the pre-war situation are almost equally impressive. The size of holdings still remains as small as before; indeed, the average has slightly diminished. Production per man-year has not advanced in spite of the real stimulus provided by more widely spread ownership and the introduction of new methods.[1] Although the income of farm households now compares more favourably than before the war with that of the city dwellers, a wide discrepancy remains. Under-employment among the rural population is still heavy. It was estimated in the early 1950's that about 37 per cent. of the agricultural population worked less than 34 hours a week.[2] The functional relationship between agricultural over-population and industrial organization has as yet been only mildly affected by the changes of the last two decades. Surplus workers from the countryside press into occupations in the small-scale secondary and tertiary industries, and this great annual flow of recruits (400,000–450,000 persons a year) [3] helps to keep wages low in those industries and inhibits the growth of powerful labour organizations among them.

[1] Labour input per *tan* in 1954 was the same as in 1935 for rice production and only about 4 per cent. less than in 1939 for wheat (U.N., *Economic Survey of Asia and the Far East, 1955*, p. 132 n.).

[2] *Data from Bureau of Statistics*, Prime Minister's Office.

[3] *Economic Survey of Japan, 1955–6*, p. 96.

FORESTRY

Nearly three-fifths of the area of Japan consists of forest land. This land has long been the source of most of the materials required for building, fuel, and pulp, and for an extensive export trade in hardwood and plywood. Forests have also been necessary for the conservation of water and for preventing soil erosion, and they make essential contributions to the resources of the arable farmers, in providing fuel, manures, and animal feeding stuffs.[1] Before the war over two-fifths of the forest land was the property of the government or the Crown; nearly a fifth was owned by public corporations; and the remaining two-fifths was in private ownership.[2] A good deal of the land in this last category was the property of the agriculturists and was held either individually or jointly by the farming communities. Although the government took over the Crown forests in 1947, the forest lands were excluded from the scope of the Land Reform, and the private landlords who retained their forests were still able to exert some influence over the agricultural life of their neighbourhood.

In this branch of the rural economy the main problems that arose after the war were the outcome of the over-cutting that had taken place during the previous twenty years. Even before the war the efforts of the government to reduce the country's dependence upon imports led to deforestation, and during the war extensive areas were cleared. The loss of Karafuto (Southern Saghalien) after 1945, the enormous demand for timber for reconstruction, and the difficulties of importing forced the Japanese to rely on home-produced supplies. By 1950 7¾ million acres out of a total forest area of 62 million acres were considered to be in need of reforestation.[3] The government subsequently instituted ambitious schemes for replanting and for improving communications with inaccessible forest areas in Hokkaido, but it was difficult to find capital needed for the execution of these plans. Even in the middle 1950's the rate of

---

[1] National Research Institute of Agriculture, *Summary Reports of Researches, 1946–8*, pp. 17–18.

[2] Ministry of Agriculture and Forestry, *Statistical Abstracts*.

[3] E. A. Ackerman, *Japan's Natural Resources and Their Relation to Japan's Economic Future* (Chicago University Press, 1953), p. 335.

growth was still behind the rate of cutting. The consumption of these capital resources was particularly heavy in the privately owned forest land.[1] It was a cause for anxiety not only because of its effects on future supplies of timber but also because of the erosion of land that has resulted.[2]

FISHERIES

The Japanese fishing industry is one of the greatest in the world. Its share in the world's total catch, today as before the war, is about 16 per cent. and its importance in the domestic economy is illustrated by the size of its contribution to the national income, 2·6 per cent. in 1954 compared with agriculture's contribution of 16·5 per cent. Fish is an essential constituent in the Japanese diet and provides on an average about four-fifths of the calories supplied by animal food.[3] It is a leading item in the country's export trade; in 1955 the value of the fish exports was 43,700 million yen ($106 million), over 6 per cent. of the total exports. The industry consists of several distinct branches, namely, the coastal fisheries, the deep-sea fisheries that operate in the northern waters, and the whaling industry. Fishing gives employment, full-time or part-time, to about 1½ million persons. These are engaged in almost a quarter of a million management units, most of them family enterprises. Only a minority are specialists. In 1954, of the total of 236,000 fishery households, fewer than 34,000 were occupied full-time in this industry. The rest consisted, in about equal proportions, of households for which fishing was the chief though not the sole occupation, and of those for which it was a subsidiary occupation. Most of the non-specialists were farmers for whom fishing was a leading source of non-agricultural income.

The war brought serious disturbances to this industry, some temporary, but others of longer duration. During the early years of the Pacific War the output of the coastal fisheries rose

---

[1] *Economic Survey of Japan, 1955–6*, p. 104.

[2] The problem is not new. From Otsu on Lake Biwa one can see eroded areas on the neighbouring mountains from which timber was cut for the building of the Horyuji temples in ancient times.

[3] *Oriental Economist*, June 1956, pp. 272–3.

steeply, for the authorities were then making every effort to free Japan from dependence on imported foodstuffs. Towards the end of the war the output declined, partly through the over-fishing of the coastal waters, but mainly through the lack of craft and manpower. The deep-sea fisheries contracted their operations from the beginning of the war and by 1945 their production was negligible. The general trend is measured by the index of fishery production (1933–5 = 100), which showed a rise to 194 in 1942 and subsequently a fall to 83 in 1945. After the war output for a time fell even lower, for the coastal waters had been over-fished, craft remained scarce, and the Occupation authorities placed restrictions on Japanese fishing in distant waters. The Japanese government tried to repair some of these deficiencies by encouraging the reconstruction of the diminished fishing fleet, and manpower was soon restored as fishermen were demobilized and other ex-service men took up fishing in the absence of alternative occupations. But for some time SCAP continued to limit the area of operations, and the loss of Karafuto and the Kuriles together with Russian restrictions on fishing in northern waters enforced a concentration on coastal areas. Consequently, the over-fishing of these waters persisted, and after 1950 the Japanese government felt obliged to reduce the licences issued to fishing vessels in order to prevent further depredations. Even when the Peace Treaty of 1952 restored to Japan full control over the coastal fisheries, onerous restrictions imposed by other governments (China, South Korea, and Russia) continued. As a result, while the output of the coastal fisheries in 1952 and subsequent years rose well above the pre-war level, the output from the more distant fishing grounds made a much slighter recovery. Yet, despite the obstacles before it, the Japanese fishing industry by the middle 1950's was substantially greater than before the war. In 1955 the index of production reached 186, little short of the maximum output of the war years. By this time the industry had been equipped with improved craft and efforts to divert operations from the grounds where Japan suffered restrictions had proved successful. But this enlarged output has been obtained only by increased effort on the part of the multitude of fishing households. Any further expansion, and an alleviation of the poverty of those engaged in the industry, can be achieved only if additional opportunities become available for fishing in distant waters. Such opportunities depend to a large extent on the outcome of negotiations with foreign governments about the rights of Japanese fishermen in territorial waters.

CHAPTER V

Industrial Reconstruction

THE dependence of Japan on imports of raw materials and foodstuffs means that her future well-being is likely to be determined by her success in exporting finished manufactures. Since, moreover, primary production is already overmanned, the manufacturing industries and the trades that serve them will be called upon to absorb an increasing proportion of her labour supply. In our examination of this supremely important sector of the economy, we shall begin by discussing the effects of the war, the process of recovery after 1945, and the broad changes that have occurred in the structure and composition of industry. Against this background we shall then consider certain of the leading trades with the object of throwing light on their size and efficiency, their organization and their technical equipment.

It was shown in Chapter II that the recovery of industrial production after the war was slow and that it was not until 1951 that the index of the volume of production rose above the level attained in the period 1934–6. After 1951, however, Japan's industry moved forward at a rapid pace. From 114 in that year the index increased to 155 in 1953 and to 167 in 1954, in spite of the check administered by the deflationary policy. In the course of 1955 the rate of increase rose sharply. The average for that year was 181 and for 1956 219. The use of this index, based on the average of the years 1934–6, is liable to lead to an exaggerated idea of the extent of the post-war industrial growth as compared with that of other countries, for the middle 1930's was a period of very rapidly increasing output in Japan. If 1937 (when Japan's Second World War began) is taken as the base, the rise is reduced to about 40 per cent. for 1955 and 68 per cent. for 1956.[1] Even this more modest increase is impressive

---

[1] If the output of the public utilities, which are excluded from this index, is brought in, the advance between 1937 and 1956 comes to nearly 77 per cent. The difference is accounted for chiefly by the very steep expansion in the production of electricity. See Statistical Appendix, p. 193 below.

and compares favourably with what has been achieved in many countries of Western Europe.

The movement of the general index gives no indication of the profound structural changes that have occurred in Japanese industry during the last twenty years. Yet, from some points of view, these are as significant as the growth in the total output. Attention was drawn in Chapter I to the pre-war tendency towards an increase in the relative size of the durable-goods industries. This tendency was greatly strengthened during the war and after the post-war collapse it was resumed. The changes can be measured. Between 1937 and 1955 the output of durable goods increased by over two-fifths, while that of non-durable goods increased by little more than one-third. These proportions are indicative of changes in the importance of certain individual industries to which attention must be directed. Before the war the predominance of textiles, though less overwhelming than it had been a decade earlier, was still unchallenged. In 1936 the textile trades as a whole were responsible for about 29 per cent. of the value of factory production and for about 38 per cent. of total factory employment.[1] During the war the size of the textile trades diminished, and after 1945 their recovery was very slow. In 1951 the volume of textile output was only half that of 1937 and in 1956 it was still 13 per cent. less. This absolute decline was naturally accompanied by a steep fall in the relative importance of this group of trades. In 1955 textiles accounted for under 18 per cent. of the value of factory production and for only 22 per cent. of total factory employment.[2]

The decline was common to all the textile industries except rayon. The largest of them, the raw-silk trade, suffered the heaviest fall. The war destroyed its foreign markets and robbed it of labour and raw-material supplies. In 1946 output was less than a seventh of the pre-war amount and subsequently there was only a modest revival, for the great American market had been permanently lost. Even in 1954 output was only a third of that in 1937. In the 1930's cotton ranked with raw silk as a

---

[1] Factories in this context are workplaces with 5 workers and over. The corresponding proportions for 1930 were 37 per cent. and 51 per cent. The figures exclude the production and employment of publicly owned establishments (Department of Commerce and Industry, *Factory Statistics*).

[2] See Statistical Appendix, p. 196 below.

major branch of the textile industries. This too followed a downward course in the early 1940's and after the end of the war output remained very small for several years. Raw materials were hard to come by. Equipment had been scrapped, bombed, or moved overseas, and capacity could not quickly be restored. The output of pure cotton yarn in 1956 was under two-thirds of the 1937 output and the production of pure cotton fabrics had declined by more than a quarter.[1] But cotton yarn and manufactures cannot be treated in isolation from rayon and staple-fibre goods, for firms in the cotton industry, in Japan as elsewhere, use staple fibre in their spinning mills and filament rayon and spun-rayon yarn in their weaving sheds. These products first became of considerable importance during the middle 1930's when Japan was trying to dispense with cotton imports so as to economize foreign exchange. Their output grew very fast in the early years of the war, but subsequently declined as resources were concentrated on war production. Post-war recovery in rayon has been carried farther than in cotton. It is true that in 1955 the output of filament and of filament fabrics was only three-quarters of that reached in 1937, but the output of staple-fibre yarn and spun-rayon fabrics was then much greater than before the war. For instance, in 1955 nearly 900 million square yards of spun-rayon fabrics were produced compared with 263 million square yards in 1937. Yet if the rayon and the cotton output are aggregated, the output in 1955 (in terms of yarn) was only about 70 per cent. of the pre-war output. For the remaining textiles, woollen and worsted goods, silk fabrics, and spun-silk yarn and fabrics, output has not yet fully recovered, and that of silk goods is much less. The production of pure synthetics (chiefly nylon and vinylon), though still small relatively to these other textiles, expanded rapidly after 1950, and in 1955 it equalled the production of raw silk (in weight).

The absolute decline in the output of this formerly predominant sector of Japan's industry provides a key to the understanding of many of her economic problems. Other countries that manufacture and export these goods, notably Great Britain,

---

[1] Data for textile production and capacity from Toyo Spinning Co., Institute for Economic Research, *Statistical Digest of Japanese Textile Industry* (Osaka, 1956), and from All-Japan Cotton Spinners' Association.

have also sustained a decline in this section of their industry since the war, but Japan's losses in textiles bore more hardly on her because of her previous specialization. These losses, moreover, were spread over a very wide range of textile goods. Even the remarkable recovery achieved during 1955 and 1956 has not yet restored this group of industries to their pre-war size.

That it has been possible for Japan, in spite of this setback, to make a substantial advance in her total industrial output testifies to her economic versatility. Like other countries that specialized in textiles she has found her main compensation in the metal and machinery industries. The output of these industries, which was growing before the war, increased enormously during the years of hostilities only to share in the general collapse after 1945. Until 1950 recovery was slow. During the subsequent period of general industrial revival the trades soon grew beyond their pre-war limits and by 1955 their output was two-thirds greater than in 1937. The production of chemicals also was much greater in that year than before the war. These three groups of industries (metals, machinery, and chemicals) were responsible in 1955 for 43 per cent. of the total factory labour force, compared with 39 per cent. in 1936 and 24 per cent. in 1930.[1] In absolute figures the numbers engaged in metals and machinery rose from 683,000 in 1936 to 1,458,000 in 1954. Among the particular trades in these groups which made outstanding progress are the iron and steel, non-ferrous metal, and the electrical and mechanical engineering industries. Motor-vehicle manufacture, which before the war was a very small industry mainly conducted in assembly plants owned by American manufacturers, had a large output by the middle 1950's. A great increase has occurred in the output of instruments of various kinds, such as clocks and watches, radios, and scientific instruments, while important new trades engaged in manufacturing cameras, binoculars, and sewing machines have come into existence. In the chemical industry the chief growth has occurred in the production of sulphuric acid, ammonium sulphate, refined oil and various derivatives of the refining process, and plastics. In the ceramics group, the pottery and glassware industries have not regained their pre-war size, but sheet-glass and cement manufacture are much larger

[1] See Statistical Appendix, p. 196 below.

than in 1937. The food and drink, timber, and rubber industries have also expanded. In mining the growth has been much
smaller than in manufactures, largely because the coal industry,
the chief branch of mining, has scarcely regained its pre-war
output. On the other hand, the production of electrical energy
doubled between 1937 and 1955.

This brief review of the changing structure of Japanese industry shows that there has been a marked advance in all major
sectors, except textiles and mining. Japan has shown resilience
in the post-war period as in earlier times, in adjusting herself to
changes in economic opportunities, but the presence until 1955
of much unemployment means that only within the last few
years can she be regarded as having accomplished a reasonably
successful transference of resources. At first sight the trends of
the post-war period might seem to be merely a resumption of
those of the 1930's which the war interrupted; but in fact there
are important contrasts between the two periods. It is true that
between 1929 and 1937 the metals and machinery group grew
in importance at the expense of textiles, but these were relative
changes and at that time both groups of industries were expanding in absolute terms. By the later 1930's, moreover, Japan had
probably reached a condition that approached full employment. In the post-war years the advance of the metal,
machinery, and chemical industries was insufficient—at any
rate until very recently—to offset the absolute fall in textiles and
to take up additional manpower in search of employment.
Over much of the period, it appears that there was considerable
unused capital equipment even in the heavy industries. By the
middle of 1956, however, equipment was probably being
worked to capacity in most branches of manufacture.

The long delay in achieving this adjustment was in large
measure responsible for the persistence of certain features of
Japan's industrial organization that were prominent before the
war. We have already referred to the dichotomy, common to
other old-established societies which have undergone a rapid
economic development, between the sector composed of highly
capitalized large-scale plants with modern techniques, and that
made up of the multitude of small workshops which operated
without elaborate equipment. In the former were to be found
the great establishments in the engineering and the heavy indus-

tries, the large, highly mechanized plants in the cotton-spinning, woollen, and rayon industries, and also a number of factories in certain traditional industries which had adopted modern techniques, for example, the *tabi* manufacturing industry. The small and medium workplaces were found both in old industries that served the Japanese consumer (such as the manufacture of certain foodstuffs, silk and rayon fabrics for Japanese dress, and pottery for domestic use) and in modern industries to which the small-scale organization could be economically applied (such as the manufacture of some kinds of electric lamps and of parts for bicycles and other engineering products). On the commercial and financial side these two sectors of the economy were linked through the great trading companies and banks of the *Zaibatsu*, for these formed the channel through which the small producers secured access to markets, finance, and technical knowledge. Yet, in spite of this link, the two sectors remained strongly contrasted with one another in the productive methods and type of labour which they employed. It was to be expected that as Japan's industrialization proceeded, this dichotomy would gradually disappear. But as long as the over-populated countryside was able to provide an abundant supply of labour for industrial and commercial occupations, the process of assimilation was bound to be delayed. In 1939 24 per cent. of the manpower employed in industry was to be found in workplaces with under five workers and 46 per cent. in those with under 30 workers.[1]

The economic circumstances of Japan since that time have preserved this dichotomy. Indeed, in many respects, it has become more pronounced. In spite of the dissolution of the *Zaibatsu* and of other changes in economic organization which will be examined later, and notwithstanding the structural changes considered above, the gulf between the two sectors has remained very wide. It is difficult to find comparable figures for the post-war and the pre-war periods, especially for the very

---

[1] E. P. Reubens, 'Small-scale Industry in Japan', *Quarterly Journal of Economics*, August 1947, p. 587. Mr. Reubens produces evidence to show that pre-war estimates exaggerated the relative importance of the smallest workplaces (i.e. those with under 5 workers). Lockwood (p. 112) agrees that these earlier estimates (based on the Census of 1930) are unsatisfactory as *measures of actual employment*, but he holds that the Census figures are 'broadly representative of the labour force in terms of chief occupation'. See p. 12 above.

small workplaces. Such information as is available, however, suggests that while there has been an absolute increase in output and employment in all the size-groups in manufacturing industry,[1] the smaller and medium-sized establishments have remained of overwhelming importance in respect of numbers employed. In 1955 42 per cent. of the total employment in manufacturing industries was in workplaces with under 30 workers and 73 per cent. in workplaces with under 300 workers. The figures for very small workplaces moreover do not include the large number of retailers engaged in manufacturing their own supplies. These are especially numerous in the food trades. Such figures are not, of course, an accurate guide to the contributions of the several size-groups to the national product. Labour productivity is far higher in the large firms than in the others and the disparity has probably been increasing. For example, in 1955, while units employing over 300 workers in manufacturing industry were responsible for only 27 per cent. of total manufacturing employment, they turned out 48 per cent. of the total industrial production (measured in values added).[2] The effect of these contrasts in productivity on the pattern of wages will be considered in Chapter X.

The survival of the small firms and of disparate conditions of employment can ultimately be explained by the nature of Japan's factor-endowment. She is deficient in natural resources and capital, while her labour supply in search of industrial employment is large and rapidly growing. Capital has been applied lavishly to certain industries where technical conditions require a heavy investment in equipment. But where the nature of the product permits manufacture by less highly capitalistic methods, production has been left to small and often, though not invariably, ill-equipped workplaces. Before the war the high concentration of new investment in certain fields was associated with the development of munitions manufacture. Similarly, during the post-war period the demands under the American procurement programme stimulated investment in the heavy industries. In the early 1950's, moreover, the government was directing a high proportion of new investment into the large-scale basic industries and much private investment was going in the same direction. This policy

---

[1] Excluding building.   [2] *Oriental Economist*, February 1957, p. 82.

must have increased the disparities between the two sectors of Japanese industry.[1] It raised issues of general economic policy that will be discussed later.

We now turn to consider certain general factors that have affected industrial efficiency and we shall attempt to compare post-war with pre-war standards in this respect. Certain estimates have been made of the changes since the war in productivity (output per man year, or output per man month). In the immediate post-war years labour productivity was undoubtedly very low, and up to the end of 1952 it is probable that in both mining and manufacturing it was still less than before the war. At this time, however, a rapid recovery was taking place, and the official estimate is that in 1953 labour productivity in manufacturing was about 10 per cent. greater than in the middle 1930's (1934–6) and in 1954 about 15 per cent. greater.[2] Quantitative estimates of this kind are liable to even greater errors in Japan than elsewhere, for they do not take account of the large sector of industry in the hands of small firms where conditions make measurement impossible. So, although the conclusion that productivity rose rapidly after 1952 in the large-scale industries is borne out by general observation and expert opinion, it may be doubted whether for industry as a whole productivity in 1954 was as much as 15 per cent. greater than before the war.

Estimates for particular industries may have greater validity. The Japanese Employers' Federation (*Keidanren*), after investigating twelve industries, found that labour productivity in 1955, as compared with a pre-war peak, was substantially higher in sheet glass, cotton yarn, and ammonium sulphate, and slightly higher in cement, steel, and electricity, but that it was less in paper, bicycles, leather, rubber goods, and coal. These figures are believed to underestimate the post-war performance, compared with pre-war, because temporary employees were included in the post-war calculation but not in the pre-war.[3] Nevertheless, although the sample is limited, the results of the

---

[1] The weakness of the *Zaibatsu* trading companies since the war has been detrimental to efficiency in many small-scale industries, since these companies formerly provided a channel for the infusion of new techniques. See ch. ix, below.

[2] Estimate of Ministry of Commerce and Industry. Labour productivity in mining was still much less than pre-war at this time.

[3] *Oriental Economist*, June 1956, pp. 274–6.

investigation suggest that performance has been very uneven and give little ground for supposing that any considerable rise in productivity throughout industry has occurred. But the present position is less interesting than the trend, and perhaps the most significant fact brought out by the investigation is that over industry as a whole a very rapid increase in productivity took place between 1953 and 1955. Since then it has continued.

The results yielded by these statistical exercises would not be convincing unless they were borne out by other evidence. In 1952 Japan supplied the World Bank with data about the position of her capital equipment.[1] These showed that a high proportion of her equipment in the heavy industries was old and obsolete, or was of an inferior quality installed during the war years. Such a conclusion was in accord with the opinion of foreign observers that the gap between Japan's technique and that of the leading Western nations had widened between 1937 and 1952. After 1952, however, much re-equipment was undertaken or planned. Japan used part of the proceeds of American procurement expenditure in importing new machinery, and her rate of industrial investment rose sharply. During this period much new plant was installed in the electricity-generating, iron and steel, engineering, and large-scale textile industries. The deflationary monetary policy introduced in 1954 to correct the adverse trend in the balance of payments compelled firms to seek economies and to reduce staff swollen during the period of boom. By the middle of the next year the new plant and the manpower economies began to yield substantial results in improved productivity. But these improvements were not universal. The great mass of small and medium-sized firms had benefited little from the investment boom and most of them still operated with technically inferior machinery and workplaces.

Although technical efficiency is an important constituent in economic efficiency it is an error to equate them. For this reason international comparisons of productivity when used as a guide to industrial policy are liable to be misleading. Where skilled labour is plentiful and capital scarce, economic efficiency is reached by other means than those employed in countries where the proportions are different. *A priori*, one would expect

[1] Cf. *Oriental Economist*, March 1954, p. 125.

that Japan's advantages in competition with the advanced Western nations would lie chiefly in the labour-intensive industries. This conclusion, however, is rather less well established than before the war, for industrial costs have been affected by changes in the labour market. In certain industries the development of trade unionism may have robbed the wage system of some of its former plasticity, while improvements in industrial welfare introduced during the period of the Occupation have raised costs. For example, the normal working hours in factories during the middle 1950's were about 15 per cent. lower than before the war, and the employers have had heavier expenses in the form of social security contributions.[1] The higher cost of labour per hour has not everywhere been offset by corresponding increases in productivity, although, as we have seen, there are wide differences between the several industries in this respect.

Some costs have been raised not only by social and economic developments within Japan, but also by external changes. The loss of her empire and of her special position in certain countries has robbed her of access to cheap sources of supply. For example, in the iron and steel industry raw-material costs have been raised because the producers have been obliged to obtain much of their ore and coking coal from the United States instead of from China and other parts of Asia. Again, the chemical industry has been deprived of the cheap supplies of salt which it used to obtain from China.

This general account of the changes in Japanese industry will now be supplemented by a more detailed examination of some of the leading trades. We shall deal first with the textile industries, secondly with the engineering industries (shipbuilding, electrical engineering, motor vehicles, bicycles, and sewing machines), and finally, with the iron and steel, fuel and power, chemicals, and a few miscellaneous trades. In each of them we shall be concerned with the changes that have taken place in size, organization, and markets.

[1] In the early 1950's the employers' expenditure on welfare (legal and extra-legal) in manufacturing industry (establishments with 30 or more employees) represented on an average 12 per cent. of the cash wages; in mining the ratio was 34 per cent. Data from Ministry of Labour.

CHAPTER VI

The Textile Industries

IT has been shown that the textile industries have not shared since the war in the development of the economy as a whole and that, in spite of their recent progress, they have failed to regain their pre-war size. Yet although they are relatively less important than they were, they still form the chief branch of Japan's manufacturing industry. In examining them, we shall be especially concerned with the silk, cotton, and rayon trades.

The depression in the silk industry during the 1930's was the source of many of Japan's most serious economic problems, for its incidence was felt not so much in the main industrial centres but rather in the countryside. Two million farming families relied upon the sale of their cocoons for the greater part of their money income, and in the chief silk-raising districts the filatures provided much employment for the daughters of the farmers. As silk formed such a large item on the export list, a fall in silk prices meant inevitably a serious disturbance in the balance of payments. These problems returned in an exaggerated form to post-war Japan. During the war capacity was much reduced not merely in the reeling branch but, more seriously, in the cocoon-raising branch, for many mulberry trees were uprooted to make room for food crops. The capacity could doubtless have been restored, although in any event the process would have been slow. After the war, however, it was seen that the great export market had gone and that the loss had to be accepted as permanent. The American hosiery industry had changed over to nylon. All that was left was the relatively small demand from domestic and foreign weavers. The decline in the industry is shown by comparative figures of production. In the period 1934–6 the average annual cocoon production amounted to 84 million *kan* and raw silk production to 729,000 bales.[1] In 1954 the corresponding figures were 27 million *kan* and 258,000 bales. As home consumption by the middle 1950's had been restored to the pre-war level, the whole loss was sustained

[1] *Kan* = 8·27 lb. Bale = 132 lb.

in the export market. In 1934–6 the annual average export amounted to 522,000 bales, in 1954 to 76,000 bales. Silk is exported in forms other than raw silk, notably as fabrics. But the production and export of fabrics also have fallen steeply. In 1934–6 the annual average export was 85 million square yards, in 1954–5 it was only 28 million square yards.[1]

The decline in world demand for raw silk, though the chief cause of the collapse of Japan's sales, was not the only cause. Before the war she supplied nearly three-quarters of the silk that entered into international trade. In recent years China has become a more dangerous competitor, and Japan's proportion of the diminished total has fallen to little more than half. The worsening of her position has occurred mainly because the fall in demand has been especially great in the types of goods and markets on which Japan formerly specialized. But the rise in her costs has also contributed to the result. Since food prices have been high, there has been keen competition for land formerly used for mulberries. This has raised the price of fodder for silkworms. At the same time new demands have arisen for the labour once used in the tedious process of cocoon raising, and finally, productivity, which declined during the war, has been slow to recover. Only recently was the cocoon yield per *tan* of mulberries restored to pre-war levels.[2] For these reasons, the reelers found that cocoon prices rose disproportionately to the price of reeled silk after the war. They responded to this pressure on their profit margins by efforts to reduce their reeling costs. Innovations such as the partial adoption of automatic machines, which reduced the labour force required, had the effect of raising labour productivity in reeling. By 1954 the output of silk per operative month was twice that obtained before the war.[3] Costs were also reduced by the adoption of a two-shift system. These measures have gone some way to offset the increasing cost of labour and the higher cocoon prices, but many of the producers have been persuaded by the uncertain prospects of the industry to take up other lines of production.

This reallocation of resources among the firms that make up

---

[1] Data from Central Raw Silk Association of Japan.

[2] *Oriental Economist*, May 1955, p. 242.

[3] Ibid. p. 242; cf. also Japan Silk Association, *The Raw Silk Industry of Japan* (Tokyo, 1953), pp. 43–52.

the industry has produced structural changes that deserve notice. At the present time the industry, as before the war, includes a few large concerns with numerous mills such as Katakura, which in 1954 operated 34 mills equipped with 1,140 automatic reeling machines and nearly 7,000 non-automatics.[1] Concerns such as these have been responsible for most of the innovations in productive technique. The majority of the producers, however, operate single mills of medium size with between 100 and 200 reeling machines and there are many small power-driven filatures, besides establishments and households engaged in the hand-reeling of silk chiefly for the home market. The relative importance of these several groups has been changing during recent years. The rise in labour costs has had comparatively little effect on the hand reelers who employ few hired workers and are untroubled by the provisions of the Labour Standards Law. The large filatures, for their part, have been able to meet the rise in wages and other costs, at any rate in some degree, by the substitution of capital for labour. So the main burden of the contraction has fallen on the medium-sized filatures, and in the middle 1950's there was considerable over-capacity in this branch of the industry, an over-capacity which seemed likely to increase as further technical improvements were introduced. Thus, whereas before the war the optimum unit in silk reeling, from an economic standpoint, was the firm with a medium-sized filature, at the present time the tendency is to concentrate an increasing part of the industry in the hands of either large concerns with highly mechanized plants, or very small hand-reeling establishments. About a quarter of the total labour force in the middle 1950's was to be found in the latter branch of the industry.[2] This branch then produced twice its annual average output of 1934–6, while the output of the machine-driven plants had fallen by over two-thirds.[3]

The other chief branch of textiles, cotton, can, like silk, attribute its decline to a loss of export markets, and we must refer to its experiences in this field before describing the structural changes in the industry. Before the war cotton goods, chiefly

[1] Bank of Japan, Foreign Capital Research Society, *Japanese Industry* (Tokyo, 1954), p. 64.

[2] Society for Economic Co-operation in Asia, 1954, *The Smaller Industry in Japan* (Tokyo, 1954), p. 15.

[3] Asia Kyokai, *The Smaller Industry in Japan* (Tokyo, 1957), pp. 101–3.

piece-goods, were sold mainly, though by no means exclusively, in Asian countries. During the the 1930's the tendency was for international trade as a whole in cotton goods to contract as the former importing countries expanded their own production, but Japan then succeeded in enlarging her exports, chiefly at the expense of Great Britain. After the war the general tendency towards a shrinkage in international trade in cotton persisted, and in this period Japan was among the chief sufferers. By the middle 1950's the shortage of raw materials and equipment which had been the chief handicap in the early post-war years had been overcome, and it was abundantly clear that the limit was then being set by the lack of foreign demand. Japan no longer had access to her former market in China, and her sales to the Indian subcontinent appeared to have suffered a permanent decline through the successful competition of Indian textiles. Consequently, in 1954 and 1955 cotton piece-goods exports (in quantity) were under half those of the middle 1930's, and yarn exports had fallen in the same proportion.[1]

The exports of pure cotton cannot be treated in isolation from those of yarns and fabrics manufactured from man-made fibres. Exports of rayon-filament goods, which are woven usually on silk looms, have been similarly affected to those of cotton goods and in spite of recovery in the middle 1950's they still amounted to only about half the pre-war quantity. But exports of spun-rayon yarn have lately exceeded those of cotton yarn and in 1955 exports of spun-rayon fabrics were nearly half those of pure cotton fabrics. Even if these exports of cotton and rayon goods are added together, however, they do not approach those of the pre-war period. The only other textile industry with a substantial export trade before the war was the wool-using trade. For most of the post-war period exports of wool yarn and fabrics were very low and, despite a rapid recovery since 1954, they are still much less than before the war. While the export trade has diminished, however, Japan's own consumption of textiles has increased, not merely because of the rise in the

[1] Statistical data for textiles from Toyo Spinning Company, Institute for Economic Research, *Statistical Digest*; All-Japan Cotton Spinners' Association; and K. Seki, *The Cotton Industry of Japan* (Tokyo, Japan Society for the Promotion of Science, 1956).

population but also because since 1952 consumption per head
has been greater than before the war.[1] For all fibres total
domestic consumption rose from 790 million lb. in 1934–6
(annual average) to 1,339 million lb. in 1954. To this increase
the main contributor has been the man-made fibres industry,
chiefly the stable-fibre branch, which in 1954 accounted for
nearly a third of the total compared with 10 per cent. before the
war. The total domestic consumption of cotton, wool, and hard
fibres has also grown, although in these cases consumption *per
head* has been reduced. We may conclude then that the Japanese textile industry has undergone two changes of great
significance. First, it has been profoundly affected by the substitution of man-made for natural fibres. Secondly, from being
predominantly an export industry, it has become concerned
primarily with serving the home market.

These changes are not independent of one another. As in
other countries, the substitution of man-made fibres for raw
cotton has been encouraged by the relative cheapness of the
former. But in Japan's case the weakness of the export trade,
to which the decline in textile sales has powerfully contributed,
and the precarious state of the balance of payments, have compelled her to seek the means for reducing dependence upon fibre
imports. Long-term policy is now being directed towards
strengthening this tendency. It is probable therefore that an
increasingly large share of production both for home supply and
for export will be secured by the man-made fibres industries,
including those branches of the cotton, wool, and silk industries that succeed in adapting themselves to the use of those
fibres.

The war made a heavy impact on the organization as well as
on the output and markets of the cotton and rayon industries.
Some of the changes that it produced have endured and deserve
detailed discussion. Before the war the cotton industry was
composed of several distinct branches. First, there were the
great integrated firms which operated combined spinning-and-
weaving mills and were responsible for a high proportion of the

---

[1] The increase per head was estimated at 23 per cent. between 1934–6 and 1954.
The estimate applies to textiles for industrial uses as well as those for household use
and apparel (*Survey of Japanese Finance and Industry*, January–February 1955, p. 15;
and E. Arita, 'Recent Competition between Cotton and Man-Made Fibres' in
All-Japan Cotton Spinners' Association, *Monthly Report*, July 1954).

yarn output and for practically all the output of standardized grey cloth. Secondly, there were the specialist spinning firms, some linked with large firms of cotton merchants. Thirdly, there were the specialist weavers with medium-sized and small sheds. These produced wide cloth for home and export and also narrow cloth for Japanese dress. Finally, there was the small and diminishing hand-weaving branch.[1]

Among the integrated firms production was concentrated in a very few business units. In 1935 six firms controlled nearly half the spindles and produced about the same proportion of the yarn output. Eleven firms possessed nearly two-thirds of the spindles. The mills owned by this group were nearly all large and their size was tending to increase. The whole industry had been reorganized during the preceding decade and operated almost entirely with high draft ring spindles. There was the same concentration in the weaving branch. The 'Big Six' operated over half the total looms owned by the integrated branch of the industry and four-fifths of the looms were in the hands of eighteen companies. These weaving sheds were equipped with automatic looms and the bulk of the output consisted of shirtings and sheetings for sale at home and abroad.

The specialist spinning firms, for the most part, operated smaller mills than the integrated firms, although most of their capacity was also high draft. The yarn was sold mainly to the third group, the specialist weavers. In the middle 1930's these turned out, on ordinary looms, nearly all the narrow piece-goods and about three-fifths of the wide piece-goods in quantity; in value the proportion was probably about two-thirds. The specialists themselves fell into several groups, the fair-sized firms with 50 power looms or over, medium firms with 10–49 looms (mainly power looms), and small firms with under 10 looms (mostly hand looms). Their output consisted of a wide variety of cloth, including fancy goods, and during the middle 1930's the tendency was for this section of the industry to increase in relative importance both in the home and export markets. This was an indication of the fact that Japan was suffering from increased competition in the bulk trade from

---

[1] For description of the pre-war structure see Schumpeter, *Industrialization*, ch. xvi.

India and elsewhere and was moving into the manufacture of higher-priced fabrics. In the finishing branch of the industry, some of the integrated firms had their own establishments, but much of their cloth, together with all the cloth of the specialist weavers, was finished by firms that concentrated on one of the main processes—dyeing, bleaching, or printing. Many of these firms were quite small.

In the early years of the Second World War, the tendencies of the previous decade were reversed, for the official control imposed on production and sale resulted in discrimination in favour of the large firms. Even before the outbreak of the Pacific War the government, in its attempt to reduce Japan's dependence on imports, had insisted on a large admixture of rayon staple in the production of cloth for the home market. For the export market a system was devised which linked allocations of raw cotton with exports of manufactured goods. The administration of these controls was centred on the spinning companies, and the independent weavers of fabrics for export became in effect mere subcontractors for those companies.[1] As the war proceeded, the controls were strengthened, and the cotton industry was drastically contracted and completely reorganized. Compulsory amalgamations were effected among the spinning companies with the result that production was entirely concentrated on 14 integrated groups, most of which had interests in other branches of textiles as well as in cotton spinning and weaving. Among the independent weavers and the finishers also production was concentrated in selected mills. The complex structure of the industry, formerly well adapted to the diverse markets that it served, was destroyed.

Even the firms that survived changed over in part to the manufacture of non-textile goods. The shortage of metal led to the scrapping of much equipment, and many spindles and looms were dismantled and shipped to the continent or the South Seas where the government hoped that they would be used for serving local markets. At the end of the war the number of operable spindles had been reduced from over 12 million to little more than 2 million. The looms owned by the spinning firms had fallen from 108,000 to 24,000 and those of the independent weavers from 255,000 to 112,000.[2]

[1] Seki, *Cotton Industry*, p. 193. [2] Ibid. p. 312.

The reconstruction of the industry after 1945, though encouraged by SCAP, was impeded by the shortage of raw materials. In 1946 imports of raw cotton were financed by the Commodity Credit Corporation and later other loans from American sources, official and private, were provided. Imports of Indian cotton began in 1947 and of Egyptian in 1948. For several years the industry remained subject to rigid official control. The financial arrangements with the Americans were administered by the government and the Bank of Japan, and until February 1949 the exports of piece-goods against which the loans were made were conducted entirely through a government agency. The government also controlled the reorganization of production. At first spinning was confined to the 10 large spinning firms that had survived the war. Then in 1947 25 new firms (*shinbo*) were allowed to produce yarn and after 1950, when the restrictions were much relaxed, numerous small-scale spinners (known as the *shin-shinbo*) began production.[1] The controls were finally abolished in 1951.

Meanwhile there had been a growth in production and equipment and this continued at an accelerated pace after the outbreak of the Korean War. By 1952 the number of spindles reached $7\frac{1}{2}$ million, of which 64 per cent. were owned by the 'Big Ten', 21 per cent. by the *shinbo*, and 15 per cent. by the *shin-shinbo*. The growth of the industry was checked by the textile recession of 1952, but it was soon resumed and by the end of 1956 there were about 9 million operable spindles. In the weaving branch the number of looms owned by the spinning–weaving concerns rose from 24,000 at the end of the war to 72,500 in 1952 and to 77,000 at the end of 1956. The growth in the number of looms owned by the independent cotton weavers was from 104,000 in 1946 to 226,000 in 1952 and 297,000 in 1956. Even after this recovery, equipment as well as production was still far short of the pre-war amount.

Although the old structure of the industry has been in some measure restored since 1952, certain important contrasts remain. Despite the diminished output of yarn, there were more spinning firms in 1955 than twenty years earlier. This is explained by the entry of the small firms of specialist spinners in

[1] Seki, *Cotton Industry*, pp. 37–47.

the early post-war period.[1] Yet although these newcomers for a time threatened the predominance of the large spinners, they lost ground during the textile depression of 1952. By the middle 1950's the 'Big Ten' had over three-fifths of the total spindles and nearly two-thirds of the looms owned by the integrated concerns. Within the spinning-weaving section the high concentration of output on a few firms has not been disturbed by the changes of the last twenty years.[2]

On the other hand, the specialist weavers appear to have increased their proportion of the pure cotton cloth output. In 1955 they accounted for about two-thirds of it (in quantity) compared with under three-fifths in the middle 1930's. This was a corollary of the change in the character of the output and particularly of exports. Exports of standardized goods—the products of the great integrated mills—have declined to a much greater extent than those of cotton fabrics as a whole. For example, the trade statistics show that post-war exports of grey cloth compared much less favourably with pre-war exports of those goods than did the exports of bleached, dyed, yarn-dyed, and printed fabrics. The rise in the relative importance of the specialist weavers is in continuance of the pre-war tendency, and as the specialists are mostly medium-sized or small firms, the effect has been to diminish the degree of concentration on the weaving section of this industry. It would be misleading to examine these structural changes wholly by reference to the output of pure cotton goods. Both the integrated and the specialist weaving sections of the cotton industry now use yarns and fibres other than cotton far more extensively than before the war. Besides pure cotton goods their output consists of spun-rayon cloth, filament-rayon cloth, and cotton mixtures. These varieties form a much higher proportion of the specialists' output than of the integrated firms' output. This is another reason for the relative improvement in the position of the former.

Yet, although the great integrated concerns in what is commonly regarded as the cotton industry itself appear to be less

[1] The newcomers into the spinning industry came mainly from other branches of textiles. They included independent weavers, knitted-goods manufacturers, rayon-staple spinners, silk spinners, rope makers, and textile-machinery manufacturers (Seki, *Cotton Industry*, p. 131).

[2] In 1935 the 'Big Six' owned 48 per cent. of total Japanese spindles and 53 per cent. of the looms owned by spinning-weaving concerns.

important than formerly, it would be an error to suppose that they have had to content themselves with a more modest place in the textile industry as a whole. In fact they have to a large extent compensated themselves for the decline in cotton by moving to other interests. This brings us to a consideration of the structure of the man-made fibres industry. As in other countries the manufacture of filament rayon and staple fibre is an activity of very large firms and large plants. In Great Britain the industry is in the hands of firms that are financially distinct from those in the natural-fibres industries, although of course staple fibre is spun in cotton mills and rayon and staple-fibre yarns are used in the weaving branches of the cotton, wool, and silk trades. In Japan, on the other hand, cotton firms have had an important share in the actual manufacture of filament rayon and staple fibre. This is what might be expected, for new developments in large-scale industry in Japan have usually proceeded from existing large firms. For many years past it was common for large cotton firms to have interests in the wool and silk-spinning trades, and when rayon was introduced, they played a leading part in the development of the manufacture. In 1955 cotton-spinning firms owned over two-fifths of the rayon capacity. The rest was in the hands of large firms either specialized to the man-made fibre production or closely associated with chemical firms. Cotton firms have also been active in the manufacture of synthetic fibres which by the middle 1950's was a rapidly growing industry.[1]

The complexities of organization in the textile industries may be illustrated by a few examples of leading firms. The Toyo Spinning Company in 1954 was one of the three largest firms in the cotton industry. It had 600,000 operable spindles and over 7,000 looms. Apart from its output of finished cotton goods, it was also one of the largest producers of woollen and worsted yarn, woollen fabrics, rayon filament, staple fibre, and spun-rayon yarn. Kanegafuchi, a peer of Toyo Spinning in cotton, had a similar range of interests. It owned mills engaged in the production of raw silk, spun-silk yarn, silk cloth, staple

---

[1] It may be questioned whether Japan possesses relative advantages for international trade in pure synthetics comparable with those she long enjoyed in other textile trades, for synthetic-fibre production, being capital-intensive, must make heavy demands on the country's scarce investment resources. However, Japan will doubtless continue to foster this production so as to reduce her dependence on imported natural fibres.

fibre, spun-rayon yarn and cloth, woollen and worsted yarn, woollen cloth and felt, and vinylon. Its employees numbered 30,000. The chief specialist firm in the rayon industry at this time was Teikoku which produced rayon filament, staple fibre, spun-rayon yarn, and rayon fabrics. Toyo Rayon, in the seven factories where it employed 17,000 workers, had a similar range of interests; it is also the sole manufacturer of nylon in Japan.[1]

During the pre-war decade Japan's cotton industry had become technically very efficient, at any rate in the main processes of spinning and weaving. Practically all the spinning mills used high drafting and the equipment of the weaving sheds owned by the integrated firms consisted almost entirely of automatic looms. The destruction of most of this equipment during the war presented the firms with a difficult problem of reconstruction. But in the process of solving this problem, the leading producers were able to equip themselves with up-to-date machinery, for after 1952 heavy investment in new plants, both in the cotton and in the man-made fibres industries, was undertaken. The government in an effort to render Japan less dependent upon imports of raw materials gave special encouragement to the rayon and synthetic-fibre industries by providing finance at low rates of interest and by reducing the tax burden.[2] In the cotton industry many detailed technical improvements were effected, notably the conversion of carding engines, drawing frames, and roving frames to large package types, the change-over of roving frames to the simplex system, and the introduction of super-high drafting and of pneumatic cleaners.[3] As a result productivity has considerably increased. A comparison with pre-war standards is obviously difficult. It appears, however, that although in the late 1940's production per man hour was very low in cotton spinning, by 1950 it had probably surpassed the pre-war level. Subsequently, and especially after 1952, the advance was rapid, and production per man hour in the middle 1950's may have been between a quarter and a third greater than before the war.[4] In the specialist weaving

[1] Data supplied by firms mentioned.
[2] *Oriental Economist*, February 1956, p. 74. [3] Ibid. May 1955, p. 240.
[4] The difficulty of comparing productivity in pre-war and post-war periods is caused by the change in the type of yarn produced. The relative decline in the production of the standardized cloths has been accompanied by a corresponding relative fall in the output of coarse yarns. The average count produced in the

section it is more difficult to estimate movements in productivity or efficiency. As already shown, a high proportion of the new capital investment has been directed into the large plants, and it is improbable that any striking technical changes have occurred in the small and medium-sized mills of which this branch is composed. This applies to mills engaged in weaving filament rayon and silk as well as to those concerned with cotton and spun rayon.

Although technical efficiency has again reached high levels in many branches of textiles, in other respects the industry, especially the pure cotton branch, has yet to recover its pre-war competitive strength. Before the war expert buying of cotton, and skill in blending, kept raw-material costs low, and cheap labour was available for the processes preparatory to spinning. After the war the exchange and import controls deprived the spinners of their former opportunities for the selective buying of cotton. These difficulties were accentuated by changes within the merchanting section of the industry. That section, which was formerly dominated by a small number of great firms engaged both in importing raw cotton and exporting piece-goods, sustained grave damage from the war. Its overseas organization was destroyed and its financial resources depleted. For many years after the war recovery was impeded by controls over foreign exchange and imports. The place of the big firm was taken by numerous small merchants who lacked both the experience and the financial resources of their predecessors. Recently a tendency to concentration among them has appeared, but Japan's merchanting organization in the textile trade cannot yet compare in its efficiency with that in existence before 1937. Other adverse factors have also been present. Textile wages, especially in the large mills, have been comparatively high since the war and the cost to the employers of providing welfare facilities considerable.[1] The consequent rise

---

middle 1950's was much higher than before the war. This is one reason why American-type cotton has been substituted for Indian cotton. See, however, *Economic Survey of Japan, 1954–5*, p. 57, and *Oriental Economist*, June 1956, p. 275.

[1] Textile workers appear to have moved up the wage ladder since the war. In 1935 the average daily wage of cotton spinners (females) was only 20 per cent. of that of steel rollers and 18 per cent. of that of lathe operatives (males). In 1954 the corresponding ratios were 30 per cent. and 37 per cent. (Data provided by Tokyo Chamber of Commerce.) This change may reflect the improvement in the economic conditions of the farming communities from which the female cotton operatives were recruited.

in labour costs has reduced the Japanese spinners' former advantages in blending and preparatory operations. Again, certain benefits flowed from the closely-knit relations which formerly existed between producers, merchants, and shipping companies. These arrangements could not be restored after the war, partly because of the weakness of the merchants and the shipping companies, and partly through the provisions of the anti-monopoly law. There is, however, no reason to suppose that all these disabilities will be permanent.

CHAPTER VII

The Engineering Industries

GENERAL TRENDS

THE enlargement of the engineering industries during the early and middle 1930's was stimulated by investment in rearmament and in the foundation of centres of heavy industry in Manchuria. But it did not depend wholly on public expenditure or national policy concerned with strategic aims, and progress was by no means limited to the branches that directly or indirectly obtained their orders from the State. Several other engineering trades made striking advances, notably the manufacture of bicycles, light electrical apparatus, and textile machinery. On general economic grounds one would expect Japan's relative advantages to lie in the production of the lighter products, especially labour-intensive goods. Yet even in some of the heavy branches, such as shipbuilding, Japan was a cheap producer.

Throughout the industry during this time there was a remarkable growth in technical efficiency. By the middle 1930's Japan was competent to turn out the complete equipment for power stations, and she had ceased to depend on foreign countries for imports of the commoner types of machine tools. She still lagged behind Western countries in the production of some products, for example, motor cars; but her industry was rapidly extending its scope. Her relatively cheap skilled labour and her well-trained technicians enabled her to go a long way towards overcoming both her technological inferiorities to Western nations and also her disadvantages in regard to supplies of certain raw materials.

With the outbreak of the Sino-Japanese War in 1937 the expansion of this group of industries, though not of every constituent in it, was accelerated. After 1941 the new or enlarged plants of the old-established firms were joined by the plants of other industries converted to wartime production. In 1944 the output of engineering goods reached its peak. In volume it was then more than three times the output of 1937, or $4\frac{1}{2}$ times that of the middle 1930's. This growth was accomplished not merely by the expansion or adaptation of the large-scale sector of industry, but also by the enlistment of small producers, including those located in country areas, as subcontractors. As in other countries, however, the industry became distorted from the pattern of peacetime needs. The trades that served the export markets and the home civilian demand, such as the manufacture of bicycles or of textile machinery, declined as their plants changed over to munitions production. On the other hand, there was an immense expansion in the output of machine-tools and aircraft. In some respects Japan was jeopardizing her future. She had depended upon foreign countries for information about technical advances. For instance, in the electrical industry, as in several others, her producers had links with American and European firms that gave her access to new devices and scientific discoveries. The war snapped these links, and the gap between Japanese and Western standards of technical accomplishment widened.

In spite of the damage sustained by many of the large engineering plants, Japan emerged from the war with a greatly increased capacity in this group of trades and with a more widely diffused knowledge of engineering skills. Yet the task of redeploying her resources for meeting the demands of the post-war world was far more onerous than that faced by her main competitors. Having lost her former export trade, she was deprived of access to supplies of imported raw materials essential to the heavy industries. With her financial system in ruins and reserves exhausted by inflation, it was difficult for her manufacturers to obtain capital for reconstruction. The uncertainties that arose directly from her defeat were especially perplexing for the engineering firms. SCAP's policy in regard to the 'level' to be permitted to various types of production was aimed particularly at trades that were deemed to contribute to Japan's capacity for making war, such as shipbuilding. These were subjected to onerous restrictions. Similarly, the proposal to distribute plants as reparations was formulated with an eye on the heavy engineering industries, and firms could not make a start on any programme of reconstruction until the fate of their plants was known. Finally, the policy of dissolving the *Zaibatsu* added to these uncertainties, because the engineering industry had been dominated by those concerns.

The attempts of the Japanese government to deal with the financial problem of reconstruction have already been described. We have also seen how Allied Occupation policy towards industry changed when the cold war started. As 'economic democratization' and the reparations problem fell into the background, the reconstruction of engineering made some headway. After the outbreak of the Korean War, and with the final abandonment of the early post-war plans for removing plants as reparations, Japan's production of engineering goods began a rapid advance. As she was the only country with spare engineering capacity at this time, orders poured into her factories and shipyards. In 1951 the output of machinery rose far above the 1937 level. The heavy demands arising from the Korean War were sustained in subsequent years by substantial investment in plants of the textile and the heavy industries, including the public utilities. In 1953 the index of machinery production reached 267 (1934–6 = 100). The decline in American procurement and the deflationary policy of the government in 1954 led to a slight fall in output; but towards the end of 1955 the growth was resumed. In 1956 the production index stood at 397. By this time new export markets had been secured and Japan was benefiting from the various development programmes worked out for South East Asia. At the same time the rise in the national income had led to enlarged demand for durable consumers' goods on the part of the Japanese themselves.

The engineering group of industries by the middle 1950's was not only much larger than twenty years earlier but it had been affected by changes in the relative importance of its various constituents, in markets and in organization. Among the older branches of the industry some had greatly expanded, notably the shipbuilding industry. The most interesting change, however, resulted from the appearance, as substantial branches of manufacture, of trades that were of minor importance before 1937. These included the manufacture of motor cars, sewing machines, and instruments such as cameras and binoculars. The tendency noticed during the 1930's towards widening the scope of engineering production had been greatly strengthened.

In markets the changes had been equally notable. In the 1930's Japan sold the greater part of her machinery export to North East Asia, especially to Manchuria. This was a corollary of her heavy investment in that area. There was only a small export, chiefly of light engineering goods and electrical apparatus, to parts of the world that lay outside her political control. In the post-war period the North East Asian markets virtually disappeared, but the export trade of the middle 1950's was greater than formerly and far more widely extended. It included the sale of machinery to South and South East Asia and also a large trade in both heavy and light engineering products to North America.

The changes in organization were less revolutionary. Before the war the technical units in the engineering industry consisted of, first, a few very large plants, each with a wide range of products, and, second, a large number of medium-sized and small plants. The former were to be found chiefly in the heavy industries, although they also shared in the output of the lighter products. The small and medium plants were of several kinds. Some of them belonged to subcontractors who worked for the large plants. Others were engaged in producing either parts for assembly in medium-sized assembly factories or light finished goods, such as cheap electric lamps, made to the orders of merchants. The small plants suffered less than the large plants from the air raids, and after the war they were able to equip themselves with machine tools from dismantled munitions factories.[1] As at this time the rehabilitation of the large factories was proceeding tardily, the importance of the small producers in the industry was considerably enhanced. After 1950, however, most new investment was directed into a relatively small number of large plants, and during the period of deflation in 1954 the small firms were hard hit. This was especially true of subcontractors to large firms. During the boom that began in the later part of 1955, when capacity in the large plants became fully occupied, a greatly increased quantity of orders was placed with the small producers and they fully shared in the prosperity of the industry during the next year. It may well be, therefore, that the small and medium plants occupy at least as important a place in engineering production as they did during

---

[1] *Survey of Japanese Finance and Industry*, January–February 1954, p. 10.

the late 1930's. Certainly in some of the industries that have made a particularly rapid advance during recent years the small and medium producers are responsible for a very high proportion of the supply. For instance, four-fifths of the output of sewing-machine parts and three-fifths of the output of bicycle parts are made by small and medium firms.[1] Since each specializes on a particular part or component, this branch of the trade is conducted very efficiently. Even in the shipbuilding industry medium-sized subcontractors have recently made a considerable contribution to the enlarged output.

SHIPBUILDING

This generalized account will be supplemented by an examination of a few of the chief branches of the industry, namely the shipbuilding, electrical-engineering, motor-vehicle, bicycle, and sewing-machine trades. We shall begin with shipbuilding. During the 1930's the Japanese mercantile marine grew fast and at the beginning of the Pacific War it amounted to more than 6 million gross tons. The Japanese shipbuilding industry which constructed most of this fleet had been stimulated by government financial assistance rendered under a Scrap-and-Build Plan as well as by large orders for naval vessels. The annual launchings of merchant ships during the five years before the outbreak of the Second World War reached about 330,000 gross tons. During the war the capacity of the industry was vastly expanded and, apart from a large tonnage of naval vessels and wooden ships for coastal navigation, about 3,200,000 gross tons of steel merchant ships were built.[2] The last stages of the war, however, were disastrous. Nearly all the ocean-going ships were sunk by Allied action and at the end of the war shipping and shipbuilding were subjected to rigid control by the Occupation authorities. SCAP was intent upon permanently destroying Japan's ability to make war, and to this end it was proposed that the merchant fleet should be limited to $1\frac{1}{2}$ million gross tons of steel ships and that no vessel should exceed 5,000 gross tons or should have a maximum speed of over 15 knots.[3] Much shipbuilding equipment was to be

---

[1] *Economic Survey of Japan, 1954–5*, p. 70.   [2] Cohen, *Japan's Economy*, p. 196.
[3] H. Yamamoto, 'The Recovery Method of the Japanese Shipping Industry in the Post-War Period', in *Kobe Economic and Business Review* (Kobe, 1954), p. 90.

seized as reparations and the remaining yards were required
to occupy themselves chiefly with the construction and repair
of ships for coastal navigation.

Even this limited programme of work was frustrated in the
early post-war years by the lack of financial resources among
shipbuilding firms. At this time the government was the only
source of funds for reconstructing the heavy industries and it
established a Ship Corporation whose functions were the execution of a recovery programme and the supply of funds for this
purpose to the extent of 70 per cent. of the cost of building. Up
to 1948 construction remained limited to small coastal vessels.
The change in Allied policy towards Japan in that year, however, had immediate consequences for shipping and shipbuilding. By 1950 SCAP's control over these industries was finally
relinquished, and Japan was then for the first time able to
proceed with the large-scale reconstruction of her ocean-going
fleet.[1] Soon afterwards the boom in world shipping, set going by
the Korean War at a moment when Western shipyards were
fully extended, brought demands from foreign ship-owners and
Japan became an important exporter of ships. For financing this
new programme money was provided by the government,
chiefly through the United States Aid Counterpart Fund. After
1952, when this source of finance dried up, the Japan Development Bank became the chief provider of funds at low rates of
interest. Then in 1953 the government took powers which
allowed it to subsidize interest payments, above a minimum of
5 per cent., on loans made by the commercial banks to the
shipbuilders. This government assistance kept the industry active throughout the early 1950's, even after the Korean boom
was over, and a substantial export was maintained. At this
time Japan's costs were high compared with those of Western
countries, but her delivery dates were shorter than theirs and
her builders were assisted in meeting foreign competition by the
application of the 'link' system to this branch of the export
trade.[2]

Meanwhile, the industry had invested heavily in new equipment and had greatly improved its constructional methods.

---

[1] Yamamoto, loc. cit., pp. 91–94.
[2] *Survey of Japanese Finance and Industry*, March–April 1955, pp. 9–15. For a
description of the 'link' system, see p. 167 below.

Between 1950 and 1955 some 22,000 million yen were invested in new capacity.[1] The number of berths capable of constructing large ships was much increased, and the 'block' building system and modern welding technique, in substitution for riveting, were widely adopted.[2] By the middle 1950's Japan was as well, or even better, equipped than most European countries for building large tankers. At the same time technical improvements were effected by the industries that supplied materials to the shipyards. In the early post-war years the steel consumption by Japanese shipbuilders per unit of tonnage was 10 per cent. higher than that of the British shipbuilders, because of the unreliability and lack of uniformity in the steel plates.[3] By the middle 1950's this disadvantage had been removed. Thus Japan was well placed to benefit from the rise in the world demand for ships that began in 1955, and her shipbuilding industry could view with complacency the abandonment of the 'link' system. In 1956 Japan became the world's largest shipbuilder. In that year she was responsible for 26 per cent. of the world's launchings, compared with 11 per cent. in 1953. Her competitive position was considered so strong that the government early in 1957 was able to remove the subsidy which had been given for compensating builders for the high interest rates on loans, while the Development Bank imposed more onerous terms.

Most of the ships were built by a few large firms, notably the Mitsubishi Shipbuilding and Engineering Industries and other successor firms of Mitsubishi, Hidachi, and Kawasaki, although these firms, as always, made widespread use of subcontractors located in premises adjacent to the main plants. In addition, there were in the 1950's, as in earlier times, many medium-sized yards which have lately been occupied in building small vessels of from 500 to 4,000 gross tons for South East Asian countries and the Soviet Union. There were hundreds of small yards engaged in building wooden boats for the fishing industry. The small yards and the subcontracting firms benefited greatly from the

---

[1] *Oriental Economist*, January 1957, p. 22.

[2] Yards capable of building ships over 20,000 gross tons increased from 14 in 1954 to 20 in 1956; among these 13 were capable of building ships of 30,000 tons and over compared with 6 in 1954 (ibid. December 1956, p. 595).

[3] Society for Economic Cooperation in Asia, *The Major Industry and Its Technique in Japan* (Tokyo, 1954), p. 26.

boom, especially as the 'block' system required that much of the work should be given out to specialist firms.[1] This had a significant effect in fostering what had previously not existed in the Japanese engineering industry (or any other), namely a single labour market for small and large firms alike. In the early 1950's the wages paid to skilled employees in small and medium engineering establishments were at least 30 per cent. lower than those paid by large firms; by 1956 these disparities had largely disappeared. The condition of over-capacity and under-employment that had long persisted gave place to a pronounced shortage of skilled workers, especially welders, and systematic training schemes were therefore organized both by the industry and by the central and local governments.

Thus, within a few years Japan's position as shipbuilder was completely transformed. In the early 1950's she was a high-cost producer and the activity of her industry depended on various types of subsidies and upon her possession of idle capacity at a time when the builders of other nations were fully occupied. In those years it seemed reasonable to suppose that her prosperity as a shipbuilder could not outlast the boom, for the high cost and the inferior quality of her steel made her long-run competitive position unfavourable. Yet by heavy investment in new plant and by revolutionizing her organization and technique she attained by 1956 a level of technical efficiency that matched, and in some respects exceeded, that of her rivals abroad. Despite many natural disadvantages, she became the largest producer and exporter of ships. Her relative strength will not be fully tested until the boom is over, but it is probable that, in spite of periodical setbacks that must be regarded as inevitable, she will retain a high, though possibly not a pre-eminent, position in the world's shipbuilding industry.

ELECTRICAL MACHINERY AND APPARATUS

The manufacture of electrical machinery and apparatus, which first became a considerable branch of industry in the years just before the First World War, grew rapidly in the next two decades. By the eve of the Second World War Japan was not only capable of supplying most of the products required for

[1] *Fuji Bank Bulletin*, December 1956, pp. 26–27; *Economic Survey of Japan, 1955–6*, p. 53.

industrial and domestic use, but she also had a large export trade in a few types of apparatus, such as electric lamps. The growth of the industry and the extension in the range and quality of its goods were accompanied by a rise in the output of electric power to which it made an essential contribution.

Many of the chief firms were originally offshoots of *Zaibatsu*-owned undertakings in shipbuilding or mining.[1] At the outset these concerns were engaged mainly in turning out electrical goods for other constituents in the same *Zaibatsu*, but after a time they turned to production for the market. The members of the electrical industry from its first years established close relationships with foreign companies from which they obtained technical knowledge and sometimes capital. The Tokyo Electric Light Company, an affiliate of Mitsui, before the First World War had close links with the General Electric Company of the United States, and during the early 1920's several other leading companies entered into relations with foreign manufacturers, e.g. Mitsubishi with the Westinghouse Electric Company and Furukawa with Siemens-Schuckert. In the inter-war period a high proportion of the production of machinery and apparatus (about three-fifths of the total) was in the hands of six great concerns, most of which produced not merely a wide variety of equipment for power stations and factories but also light electrical apparatus.[2] Nevertheless, small and medium-sized firms found a place in the industry both as subcontractors to the big firms and also as specialist producers. For instance, at that time, the electric-lamp industry comprised three types of producer: first, the Tokyo Electric Light Company which manufactured high-grade lamps, together with most of their components, in a few large and well-equipped factories; second, about a dozen medium-sized firms which produced standard types of lamps from parts and materials bought from specialist suppliers; and finally, numerous small factories and workshops engaged in making cheap lamps, miniature bulbs, and automobile bulbs. The output of the first two groups was sold

---

[1] Mitsubishi Electrical Manufacturing Company was formed to take over the electrical business of the Mitsubishi-Nagasaki Shipbuilding Company, and the Hidachi Electrical Company was formed to undertake the repair of electrical machinery used by the Hidachi Mining Company.

[2] *Survey of Japanese Finance and Industry*, July–August 1954, p. 3.

mainly in the home market, but most of the output of the small producers was exported.[1]

During the early part of the war the capacity of the industry was much enlarged, and the 'Big Six' (reduced to five in 1939 by the amalgamation of the Tokyo Electric Light Company and the Shibaura Engineering Works) built several new factories and absorbed a number of small firms. In the later years of the war the capacity of most of these factories was concentrated on the production of munitions and the output of many types of electrical apparatus declined. In the period of economic chaos that followed the war the industry encountered many difficulties. The dissolution of the *Zaibatsu* struck a particularly heavy blow at this industry which was so intimately bound up with their interests, and the shortage of investment funds meant that there was little demand for the kind of equipment required for the generation and transmission of power. A high proportion of the diminished output consisted of apparatus for domestic use and much of it was turned out by the small producers. Revival in the heavy branches did not begin until 1951 when it was at last possible to proceed with plans for developing the electricity-power supply. From then onwards recovery was rapid.[2]

By this time the industry had largely re-established the forms of organization and the system of inter-firm relationships which the war had destroyed. One of the obstacles to the recovery of the industry in the immediate post-war years was the backwardness of Japan's technique. She had depended upon foreign associates for access to new devices and discoveries, and when she was deprived of this assistance during the war her standards of technical proficiency were lowered. During the early and middle 1950's, however, the former links with foreign companies were rejoined and new ones forged. The flow of technical information to Japan was thus resumed, under contracts with such firms as Escher Wyss, Westinghouse, International General Electric Company, Siemens-Schuckert, Brown Boveri. At the same time the fabric of financial and commercial relationships that was so seriously damaged by the dissolution of the *Zaibatsu* was to a large extent repaired. By the middle

---

[1] Schumpeter, *Industrialization*, pp. 544–8.
[2] *Survey of Japanese Finance and Industry*, July–August 1954, pp. 3–10.

1950's Tokyo-Shibaura Electric had established close links with the Mitsui Bank, and Mitsubishi Electric with the Mitsubishi Bank. As a Japanese commentator has said of this industry, 'the pre-war relationships with the *Zaibatsu* have been continued under a changed form in the post-war period'.[1] It seems also that with recovery in the heavy branch of the industry, the early post-war tendency towards an increase in the relative importance of the small producers was reversed.

The electrical-machinery industry, at any rate the branch concerned with generators, transformers, and motors, has always found its chief markets at home. But it might have been expected that Japan would possess considerable relative advantages in the manufacture of light electrical apparatus in which she could make use of her abundant supply of skilled labour. It might also have been thought that the development plans of South Asia would bring her substantial orders for generating and transmission equipment. So far, however, in spite of recent improvements, Japan's costs have been high in this group of products compared with those of Western countries. In much of this industry it is probable that the gap between her technical standards and those of the leading Western producers is a more serious obstacle to successful overseas competition than in many other trades. Even in the lighter branches Japan's exports have been small for the greater part of the post-war period. They began to grow after 1954 chiefly through increases in foreign sales of wireless equipment and insulated cables. The export of electric lamps, especially miniature lamps, has again become a large trade. However, this industry does not rank as a major exporter. For instance, in 1955 the total value of all exports of electrical machinery and apparatus was considerably less than that of either toys or sewing machines.

MOTOR VEHICLES

Up to the middle 1930's the Japanese motor-car industry was of small account and the country relied upon imports for most of its needs. Even the small domestic production consisted mainly of cars and lorries assembled from imported parts by local branches of Ford and General Motors. Apart from these,

---

[1] *Survey of Japanese Finance and Industry*, July–August 1954, p. 8.

Japan-made cars were few in number (under 10,000 a year) and poor in quality. In 1936 manufacturing equipment was bought from the United States and American engineers were engaged by Japanese firms to develop the industry. After the outbreak of the Sino-Japanese War the government made determined efforts to free Japan from dependence on imports, and both in Japan and in Manchuria the leading *Shinko-Zaibatsu*, Aikawa of Nissan and of the Manchurian Industrial Development Company, organized the expansion of the industry. By the time of the Pacific War Japan had become almost self-sufficient in the supply of lorries, although little progress had been made in the production of passenger cars. In 1940 the output of cars and lorries together reached about 50,000. After the war the industry had to be created anew. There was an abundance of engineering capacity which could be diverted to this manufacture. The Korean War brought an increased demand for vans and lorries, and from then onwards growth was very fast. In 1953 the output was nearly 60,000 vehicles apart from a substantial production of motor cycles, three-wheelers, and motor scooters. A large new industry employing over 100,000 workers in the motor factories themselves had been built up. In 1956 the output reached over 100,000 vehicles. Of these about three-quarters consisted of vans and lorries. Light vehicles, suitable for Japanese roads, predominated.

The new industry started its career after the war with grave deficiencies in up-to-date equipment and technical knowledge. As in the electrical-engineering industry remedies were sought after 1952 by manufacturing arrangements with foreign producers, such as Renault, Austin, Hillman, Willys Overland, and the Kaiser Motor Company. These arrangements enabled foreign-style cars to be produced by the Japanese under licence. In addition, several Japanese firms began to turn out light cars, trucks, and passenger vehicles of their own design. Some of these even found export markets. The re-equipment of the industry and the reorganization of productive processes went ahead rapidly after 1952. In the middle 1950's the Japanese manufacturers were still handicapped by the high cost and poor quality of certain types of steel, as well as by their relatively small scale of output. So their products compared unfavourably both in quality and price with those of Western firms. For example, even in 1956 Japanese-made trucks were 30 per cent. higher in price than their foreign-made equivalents and for passenger cars the comparisons are even less favourable.[1] The chief producers were Toyoda, which began its career as a loom manufacturer, and Nissan, formerly operated by Aikawa. As in most new industries that require large capital resources and modern technique, control in this industry has been concentrated in established firms already prominent in other branches of engineering.[2] This concentration at the centre, however, is quite consistent with the continuing importance of very small producers who work as subcontractors for big firms. In the middle 1950's there were more than 300 small and medium-sized factories engaged in the manufacture of parts for the motor industry. Some of these firms were efficiently conducted and, as a result of a high degree of specialization, their productivity, by Japanese standards, was high. A number of them produced parts needed in the maintenance of imported cars. Thus, as was usual in the establishment of new industries by large firms, opportunities were at the same time created for many small producers who indeed had an essential contribution to make to development.

BICYCLES

During the 1930's Japan was the world's chief producer of bicycles. In 1937 her output was 2¼ million. Half of them were exported and, in the machinery and vehicle group, cycles were the most important item in the export list. The industry declined during the war, for the plants and the labour force were diverted to war production. After 1945 recovery was not long delayed, and by 1950 the pre-war output had been surpassed. In 1953 output reached over 2,800,000.[3] The rapid recovery in production can be attributed in part to the fact that war factories, now without markets, had ample supplies of machine tools which either could be diverted to cycle production *in situ* or could be sold to former manufacturers of cycles or cycle components. The new equipment permitted the production of

---

[1] *Oriental Economist*, February 1957, p. 84.

[2] Among the other producers are the Fuji Precision Machinery Company (a successor of the Nakajima Aircraft Company) and a Mitsubishi subsidiary.

[3] These figures cover finished bicycles and parts equivalent to finished bicycles.

cycles of an average quality superior to those made before the war.[1]

During the 1930's the cycle industry was composed of a small number of substantial and medium-sized firms engaged in the manufacture either of the completed cycle or of parts, and also of numerous small specialist workplaces, each of which undertook the production of a component or the performance of a process of manufacture or assembly, to the orders of wholesale merchants. The very cheap bicycles produced for export (mainly in the form of parts) came from these small producers. By the middle 1950's the organization had been considerably modified, though by no means transformed. The number of workplaces was fewer than before the war and the importance of the very small manufacturers had declined. This occurred partly because of the loss of foreign markets for very cheap bicycles and partly because of the competitive advantages enjoyed by the larger factories equipped with efficient machine tools. Nevertheless, although factories with 100 workers and over employed about half the total labour force engaged in workplaces with 10 or more employees, a large section of the trade remained in the hands of specialist manufacturers of parts or assemblers, some of whom operated on a very small scale.[2] It is estimated that in 1954 there were 400 factories with 10 or more workers, besides probably 1,000 domestic workshops. The town of Sakai, near Osaka, was dotted with cycle workshops and small factories. The low administrative expenses and cheap labour recruited by these producers compensated in some measure for their inferiority to the large factories in equipment and technique.

The recovery in foreign trade did not keep pace with the rise in output. In the early 1950's exports were less than a third of the pre-war quantity, and they accounted in 1953 for only a tenth of the total production. Little further progress has been made since then. Before the war Japan's competitive strength in this trade was displayed chiefly in the manufacture and sale of the cheap, low-grade bicycle to West Africa and other countries where incomes were very small. The demand for that type of

---

[1] Society for Economic Cooperation in Asia, *Smaller Industry in Japan*, pp. 39–40.
[2] Ibid. pp. 40–41.

product has fallen away since the war, and in the market for higher-grade bicycles her relative advantages are less conspicuous.

SEWING MACHINES

While the cycle industry is an old-established industry that has been concerned with recovering its pre-war markets, the manufacture of sewing machines is new. Before 1935 output had been insignificant, and the home market both for industrial and for household sewing machines was supplied by imports from the United States. In the years just before the war Japan's production began to expand. It reached a peak in 1940 when 150,000 machines were produced. Like other industries that served a civilian market, sewing-machine manufacture declined precipitately during the war and only machines for industrial use continued to be made. Immediately after the war, however, a remarkable expansion began. By 1947 production was already near to the pre-war peak and in 1951 over a million machines were produced.[1] In 1956 output reached 1,720,000 units. At first most of the output went to the home market, but after 1948 a substantial export trade began. It reached 840,000 units in 1951 and 1,180,000 in 1954, or 86 per cent. of the total output. The value of this trade was exceeded, in the machinery group, only by that of ship exports. Thus this new industry depended predominantly upon demand from abroad. At a time when Japan's export trade as a whole was stagnating, foreign sales of these goods increased from year to year. A high proportion of the exports was sent to the United States.

This remarkable development must be explained. It can be well understood that the home demand for sewing machines should have been very high for some years after the war, for the Japanese had to restock their wardrobes and the increasing use of Western-style dress called for a large supply of sewing machines. This, however, does not account for the growth of exports. At the end of the war, as we have already seen, Japan had a surplus of engineering capacity. For many years none of this could be used for munitions and restrictions had been imposed on various other types of production. Japan

[1] *Survey of Japanese Finance and Industry*, September–October 1955, pp. 1–2.

therefore had ample capacity and skilled labour to devote to the manufacture of products of this kind. In the chief manufacturing countries of the West, on the other hand, engineering capacity was fully stretched and the post-war demand for durable consumer goods such as sewing machines could not be satisfied. A ten-months strike at the American plants of the Singer Sewing Machine Company in 1949 gave Japan her opportunity to enter that market.[1]

In the conversion of her productive capacity to new uses after the war, Japan showed a characteristic adaptability, and sewing-machine manufacture fully demonstrated this quality. In recent years as in the past capacity for adaptation was in some degree bound up with the form of industrial organization in Japan. It was not merely the pre-war sewing-machine makers who reconverted their factories to this production. The industry enlisted many new recruits. Some of them consisted of large firms engaged in various branches of engineering (e.g. the Mitsubishi Electrical Company). Some were firms hitherto engaged on quite different types of production, such as the Fukusuke Tabi Company.[2] Others were small firms of engineering subcontractors who turned to the production of parts for sewing machines. These small firms were very numerous just after the war, and although there was a reduction in their number in later years, even in the middle 1950's four-fifths of the sewing-machine parts were then being manufactured by specialist makers of parts.[3] This organization had been fostered by the government which instituted standards for sewing-machine parts and introduced a system of inspection which saw that they were maintained. At the same time certain firms became the focus of a co-operative system of production in which numerous producers participated.

As in other branches of the Japanese economy, this combination of large-scale organization at the centre with a wide diffusion of the actual processes of production led to the emergence of a highly efficient industry. The several types of producers of which it is now composed may be classified as follows: first, a few large integrated concerns which produce a high proportion

---

[1] *Survey of Japanese Finance and Industry*, September–October 1955, pp. 2–3.
[2] *Tabi* are Japanese-style socks.
[3] *Economic Survey of Japan, 1954–5*, p. 70.

of the parts they require, secondly, medium-sized firms which process the arm-beds and assemble the products, and thirdly, the assembly firms which buy parts from small specialists. With one exception, these assemblers also are very small firms. The proportion of the trade served by the second two groups recently increased, and by the early 1950's they were responsible for most of the output of household machines, while the large firms tended to concentrate on industrial machines.[1] Co-operative organization played its part in the conduct of the export trade as well as in the organization of production. When low-priced Japanese exports gave rise to a threat that anti-dumping duties would be imposed in the United States, the industry formed an association for handling exports jointly so as to prevent offers of goods at exceptionally low prices.

[1] *Survey of Japanese Finance and Industry*, September–October 1955, pp. 3 ff.

CHAPTER VIII

Iron and Steel, Fuel and Power, and Some Miscellaneous Trades

IRON AND STEEL

THE modern Japanese iron and steel industry, in its origins and development, was a product of State initiative. The first iron and steel works of a Western type, the Yawata Works, was founded in the early years of the present century by the government and was operated as an official undertaking. Most of the other firms that entered the industry in the first few decades of the century also depended in varying degrees upon government financial assistance or protection. The predominance of Yawata, moreover, was never shaken. When Japan launched her rearmament programme during the 1930's it was considered desirable to extend government control over industries of strategic importance. The iron and steel industry was an obvious subject for the application of this policy. Accordingly, in 1934 the Nippon Seitetsu[1] was formed to take over and operate the Yawata concern along with six other important enterprises. The State held most of the capital in this new company and the various *Zaibatsu* the rest. At the time of its formation the Nippon Seitetsu was responsible for nearly all the country's output of pig-iron, more than half the ingot-steel output and over two-fifths of the finished-steel output of Japan and Korea. After the outbreak of the Sino-Japanese War in 1937 a great expansion of capacity was undertaken both by the official concerns and by outside companies. Nor was growth limited to Japan Proper. In Manchuria also there was a steep increase in capacity, especially of pig-iron capacity, under the leadership of another government concern, the Showa Steel Company. The aim of the policy was not merely the expansion of output, but also the creation of a well-articulated industry in which the producers in Japan Proper were supplied with pig-iron and ore from Manchuria (together with some ore from Karafuto) and coking

[1] Japan Iron and Steel (Co.).

coal from North China, while firms in Japan Proper produced
the finished steel required for Manchurian as well as for domestic development. At this time Japan was also obtaining ore
from Japanese-owned mines in Malaya, scrap from the United
States, and pig-iron from India.

The policy of expansion and integration was pressed much
further after the outbreak of the Pacific War. The result was
the creation of a great industry, by far the largest iron and steel
industry outside Europe, the United States, and Russia. In the
early 1930's Japan's output had been quite small; in 1932 it
was about 1 million tons of pig-iron and under $2\frac{1}{2}$ million tons
of ingot and cast steel, while the Manchurian and Korean output did not exceed half a million tons of pig-iron a year. By
1943 Japan's output of pig-iron amounted to nearly $4\frac{1}{2}$ million
tons and her output of ingot steel to over $7\frac{1}{2}$ million tons.[1] The
Korean and Manchurian output by then had risen to about $1\frac{1}{2}$
million tons of pig-iron and half a million tons of steel.[2] The
successful execution of this expansionist programme depended
upon the maintenance of the lines of communication between
Japan on the one hand and North and South East Asia on the
other. When towards the end of the war these lines were cut by
the Allies, the Japanese industry was deprived of most of its raw
materials and semi-products. By the end of the war most of the
plants in this industry were still intact, but production had fallen
very low through a shortage of material supplies.

For several years after the war recovery was slow. Imports of
raw materials were narrowly limited by the shortage of foreign
exchange and by the policy of the Occupation authorities who
contemplated permanent restrictions over the future size of this
as of other strategic industries. At the same time domestic supplies of fuel were small because of the deterioration of mining
equipment and the dispersal of coalminers. In 1946 the output
of pig-iron amounted to only about 200,000 tons and of steel to
560,000 tons. During the next year the Occupation authorities
allowed coking coal and ore to be imported from the United
States and elsewhere, and the government provided subsidies

[1] Economic Counsel (Planning) Board, *Japanese Economic Statistics, Industrial
Production* (various years); and Japan Iron and Steel Federation, *Statistics of Iron
and Steel Industry of Japan* (various years) for statistical data in this section.

[2] Jones, *Manchuria*, p. 153.

for reconstruction from the Reconstruction Finance Bank. These measures made a revival possible. By 1949 output had risen to 1½ million tons of pig-iron and over 3 million tons of steel, broadly equivalent to the output of 1933 and 1934. The institution of the Dodge Deflation Plan threatened to check the recovery, but after the outbreak of the Korean War in June 1950 the advance was resumed at a much increased rate. Japan's iron and steel industry, along with her other heavy industries, was among the chief beneficiaries of the boom that the war engendered, and large orders were placed by the Allied governments as well as by private customers. Even when the general boom collapsed, the home demand for iron and steel persisted and output continued to rise. By 1953 it was higher than the wartime peak and after a slight fall in 1954 it rose again. In 1956 pig-iron output reached 6·3 million tons and ingot and cast-steel output 11·1 million tons. This represented an increase over 1937 of 90 per cent. in the case of steel and 160 per cent. in the case of pig-iron. Among the finished-steel products, the advance was especially great in sheets, plates, and tubes. At the same time the quality was improved and the range of products extended to take in special steels and highly fabricated goods.

The war had important effects on the industry's organization, its sources of raw-material supply, and its markets. As we have seen, before and during the war, output in Japan Proper was very highly concentrated in the government-owned Nippon Seitetsu and in a small number of other concerns owned for the most part by the *Zaibatsu*. The Occupation policy of destroying concentrations of economic power led to the break-up of the former and to the destruction of the economic empires of which the outside iron and steel companies were members. The properties of the Nippon Seitetsu were distributed between the Yawata Company, which had been the nucleus of the combine, and a new concern called the Fuji Iron and Steel Company. The shares owned by the government were sold on the market, and many of them passed into the hands of banks and financial institutions formerly part of the *Zaibatsu*. As a result of this and of other measures of reorganization, there emerged in the post-war world three major integrated producers, Yawata, Fuji, and the Nippon Kokan Company, a concern which before the war had been specialized to tube production. In 1953 these three concerns between them produced over four-fifths of the country's pig-iron, 55 per cent. of the ingot steel, and about the same proportion of the finished steel.[1] The rest of the industry was in the hands of some ten concerns of which the largest were the Kawasaki Steel Corporation, Sumitomo Metal Industries, and the Kobe Steel Works.

The second group of steel firms was, in general, less well-equipped than the three leaders. They had formerly obtained their pig-iron from abroad, especially from Manchuria, and the collapse of the Japanese empire and the shortage of foreign exchange meant that after the war they had to look for supplies within Japan itself, either among the integrated concerns or the smaller pig-iron producers. Their difficulties were increased because foreign scrap, used extensively in their furnaces before the war, could not easily be obtained. Further, many of their finishing plants had been located for the convenient handling of Manchurian semi-products and for this reason also the change in Japan's economic position left them seriously handicapped. The responsibilities of the war and of the Peace Settlement for the weakness of this section of the industry must not, however, be exaggerated. Technical advances which had increased the advantages of vertically integrated plants would anyhow have rendered obsolete the former relationship between the Manchurian and Japanese branches of the industry. Yet this fact merely emphasized the inadequacies of the specialist steel producers in the post-war world.

There were other difficulties common to the industry as a whole. All the producers met with serious obstacles in acquiring raw materials. Before the war Japan had depended upon imports for 87 per cent. of her ore and for a high proportion of her coking coal. At that time nearly 40 per cent. of her ore came from China, Manchuria, and Korea; Malaya supplied most of the remainder. For imports of coking coal Japan depended

---

[1] Yawata was the largest producer with 1·4 million tons of pig-iron, 1·9 million tons of ingot steel, and 1·6 million tons of finished steel. Fuji, which had a high proportion of newly-built equipment, produced 1·65 million tons of pig-iron, 1·45 million tons of ingot steel, and 1·2 million tons of finished steel. Nippon Kokan's output was ·8 million tons of pig-iron, ·9 million tons of ingot steel, and ·6 million tons of finished steel. These figures are for 1953 (S. Kawata, *Japan's Iron and Steel Industry* (Tokyo, Tokyo Foreign Service, 1954), *passim*).

wholly upon China and Saghalien. After 1945 these sources of
supply were denied to her. Although she managed to reduce
her relative dependence upon ore imports, she still found herself
obliged to rely on distant foreign countries for from three-fifths
to two-thirds of her ore and for at least half her coking coal.
Over the greater part of the period she had to draw most of her
imports of coking coal and about a third of her ore imports from
North America. The rest of the ore imports came from Malaya,
the Philippines, and India. These changes not merely raised
the cost of raw materials but also made that cost very unstable
since it was sensitive to fluctuations in freight rates. The rise in
mining costs at home added to the steel makers' problems, and
at the same time difficulties were encountered in securing scrap.
These conditions combined to oblige Japan to effect a thorough-
going technical reorganization of her industry. In 1951 an
ambitious modernization plan was introduced by the government.[1] This plan provided for the creation of new sintering
plants (for the treatment of low-grade Japanese ore), the renova-
tion and extension of blast-furnace capacity, the construction of
new integrated plants, including a very large works of the
Kawasaki Steel Corporation at Shiba, and the installation of
new equipment for rolled products, including continuous strip
mills and plate-rolling mills. Efforts were also made to reduce
dependence on ore imports by using increased quantities of iron
sand which is abundant in Japan. Until recently this material
was smelted only in electric furnaces, but methods have been
worked out for using it in blast furnaces and in 1956 about
1 million tons were consumed.

   The government gave financial support to this modernization
programme by making loans available at low rates of interest
from the Development Bank, and by furnishing foreign exchange for the import of machinery from the United States and
Germany. By 1955 a considerable part of the programme had
been carried out. Even so much new investment was required
for the modernization of the industry which was still handicapped by being obliged to operate some equipment that was
obsolete or in bad repair. Nevertheless, a substantial improvement was undoubtedly brought about in technical efficiency.
Labour productivity had declined steeply in the early post-war

---

[1] Kawata, *Japan's Iron and Steel Industry*, pp. 62–83.

years and was slow to recover. Between 1950 and 1955, however, the output of crude steel per man year rose from 29 tons
to 51 tons, and the advance in productivity is likely to continue
as new and improved plants come into operation.[1]

An advance in productivity was necessary to offset Japan's
high material costs compared with those of other countries. In
the early 1950's the cost of coking coal per ton of pig-iron
produced in Japan was double that in England or West Germany.[2] Indeed international comparisons of steel costs in
general were then very unfavourable to Japan. It was estimated that in 1951–2 she needed twice as many man hours as
Great Britain and seven times as many as the United States to
produce a ton of pig-iron; for steel the factors were 2 and 5
respectively. The effect of these disparities on costs was not
balanced by her lower wages. Labour costs per ton of pig-iron
were 20 per cent. higher in Japan than in Great Britain and the
United States; for steel produced from molten pig-iron the disparity between British and Japanese costs was about the same,
although it was less for steel made from cold pig-iron.[3] The
differences have probably narrowed since these calculations
were made because of the technical improvements already described. Yet Japan is still a relatively high-cost producer.
Moreover, in quality some of her products (e.g. steel sheets) are
less reliable than those of Western manufacturers, although they
are improving as new plants come into operation.

During the currency of the Five Year Plan the chief progress
was made in correcting the imbalance that characterized part
of the iron and steel industry and in developing a structure
composed of vertically integrated plants. It is intended to pursue this policy further in accordance with a Second Five Year
Plan introduced in 1955. The plan is also aimed at remedying
another weakness common to many branches of the metal
trades, namely the lack of specialization among the several
plants. When this plan has been carried through, it should lead
to a substantial reduction in costs.

---

[1] In this calculation the employment series includes process workers, technical
and clerical staff in the blast-furnace, steel-furnace, casting, forging, and rolling
sections of the industry. The output series covers crude steel. No account is taken
of changes in the quality or range of products. It is difficult to compare productivity before and after the war, but it was certainly higher in 1955 than in 1936.

[2] Ibid. p. 89.   [3] *Economic Survey of Japan, 1953–4,* p. 61.

The favourable market conditions that have existed since 1950 have permitted Japan to build up a large export trade in iron and steel, a trade that has risen far above pre-war levels. In the middle 1930's the exports, which amounted to about 400,000 tons of finished steel, went mainly to Manchuria, China Proper, and Kwantung. They represented about 10 per cent. of the finished steel output. During the early 1950's the exports have been much in excess of this figure. They rose sharply after 1950 and in 1952 they reached 1,650,000 tons. After a decline in 1953 they again increased and in 1955 amounted to about 2 million tons, well over a fifth of the total output. These goods have found markets all over the world, especially in India, South East Asia, the United States, and even the United Kingdom. The significance of the exports, however, must be judged by reference to the price policy that has made them possible. The Japanese steel makers have been expected by their government to earn foreign currency to pay for their imports of raw materials, and they have therefore sold their steel abroad at much lower prices than those charged at home. For instance, in 1956 the f.o b. export price of heavy plates was £60–70 a ton compared with a home price of £90–100 a ton; for angles the respective prices were £50 and £90.[1] Japan has been remarkably successful in adjusting her iron and steel industry to profoundly changed conditions, including the disruption of former channels of material supply and the loss of former markets. Since 1952 she has done much to overcome technical deficiencies. It must be remembered, however, that her industry has been operating in very favourable market conditions at home and abroad. If steel ceased to be scarce in the outside world, and if Japan were faced with keen price competition from the United States, Britain, and Western Europe (and even from the Soviet Union), her position as the only substantial manufacturer of iron and steel in Asia would scarcely enable her to maintain her present export trade. For the moment demand remains buoyant. In the long run, however, the fortunes of the iron and steel industry are likely to depend on Japan's success in enlarging her trade in finished manufactured goods in which the ratio of the metallic to the labour content is small.

[1] Information from Japan Iron and Steel Federation.

COAL MINING AND ELECTRICITY GENERATION

Coal mining, in Japan, as in most other countries, was one of the chief industrial victims of the war. During the 1930's output had grown steadily and by 1937 reached 45 million tons. A little was exported, but on balance Japan was an importer of coal, chiefly from China. Although these imports represented under a tenth of the home supply, they were qualitatively of great importance, for they consisted chiefly of coking coal for the iron and steel industry, a commodity in which Japan was deficient. In the early years of the war the expansion of output continued, but this was at the expense of the future. It was achieved by the neglect of development work and the concentration of mining operations on the most easily won coal. When the war came to an end, the industry passed through a period of chaos. Much of the mining labour was dispersed, and for a time little could be done to repair the ravages of the war. Output in 1946 and 1947 was little more than half the pre-war output, and production per worker fell to 72 tons a year compared with 216 tons in 1935.

Recovery started in 1948 and by 1951 output approached the pre-war (1937) peak and in 1953 exceeded it. Subsequently there was a decline and in 1955 output was only 42 million metric tons.[1] This hesitancy at a time when industrial production as a whole was advancing rapidly requires examination. In coal we touch on one of the chief weaknesses in Japan's industrial structure. The thinness of the seams and the poor quality of the product have always handicapped the industry. Mining difficulties have increased through the running down of equipment and the exploitation of the best seams during the war. Attempts to counter the worsened physical conditions by the introduction of power-cutting and loading machinery and by the adoption of improved systems of mining have not succeeded in raising productivity (output per man month) to the pre-war level. Thus while *hourly* production per man had been restored by 1955 to that attained in 1936, the reduction in working hours by about 30 per cent. since the war has left production per man month substantially less. In 1934–6 the average was

[1] The annual average output of the period 1952–6 was 44 million metric tons compared with 43 million metric tons for 1935–8.

17¾ tons; in 1954 only 12 tons.[1] As real wages in coal mining have regained their pre-war level, the cost per ton has risen sharply. The result is that Japanese coal prices have compared very unfavourably with those of foreign countries. During the 1950's United States coking coal could be delivered to Japanese ports at a much lower price than that charged for high-grade Japanese coal. This imposed a serious burden on the heavy industries. It persuaded the government not merely to give financial assistance towards the re-equipment of the coal mines but also to provide finance for imported coal and oil. Between 1951 and 1955 the share of domestically-mined coal in the total fuel consumption fell from 93 per cent. to 80 per cent.

In the middle 1950's the industry was in the hands of 600 firms with nearly 1,000 mines. Most of these were very small. Half the output came from 30 large mines, and the 18 leading coal-mining companies were responsible for 70 per cent. of the output. This concentration, however, was far less than before the war, for many new small mines came into existence during the last decade.

It is sometimes thought that Japan can view the worsening conditions in her coal industry with equanimity because of her resources of water power. These resources are certainly very great and they have long been extensively exploited for generating electric power. Even before the war Japan's output of electricity was not far short of that of the United Kingdom. There was a further increase during the early years of the war. Then followed a period of stagnation which lasted until 1949. In that year development was resumed, financed by loans from the United States Aid Counterpart Fund. In 1952 the government drew up an elaborate plan for the construction of new generating stations. It provided large funds for this purpose, and the industry also obtained foreign loans from the World Bank and from financial houses. Elaborate works were set in hand and much equipment was imported from the United States. In 1955 production reached 64,000 million kwh., well over twice the pre-war output.

Japan cannot depend wholly on water power for the generation of electricity. She needs thermal plants to maintain output during the winter months when the rainfall is inadequate. In

---

[1] Data from Ministry of International Trade and Industry.

recent years the amount of electrical energy produced by coal
was nearly a quarter of the total. So the high price of coal
affects the cost of electricity despite the predominance of water-
generated supplies. Further, the cost of production at the new
hydro-electric stations has been very high—twice that at stations built in pre-war days—because of the high rates of interest
paid on loans. In so far as these interest charges have been
reduced by government assistance, or by loans made at less
than the market rates, this merely means that the industry has
been subsidized at the expense of the taxpayer. The real cost
of Japan's power is thus much greater than before the war.

The post-war period has seen a change in the organization of
the industry. During the 1930's the generation of electricity
was becoming increasingly concentrated in a few very large
concerns, several of which had raised capital in the United
States or Great Britain. After the outbreak of the Sino-
Japanese War, the government took control of the generation
and transmission of electricity and set up a semi-official corporation, the Japan Electric Power Generating and Transmission Company, to execute its policy. Such a concentration
of economic authority was repugnant to the Occupation
authorities. In 1951 the semi-official concern was dissolved, and
its generating and transmission properties were distributed
among nine regional supply companies which had hitherto been
engaged only in distribution. In September 1952, however, the
government, intent upon stimulating a more rapid growth in
the industry, and conscious that private capital was unlikely to
be available, created a new instrument for its purpose, namely
the Electric Power Development Company. Nearly all the
capital of this concern was held by the government. Among its
first tasks was the construction of a vast new generating plant
on the Tenryu River. Thus in some degree the former concentration of authority has been restored. Japan was compelled by the Americans to accept a more widespread diffusion
of economic power, but the principles of economic liberalism
yielded readily to circumstances when rapid economic development proved to be incompatible with them.

CHEMICALS

The chemical industry was one of the most rapidly growing branches of manufacture both in size and range during the 1930's. Whereas at the beginning of that decade Japan depended upon imports for a substantial proportion of her chemical fertilizers and chemical products needed by her textile industries, on the eve of the Second World War she had become almost self-sufficient. For many years the government had interested itself in the development of the industry, largely for strategic reasons, and some branches owed their initial growth to official assistance or protection. Nevertheless, by 1937 Japan had become fully competitive with foreign countries in most classes of chemicals, and she had worked up a fair-sized export trade in a few of them, e.g. the sale of dyestuffs to China. At that time the chief products of the industry consisted of nitrogenous fertilizers (especially ammonium sulphate), which were essential to the maintenance of the agricultural output, sulphuric acid used in the manufacture of various chemicals and for processes in the textile and metal industries, caustic soda and soda ash for the rayon, glass, and soap trades, and dyestuffs and pharmaceuticals.

By the end of the Second World War the output of these goods had been much reduced because of bomb damage, the shortage of power and raw materials, and the conversion of many plants to the manufacture of explosives. The recovery of the industry was very uneven. The restoration of plants in the ammonium sulphate and other chemical-fertilizer trades was given priority by the Occupation authorities in the interests of food production, and funds were provided for this purpose by the government's financial agencies. So this section of the industry was one of the earliest to recover, and by 1949 the pre-war output had been surpassed. Expansion continued for several years, and in 1955 the output of ammonium sulphate was more than twice the annual average output of 1936–7. By that time Japan not merely satisfied her own needs for nitrogenous fertilizers, but she had also worked up an export trade of about half a million tons a year. It might have been inferred from this that she had become a cheap producer. In fact, however, although labour productivity in the manufacture of ammonium sulphate in 1955 was well above the pre-war level, advances in other countries

were even greater and Japan was by no means a low-cost manufacturer. During the early and middle 1950's her domestic
prices were well above the international price, and exports were
only possible because the producers practised a discriminatory
pricing policy.[1] The producers, having a home market protected
against outside competition by the operations of exchange control as well as by import duties, did not hesitate to dump their
surplus output abroad. This policy was all the easier to follow
because production was in the hands of a small number of large
firms organized for export purposes in a joint selling company.[2]
Even so, the export trade in this product has not extended significantly beyond neighbouring countries (Korea, Formosa, and
China) where Japan enjoys freight advantages in her competition with Western producers.

The ammonium-sulphate industry is based upon domestic
supplies of raw materials and power. Other branches of the
chemical industry, however, depend upon imports, for example
the manufacture of caustic soda and soda ash on imports of salt.
Before the war salt could be obtained cheaply from China, but
as this source of supply was cut off, Japan was obliged to find
others at a much greater distance, for instance, India, Aden,
and North Africa. In consequence, the price of Japan's soda
products during the 1950's was above the world price and output failed to regain the pre-war level until 1954. The dyestuffs
industry was another branch to suffer from the change in
Japan's position *vis-à-vis* China. In that case, however, it was
the loss of China as a market that hampered recovery.

In compensation for these difficulties, Japan has greatly extended the *range* of her chemical manufactures since the end of
the war. Apart from an increased variety of chemical fertilizers,
she has created important industries engaged in producing
new types of pharmaceuticals and plastics. These innovations
were stimulated by the establishment of technical and financial
relations between Japanese and foreign firms.[3] For example,

[1] *Survey of Japanese Finance and Industry*, July–August 1955, pp. 11–12; July–
August 1956, pp. 5–6. The greater part of the output since the war has been produced by the gas process, the use of the synthetic process having been handicapped
by the shortage of electric power.

[2] *Sumitomo Bank Review*, July 1955, pp. 21–22.

[3] Bank of Japan, Foreign Capital Research Society, *Japanese Industry, 1954*, pp.
40 ff.

companies jointly capitalized by Japanese and Americans were formed to manufacture plastic materials, and foreign techniques were imported by arrangement with American and European firms in connexion with the production of various insecticides. In this way Japan was able in some degree to overcome the technical inferiority which was one of the most serious legacies of the war. As to her future prospects, she is geographically well placed for serving markets in East and South Asia with heavy chemicals, and if her recent technical progress continues, her chemical industry could reasonably hope to benefit greatly from the economic development of that continent, especially if this were attended by a considerable increase in the demand for fertilizers from Asian agriculturists.

CERAMICS

Two other representative trades will now be examined, ceramics, an old-established industry which for many years possessed a flourishing exporting section, and camera manufacture, a new industry in which the distinctive excellence of Japan in producing goods that require much skilled labour is demonstrated.

Ceramics in the Japanese industrial classification comprises a number of separate trades—heavy industries, such as the manufature of sheet glass, cement, and bricks, and lighter industries engaged in the production of optical glass, glass-ware, and pottery. The last mentioned can be further divided into several branches, including electrical porcelain, tiles, sanitary ware, and table ware. Before the Second World War all these trades were well established and were expanding rapidly. Their growth continued up to the outbreak of the Pacific War but then a decline set in. The light branches had catered mainly for peacetime markets and the heavy branches were now very short of fuel. By the end of the war the volume of output had been reduced to a quarter of that of 1937, or about a sixth of that of 1940. Recovery was impeded by the continued shortage of fuel and by the lack of capital during the early years of the Occupation. It was not until this group of industries came under the influence of the Korean War boom that output rose above pre-war levels. Subsequent expansion brought the production index for the ceramics group as a whole to 175 in 1955 (average 1934–6 = 100), about 47 per cent. greater than the output reached in 1937 and roughly the same as that of the peak years 1939–40. Compared with pre-war days, the most striking advances were in sheet glass, cement and cement products, and optical glass. The contrasts in the rate of recovery of the several sections of the industry can be attributed to a number of causes that affected the economy as a whole. The steep increase in the output of cement and sheet glass can be explained by the strong demand for these products for the reconstruction of industrial plants and buildings, the creation of new power stations, and the replacement of traditional materials in building (e.g. glass for paper). The optical glass industry was a new trade serving the growing camera, binocular, and scientific-instrument industries. Its size increased very rapidly in the post-war period. Pottery and glass-ware on the other hand were slow to recover, and it was not until the middle 1950's that they again approached their pre-war output.

In the export trade also the fortunes of the different sections varied. The high freight charges on cement have given Japan considerable advantages in catering for demand from other countries in the Far East where the industry is less highly developed. Exports, financed largely by special procurement expenditure, rose steeply after the outbreak of the Korean War, and after declining slightly in 1952 and 1953, resumed their expansion. In 1956 they accounted for about a sixth of the total output, and they are likely to rise further as demand from East and South Asia grows.[1] The other main exporting trade in this group is the pottery industry, especially table-ware manufacture. In recent years the North American and South Asian markets have been the chief destinations of these goods.

The ceramics industries use mainly indigenous materials, but this advantage can easily be overestimated, for they have all been handicapped by the high price of domestic coal. The glass industry has also been affected by the increased cost of salt. At the end of the war the technical efficiency of the heavy branches had seriously declined, and in spite of heavy investments in improved plants during recent years, in cement and glass manufacture Japan's methods are still inferior to those of the leading

[1] *Fuji Bank Bulletin*, March 1957, pp. 26–38. In 1956 Japanese cement exports, at 2,100,000 metric tons, were larger than those of any other country.

Western countries and her costs are relatively high.[1] She has only been able to build up an export of those goods because the Asian markets have been insulated from Western competition by high freight charges. In the table-ware trade, on the other hand, Japan's ample supplies of cheap skilled labour with artistic aptitudes provide her with considerable advantages in competition with Western countries.

The organization of the several branches of the industry is varied. The manufacture of cement and sheet glass, as in other countries, is an activity of very large firms. In 1955–6 6 companies with 31 plants were responsible for about three-quarters of the cement output.[2] Three companies with 7 plants produced the sheet-glass output. In pottery there is great diversity. The heavy porcelain branch and part of the table-ware industry engaged in the export trade are conducted by a few large concerns. The remainder of the export trade and the whole of the domestic trade in Japanese-style ware are conducted by numerous medium-sized and small concerns. In this respect the pottery industry has not changed for many decades. Even before the war the large firms used advanced types of equipment (such as oil, gas, or electrically fired furnaces) and practised flow-production methods, while in the rest of the trade the equipment was simple. Since the war modern types of equipment have been increasingly adopted by firms of medium size.

CAMERAS

It has been suggested that Japan's relative advantages in international competition are to be found chiefly in those finished manufactured products in which the labour content is large and the raw-material content small. Among the older industries those engaged in manufacturing bicycles, toys, fancy goods, and table-ware satisfy these criteria. Since the war Japan has added a number of new products within this class, notably cameras, binoculars, and fishing tackle. Large quantities of all these goods were sold abroad during the early and middle 1950's. The manufacture of cameras will be taken as

---

[1] Japan's f.o.b. price for cement in January 1957 was 20–30 per cent. higher than that of West Germany (*Fuji Bank Bulletin*, March 1957, p. 38).

[2] Ibid. p. 29, and *Survey of Japanese Finance and Industry*, January–February 1956, pp. 4, 11.

an example. Before the war, in spite of the propensity of the Japanese to take photographs, the camera industry was small and its products of indifferent quality. During the war technique improved under the influence of the military demand. In particular, there was a marked advance in the quality of lenses. After the war the skilled labour and technical resources were quickly adapted to the creation of what was in fact a new industry. At first the inducement towards this production came from the demands of the Allied Occupation troops, but soon a substantial export trade to the United States was created. Output (in units) which had numbered about 6,000 in 1937 rose to 50,000 in 1947 and to nearly three-quarters of a million in 1955. About a quarter of them were exported. Recently a high proportion of the output consisted of high-grade cameras, and it is these which found a market in the United States as well as among American forces in Japan.[1] The reasons for Japan's success in this industry are significant for the light they throw upon her industrial potential. For cheap cameras as for other products that depend upon a mass-production technique and up-to-date mechanization, Japan cannot match the United States. But the high-grade camera calls for much patient labour for testing and inspection. This labour Japan has in abundance and it is the basis of her achievement. Similar reasons underlie her success in developing a large export of binoculars. Since her lenses are of high quality she may be expected to gain a footing in markets for other optical instruments.

The structure of the camera industry changed considerably during the period of its expansion. In the early 1950's about 90 concerns were producing cameras, but by 1956 the number fell to 50, and four-fifths of the production had become concentrated in 9 large concerns. In some plants more than 1,000 persons were then employed. The leading firms all had pre-war connexions with the optical, camera, or photographic industries, but they were small until the war brought about a vast growth in demand for optical equipment for military purposes. After 1945 the expertise and skill gained in the course of meeting that demand were applied to camera production for the civilian market.[2] Large-scale operation has advantages in this industry,

[1] *Sumitomo Bank Review*, January 1956, pp. 20–21.
[2] *Oriental Economist*, March 1957, pp. 135–42.

especially for high-grade products, because although much de-tailed manual work is involved, the manufacture calls for standardization and the use of expensive equipment. In other words this is an industry in which Japan can employ two of her chief endowments, her abundant skilled labour and her organizing capacity.

CHAPTER IX

The *Zaibatsu* in the Post-War Economy

THE industrialization of a materially backward country is usually accompanied by a high concentration of economic power either in the State or in a few private entrepreneurial groups. The reasons for this association are not far to seek. In such a country the supply of entrepreneurial ability is narrowly confined, while capital needed for development can be rapidly accumulated only if incomes are very unequally distributed or if the State can enforce savings on the necessary scale. So there is nothing surprising in the emergence of a few dominant business houses during the period of Japan's industrialization. It is true that their form, their internal organization, and their relations with each other and with the government bore the impress of the country's social and political traditions, and that the actual direction of their development was determined by opportunities afforded by national policy. Yet, in essentials, the *Zaibatsu*, though remarkable business constructions, were neither so peculiar nor so sinister as is sometimes made out.

The organization and growth of these business groups have been described elsewhere,[1] and here only a few of their most important features will be considered. Some had their roots deep in the past. Mitsui, Sumitomo, and Yasuda had been prominent in Japan's economic life long before the opening of the country. Others emerged at the time of the Restoration from among *samurai* who had formerly administered the commercial and industrial undertakings of the feudal lords and later acquired control of them; Mitsubishi is in this category. Again, some appeared from among new firms who successfully exploited the opportunities of the Meiji era. For example, Furukawa and Asano began their modern career when they came

---

[1] Lockwood, *Economic Development*, especially pp. 214–32; G. C. Allen, 'The Concentration of Economic Control in Japan', *Economic Journal*, June 1937; Mitsubishi Economic Research Institute, *Mitsui, Mitsubishi, Sumitomo* (Tokyo, 1955), pp. 3–12 and *passim*.

into possession of mines and industrial establishments previously owned by the government.

All the *Zaibatsu* benefited substantially from their official connexions. The administrative talents, technical expertise, and capital resources needed for the execution of the government's expansionist policy were not widely diffused in Japan, and the State could not dispense with the services of the few who possessed them in financing its own activities or in building up the economy. So the *Zaibatsu* gained high rewards in their role as the essential agents of the government. They received profitable public contracts. Valuable government properties were from time to time made over to them in return for financial help. They rose on the tide of economic expansion to which they themselves markedly contributed, and by the time of the First World War the ascendancy of certain houses was well established. Their economic power as it expanded enabled them to exert an influence on political trends, and during the 1920's some of them forged close links with the chief political parties. Their pre-eminence excited resentment among other groups in Japan, especially the army and the rural communities, and in the upheavals of the early 1930's their political influence was constricted. In the face of popular criticism the older and larger *Zaibatsu* tried to make themselves less conspicuous and withdrew from some lines of activity. They were now obliged to share the economic domain with certain newcomers favoured by the military. Of these *Shinko-Zaibatsu*, as they were called, the most important was Nissan. This concern originated in 1928 when G. Aikawa took over the Kuhara Mining Company and it subsequently played a leading part in the development of the heavy industries in Manchuria as well as in Japan Proper. Another *Shinko-Zaibatsu*, Nakajima, came to the front during the later 1930's when it was associated with the rise of armaments manufacture.

On the eve of the Second World War the four leading *Zaibatsu* (Mitsui, Mitsubishi, Sumitomo, and Yasuda in that order of importance) were to be distinguished from the others [1] not only by their size nor even by the wide scope of their interests, but also by the fact of their predominance in both finance and industry and trade. Their banks and their trust and insurance

---

[1] Such as Asano, Furukawa, Aikawa (Nissan), Okura, and Nomura.

companies, which included the chief institutions in these several fields, provided a channel through which the savings of the general public were directed into the industrial and commercial undertakings in the same group. Through these financial institutions the liquid resources of a great mass of concerns could be mobilized whenever the need arose, for example when heavy investment was required in some new branch of economic activity. Since there was only a small market for industrial securities among the general public, a manufacturing company that had no finance house behind it was liable to fall into a position of dependence upon a bank in another group.

In the industrial sector the *Zaibatsu* were especially prominent in the heavy industries (coal and metalliferous mining, metals, engineering, shipbuilding, and chemicals), although they also participated in the ceramics, textile, and paper industries. They had enormous real-estate interests, and the largest trading and shipping undertakings were under their control. It was not only the large-scale sector of the Japanese economy in which the *Zaibatsu* played a conspicuous part. Through their trading companies they handled the products of multitudes of small firms which they often financed, equipped, and largely directed.

The scope of the various *Zaibatsu* differed in detail. In the case of Mitsui, Mitsubishi, and Sumitomo the range of interests was extraordinarily wide—mining, numerous manufacturing industries, banking, trust and insurance, trade, warehousing, real estate, and shipping. Mitsui, the greatest of them, had been especially active in developing its trading interests and the famous Mitsui Bussan Kaisha (M.B.K.) played an outstanding part in the conduct of domestic and foreign trade. Mitsubishi also had a large trading company, Mitsubishi Shoji Kaisha, and it was especially important in the engineering and shipbuilding industries. Sumitomo's main strength lay in mining, non-ferrous metals, and electrical engineering. Yasuda was primarily a financial house, although it had large interests in textiles, electricity supply, real estate, and warehousing. The lesser *Zaibatsu* tended to confine their strength to a narrower range of interests. Asano was concerned chiefly with the heavy industries, especially iron and steel and cement, Furukawa with mining, electrical engineering, chemicals, and rubber, Okura with engineering, metals, chemicals, and trading (including heavy investments in Manchuria), Nakajima with aircraft and munitions, Nomura with banking and trust business, and Nissan with engineering and chemicals both in Japan and Manchuria. There were several other firms which were dominant in certain localities or in particular industries, notably Katakura in the raw silk industry.

One reason why the *Zaibatsu* excited the curiosity and suspicion of the outside world was to be found in the peculiarities of their internal organization. These vast and efficient businesses, equipped with all the contrivances of twentieth-century technology, rested on institutional foundations laid down in the 'feudal' past. Mitsui and Mitsubishi resembled the Fuggers of Augsburg rather than the anonymous giants of the era of the Western managerial revolution. Ownership was vested in a family or group of families, and the activities of every family member were regulated according to Japanese social practice by a family council which, in the case of Mitsui, framed its decisions in conformity with the ancient code of the house. Financial control over the network of businesses was exercised through a top holding company, usually called the *honsha*. This controlled the major operating subsidiaries under which there was an intricate network of sub-subsidiaries and affiliated companies. Major policies and the chief appointments to the *honsha* were determined in the family councils on the advice of the leading executives.[1]

Personal relations within the business hierarchy were governed by the Japanese tradition which prescribed absolute loyalty to superiors; but the extent to which the family members themselves exercised administrative authority varied from *Zaibatsu* to *Zaibatsu*. In Mitsubishi, for instance, the influence of the Iwasaki family remained very strong. In Mitsui, on the other hand, control over policy even before the Restoration had passed mainly to *banto*, or managers. But even the greatest of these *banto* could expect to retain their positions only so long as they were successful in promoting the welfare of the house.

The rivalries between the older *Zaibatsu* and the *Gumbatsu* (military)—rivalries which in the early 1930's had been accompanied by violent denunciations of *Zaibatsu* policy and even the

---

[1] Cf. T. A. Bisson, *Zaibatsu Dissolution in Japan* (Berkeley, University of California Press, 1954), p. 24.

assassination of leading *banto*—gradually gave place to co-operation between them in strengthening Japan's military power. By 1937 the *Zaibatsu* (the 'old' and the 'new' alike) had been called upon to promote the expansion of the munitions industries and to act as agents for the government in organizing the economy for war. After the outbreak of the Pacific War this co-operation became unqualified. The *Zaibatsu* alone had the resources needed for the task and as the war proceeded economic power became increasingly concentrated in their hands. While the civilian industries in which the smaller firms played an important part contracted, the heavy industries, already largely in *Zaibatsu* hands, expanded. The concentration of the banking system during the war left the *Zaibatsu* banks in an even more dominating position than they already occupied. At the same time, *Zaibatsu* personnel were closely engaged in the administration of official controls. The result was that by the end of the war these great houses had much increased their share of the economic activity of the country. Figures can throw only a dim light on the position they had then obtained. It is to be noted, however, that whereas in 1937 the 'Big Four' owned 15 per cent. and ten leading *Zaibatsu* 25 per cent. of the total paid-up capital in the heavy industries, in 1946 the proportions were 32 and 49 per cent. In finance and insurance, the corresponding figures were, for 1937 23 and 24 and for 1946 50 and 53 per cent. The ratio of the loans of the four great *Zaibatsu* banks to those of all ordinary banks rose from 44 per cent. in 1937 to 66 per cent. in 1945. It is estimated that at the end of the war Mitsui employed 1,800,000 persons in Japan Proper and probably over a million more overseas. Mitsubishi is thought to have employed about a million.[1]

It is not disputed that the *Zaibatsu* contributed 'strength, efficiency, and sureness of purpose' to Japan in her period of rapid economic development.[2] They were the chief sources of investment capital and the spearhead of the nation's enterprise. This, however, was not an aspect of their activity with which the Occupation authorities in 1945 felt much sympathy. To them the *Zaibatsu* represented a major obstacle to the construction of a liberal society and a competitive economic system. These

---

[1] Mitsubishi Economic Research Institute, *Mitsui, Mitsubishi, Sumitomo*, pp. 5–10.
[2] Bisson, *Zaibatsu Dissolution*, p. 32.

great houses had armed Japan for her conflict with the West
and they had impeded (so the Americans believed) the rise of
democratic institutions at home. Their destruction was an
essential part of the general policy of social and political reform.
If, in the process, economic efficiency were for a time diminished
and recovery delayed, that was a price which Japan must be
prepared to pay in the interests of the future welfare of her
people and of international peace. The Japanese firmly believe
that the Americans were also moved by a desire to weaken the
country's competitive strength in foreign trade, but it is doubtful if that motive ever exerted more than a minor influence over
what was done. Indeed there is evidence that once American
business circles had realized the full implications of SCAP's
policy, they became deeply suspicious of it and did not refrain
from bitter criticism. According to one commentator, they
feared that 'an active anti-monopoly program abroad [might]
presage increased anti-trust activity in the United States'.[1]

It must not be imagined that Japanese opinion was universally opposed to the American policy. Even in the ruling
cliques the *Zaibatsu* had their enemies, and their shadow frustrated the growth of independent enterprises. Socialists and
Liberals in general supported the view that the existence of the
Zaibatsu was incompatible with the emergence of democratic
institutions. But these circles, while supporting dissolution, believed that the State itself should take over and manage the
Zaibatsu properties. This proposal found widespread support
among those Japanese who realized that the disappearance of
the *Zaibatsu* would leave a 'power vacuum' that the government
alone could fill. However, the Occupation authorities were not
disposed to consult Japanese preferences. They were intent
upon dissolution.

Their policy passed through several stages. In the first days
of the Occupation the authorities proceeded on the assumption
that their purposes could be accomplished by a few sweeping
measures. Then, as the complications of the task of remodelling
the country's economic institutions were more widely understood, an elaborate series of measures was devised and vigorously applied. In the course of 1948, however, when the cold

[1] E. M. Hadley, 'Trust Busting in Japan', *Harvard Business Review*, July 1948, p.
427.

war began and the American administration became concerned with economic recovery rather than reform, its hostility towards the *Zaibatsu* and towards monopoly in general diminished. Nevertheless, the policy was not abandoned but was pursued in a modified form until the end of the Occupation. By then Japan's economic structure had suffered a profound change and some of its most prominent features had been permanently removed.

The policy was carried out by a series of related measures which were directed, first, towards destroying the power and wealth of the *Zaibatsu* families, secondly, towards the dissolution into numerous independent enterprises of the great mass of concerns within each group and, thirdly, towards the preservation of competition as a permanent condition of the economy. The *Zaibatsu* directly affected by this policy consisted of the 'Big Four' and six others. The properties of the family members were frozen immediately after the Occupation began, and the family securities together with those owned by the top holding companies were transferred to a Holding Company Liquidation Commission set up by the Japanese government in obedience to SCAP's orders. The Commission's main function was to dispose of these securities among the public in the hope of achieving a wide distribution of industrial ownership. The *Zaibatsu* family members were required to cease for ten years from participation in the businesses formerly under their control, and there was a 'purge' of most of the former leading *banto*. Next, a group of major subsidiaries which themselves had controlled a large number of undertakings was dissolved. Among the outstanding companies in this group were M.B.K. and Mitsubishi Shoji, and the fragmentation of these great trading concerns provided the chief ground for the Japanese conviction that the policy was aimed primarily at weakening their country's competitive power in foreign markets. The attack was also directed against the major subsidiaries in mining and manufacturing, although here it did not display the ruthless determination that characterized the policy when applied to the trading companies.

The dissolution, as it affected industry, was not limited to *Zaibatsu* companies. It was extended to a number of semi-official concerns, or so-called 'national policy' companies, whose existence in the eyes of the more zealous reformers constituted a serious offence against economic liberalism. Most of these concerns had been founded during the 1930's when the Japanese government was increasing its control over the economy for strategic purposes. The companies included the Nippon Seitetsu (Japan Iron and Steel Company) and the Japan Electricity Generating and Transmission Company.

In banking and finance the existing structure was only slightly disturbed, although the chief banks, in common with other *Zaibatsu* companies, were required to change their names so as to emphasize their independence of former associates. The mildness of the authorities towards the banks can be explained partly by the intricate technical problems to which dissolution gave rise and partly because the policy had exhausted itself by the time SCAP was ready to deal with this sector.

The authorities were determined that the personal and financial links between concerns formerly in the same group should be effectively severed. So restrictions were imposed on the holding of shares in other companies and on interlocking directorates. Further, the contractual arrangements that had existed between the several member companies within each group were brought to an end; these arrangements had taken the form of undertakings or agreements by which the major business decisions and appointments in a particular company depended upon approval given by another. These measures were strengthened by the enactment in April 1947 of an anti-monopoly law which prohibited or narrowly limited the rights of firms to resort to restrictive practices or to devices designed to restrain competition and to create monopolies.[1]

The results of these measures were far-reaching. The wealth and power of the *Zaibatsu* families were in fact destroyed, for although compensation in the form of government bonds was paid for the properties which they surrendered, the value of this payment was almost wiped out by a capital levy and by the subsequent inflation. The dissolution of the top holding com-

---

[1] The data on which this account of the *Zaibatsu* dissolution is based are: Holding Company Liquidation Commission, *Laws, Rules and Regulations concerning the Reconstruction and Democratization of the Japanese Economy* (Tokyo, 1949) and *Final Report on Zaibatsu Dissolution* (Tokyo, 1951); Bisson, *Zaibatsu Dissolution*; and Mitsubishi Economic Research Institute, *Mitsui, Mitsubishi, Sumitomo*.

panies of the leading *Zaibatsu* and of many of their major subsidiaries together with the breaking of the personal, contractual,
and financial links among them succeeded in producing a fragmentation of these great concerns. The leading executives were
prevented for several years from any direct participation in the
management of the successor companies which now came under
the control of relatively junior officials.

In the course of these operations a vast quantity of securities
passed into the hands of government agencies. The Holding
Company Liquidation Commission acquired shares worth
about 9,000 million yen at original paid-up values, and securities of about the same amount came into possession of the
Finance Ministry (as the result of the capital levy) and of other
public authorities. But these sums were dwarfed by the quantities of new issues which were required for financing industrial
reorganization during the inflationary period and were mainly
taken up by government agencies. In the end about '70,000
million yen of company shares was handled in disposal operations directed by the government'.[1] Of this vast amount the
securities handled by the Holding Company Liquidation Commission represented only a small proportion and the disposal
operations of that body must obviously be viewed in the light of
the conditions created by the inflation. As we have seen, the
original intention was to bring about a wide dispersal of securities as an essential condition for ushering in a liberal competitive society, and the Holding Company Liquidation Commission was the instrument chosen for this task. At the outset those
familiar with Japanese economic and social conditions feared
that the plan for disposals would encounter insurmountable
obstacles in a country where private investors had been
unaccustomed to enter the market for industrial securities. In
the event the task proved to be at once less onerous and less
significant. Disposals proceeded very slowly at first, but by 1950
some two-thirds of the shares held by the H.C.L.C. had been
sold. Many passed to the employees of the companies and a
fairly wide distribution was achieved. But an even greater
number of securities had been sold by the Finance Ministry and
other official agencies. In addition there was the great mass of
new issues. It seems probable that most of these shares were

---

[1] Bisson, *Zaibatsu Dissolution*, p. 115.

acquired by banks, insurance companies, and other institutional investors, among which the former *Zaibatsu* financial houses were especially prominent. In the final result it appears that although the policy had led to a somewhat wider dispersal of security holdings, industrial ownership at the end of the occupation still remained highly concentrated.

The dissolution policy retarded Japan's economic recovery, for it disorganized the main centres of economic initiative upon which she had hitherto relied and it introduced uncertainties into the business of decision making. SCAP's implied acceptance of this conclusion is shown by the diminishing vigour with which the policy was applied after the economic recovery of Japan became an aim of American policy. It is tempting to relate the speed of recovery in different sectors of the economy to the extent to which they had been affected by the dissolution measures, to argue that the stagnation of the export trade long after industrial production had revived was largely attributable to the destruction of the great trading companies. But this argument has little substance. The long frustration of Japan's trade revival can be attributed primarily, though not exclusively, to other causes.

We must now consider how far the formal results of the dissolution policy corresponded with changes of substance in the country's economic organization. There can be little doubt that by the end of the Occupation the once closely-knit Japanese economy had been wrenched apart. But the policy had not been equally effective in all its aspects and its incidence on the several *Zaibatsu* had varied. The effect on the position of the families had certainly been catastrophic and probably permanent. Some of their real property and personal possessions could be, and later were, returned to them. Many of these assets, however, as well as the compensation received for the securities, had been used in the payment of taxes, and the family ownership of and control over the great business aggregates were at an end. Thus it appeared that in each group the original focus of activity had been finally destroyed. Yet we must recall that long before the dissolution, effective management had been largely in the hands of officials, and the question remains whether the destruction of the families meant also the end of centralized control. In the first place, it is important to realize that the dissolution of the central holding companies and the subsidiaries still left the industrial and mining companies of the former *Zaibatsu* as the leading undertakings in their several fields, even though some of them had been split up into a number of independent firms. Similarly, the former *Zaibatsu* banks and insurance companies, though weakened, remained among the chief financial institutions of the country. Thus, except in trade where the policy of fragmentation had been most ruthlessly pursued, although the empires had been dissolved, the successor states were still dominant entities.

The problem of how far these successors were really independent, to what extent the old ties between them had actually been cut, is not easy to solve. With the 'purging' of the high executives management had passed into the hands of younger men. Yet it is acknowledged that the former chief *banto*, even in the hey-day of the dissolution policy, were consulted privately on matters of high policy by those formerly in charge of the several businesses. The Japanese tradition of the elder statesman offered powerful opposition to the designs of the SCAP reformers. Further, the authorities were powerless to dissuade the officials in charge of the successor companies from meeting together to discuss their common problems when they found advantage in doing so. Nor were the former financial links always severed so completely as had been intended. We have already noted that a high proportion of the new issues made by industrial companies during the inflationary period were acquired by banks and finance houses formerly in the same group. In the same way the financial business of these industrial companies continued to be handled as a rule by the bank with which they had previously been associated.

It was evidently found almost as difficult to destroy the cohesion of the *Zaibatsu* concerns as to compel oligopolists to compete. But general statements are liable to mislead. The several *Zaibatsu* were not equally resistant to the policy nor equally affected. Of the major *Zaibatsu* Mitsui, the greatest of them, suffered most. Its empire had centred on its trading company and this was completely shattered. The Mitsui Bank, which alone of the *Zaibatsu* banks suffered a measure of dissolution, emerged in a weaker state than its rivals. It was not able to afford as effective assistance to other Mitsui companies as that given by the Mitsubishi and Sumitomo banks to their former associates. So Mitsui's industrial companies had to go elsewhere for accommodation during the reconstruction period. Finally, either because of its size or because of a stronger impulse of personal ambition among the managers of its undertakings, the emotional ties with the house were rather weaker than was the case with the other *Zaibatsu*. Certainly, the executives to whom the control of the successor companies passed, seem to have enjoyed their independence and to have displayed reluctance in accepting restrictions upon their full liberty of action.

On the other hand, in Mitsubishi the bank rather than the trading company had been at the centre of the concern, and the bank came out of the dissolution period in a comparatively strong position. Moreover, the Iwasaki family in recent times had exerted a greater influence over the policy than the Mitsuis, and among the *banto* strong personal loyalties towards the family had persisted. For all these reasons, in Mitsubishi the old ties, though loosened, were not broken. The same was true of Sumitomo, whose centre of interest lay in heavy industry and whose constituent companies retained their identity and much of their strength. In this *Zaibatsu*, control had always been highly centralized and personal relations among the executives remained close. Sumitomo had not largely participated in foreign trade, and, having its headquarters in Osaka away from the excitements of the capital, had not become deeply involved in political affairs. So it escaped some of the virulence that Mitsui had aroused in Occupation circles. As for Yasuda, this *Zaibatsu*, which had always concentrated on banking and allied interests, was divorced from its industrial and other properties, but it was left as one of the chief forces in Japanese finance.

The dissolution policy appears to have gained its chief enduring successes among the lesser and the *Shinko-Zaibatsu*. We have seen that the lesser *Zaibatsu* differed from the 'Big Four' in that their interests were not equally spread between finance and industry. In the period of reconstruction the individual companies, therefore, were unable to seek financial help from an associated bank, and there was no focusing point for the successor companies as a body. The *Shinko-Zaibatsu*, for their part, had specialized on armaments production or on colonial and Manchurian enterprise. Japan's defeat and the loss of her empire undermined their strength. Their dissolution left in being some very important industrial concerns, such as the Hidachi Engineering Company, formerly part of Nissan, but these were without affiliations with any group.

If at the end of the Occupation the *Zaibatsu* still retained more than a shadowy existence, they were certainly not then equipped to serve as centres of initiative in the reconstruction of Japan's economy. Yet this did not mean that initiative was now widely diffused, as the Americans had hoped. On the contrary, the immediate effect of the dissolution was to produce an even more highly centralized economic system than before, at any rate so far as the large-scale sector of the economy was concerned. Responsibilities formerly discharged by the *Zaibatsu* were now concentrated in the State. Government officials stepped into the places once occupied by the great *banto*. This transference of power was confirmed by the shortage of private capital for reconstruction. As shown in Chapter III, for many years resources for that purpose could be provided only by the government or its agencies, at first through the Reconstruction Finance Bank, and later through the Bank of Japan which supplied the commercial banks with funds needed for financing industry. Thus the whole economy was reduced to extreme dependence upon the central authorities, an odd consequence of measures directed towards liberalizing the country's economic organization and based on a firm rejection of nationalization and State control.

This situation persisted until the end of 1954, but from the end of the Occupation the *Zaibatsu* began to mobilize their forces in an attempt to regain some of their lost ground. The reasons are clear. The underlying conditions that had led to the emergence of the *Zaibatsu* were still present, even in an exaggerated form. Investment capital and first-rate entrepreneurial capacity were scarce. Technical and administrative expertise was still concentrated in relatively few undertakings. Those whom the dissolution placed in charge of the chief enterprises had every inducement to seek by conjunction with former associates a solution for the problems, especially the financial problems, which in isolation they found overwhelming. Their loyalties had not been destroyed and, for the most part, they were led by habit and disposition to co-operate in rebuilding the edifices demolished by foreign edict. Events favoured them. The boom in the heavy industries that accompanied the Korean War and persisted in the years that followed was greatly to the benefit of the mining and manufacturing concerns formerly owned by the *Zaibatsu*. Then the deflation of 1954 wiped out or debilitated many new concerns that had risen on the tide of post-war inflation. As had happened in similar circumstances in the past, the *Zaibatsu* were then left with greater relative strength. Finally, industrial recovery provided the great concerns, including the banks, with resources which freed them from extreme dependence upon the Bank of Japan and the central government.

The general attitude of the successor firms towards the houses of which they were once members was demonstrated by the hasty resumption of their old names as soon as the Occupation came to an end.[1] By the middle 1950's regrouping was well under way. Personal links among former member firms were strengthened by the appointment of common directors and there was a pronounced tendency for the proportion of each company's capital held by others in the same group to increase. At the same time consultations among the leading executives became more systematically organized. For instance, a Sumitomo Club was founded at Osaka where the staffs met together frequently and discussed their common problems. The rehabilitation of the trading companies was also energetically pursued, and a number of the constituents into which each of them had been dissolved were merged. In this process Mitsubishi took the lead. In July 1954 four of the successor firms of its trading company came together; other businesses were later absorbed; and by 1956 Mitsubishi Shoji had become the largest trading firm in Japan. Mitsui encountered more serious obstacles. Nevertheless in 1952, when two of the successors of M.B.K. amalgamated, the old name was resumed. In August 1955 Dai Ichi Bussan, another former constituent, merged with two others, and later it established close links with several previously independent traders, including Katakura Industry, the largest business in the silk trade. Several of the other specialized

---

[1] Except by the Fuji Bank, the successor of the Yasuda Bank.

companies into which M.B.K. was divided have grown substantially during the last few years, and it is expected that ultimately all these concerns will join with M.B.K. Yet even when
this process is complete M.B.K. will have a long way to go
before its former importance is restored. Several of its affiliated
companies, such as Toyo Menka, the cotton trading firm, now
appear to be following an independent course. Further, M.B.K.
has not yet regained its massive business of marketing the products of small and medium producers. Its place has been supplied, though inadequately, by smaller merchant firms, co-
operative associations, and especially banking institutions established by the government. Other developments have also been
unfavourable to Mitsui. For instance, several Osaka textile
firms, such as Marubeni–Iida and Ito & Company, have
transformed themselves into large general merchants. The rise
of these undertakings may well make it impossible for the trading companies of the two major *Zaibatsu* to recover their former
share of Japan's foreign trade—one-third before the war. Yet,
consolidation has recently been proceeding rapidly. The
numerous small firms which were characteristic of Japan's trading structure in the early post-war years have been disappear-
ing, and it is probable that the conduct of foreign trade will
again be strongly concentrated, even though Mitsui and Mitsubishi have to be content with a less dominating position. This
concentration offers advantages to Japan, since capital-goods
exports which have now become prominent can be handled
most efficiently by large firms. It is significant that Mitsubishi
has set up a technical service, with headquarters in Calcutta,
for South East Asian countries, and that Dai Ichi is a leading
member of the Mitsui Plant Export Council of which eight
former Mitsui companies are members.[1]

We have shown that the *Zaibatsu* enterprise was formerly
centred upon the *honsha* or top holding companies. These, of
course, no longer exist and power within each group is now
focused on the bank. This came about partly because the shortage of capital left industrial concerns heavily dependent upon
banking advances for financing their reconstruction and partly

[1] For information about the reconstruction of the *Zaibatsu* see *Oriental Economist*,
January 1954, pp. 15–23, February 1955, pp. 72–75, April 1955, pp. 171–3, May
1955, pp. 220–30, July 1955, pp. 343–6, September 1956, pp. 439–44.

because the banks were for the most part left intact during the
dissolution period. As long as the banks merely acted as channels through which the Central Bank fed industry with funds,
it was not obvious that they would form the rallying point for
the resuscitation of the *Zaibatsu*. But as they regained their independence of the central monetary authorities, the significance
of their role was revealed. If Mitsubishi has advanced further
than Mitsui, this can be partly attributed to the greater strength
of its bank, which, unlike the Mitsui bank, escaped dissolution.

The devices available to the *Zaibatsu* in their efforts to re-
group were affected by the provisions of the Fair Trading Laws,
which were regarded as an essential buttress of the dissolution
policy. The original Law prohibited all types of business conduct normally associated with monopoly; but subsequent
amendments weakened its effect. Agreements that exercised an
unreasonable restraint on trade remained forbidden, but exceptions were permitted in the case of cartels formed to
deal with depressions, to promote rationalization, to prevent
dumping, or to foster exports. Again, although holding companies are still illegal, the restrictions on inter-corporate share-
holdings and interlocking directorates have been relaxed.
These amendments have smoothed the path to the concentration of economic power, although some legal obstacles still
remain.[1]

It is too early to speak with assurance of the future shape of
Japan's economic organization, for there is doubt about how far
present tendencies will go. A few tentative judgements, however, may be made. In the first place certain consequences of
the Occupation measures will endure. For instance, the wealth
and power of the *Zaibatsu* families themselves have been permanently destroyed, and it is improbable that control will ever
again be centred upon them or upon the top holding companies. It is true that some members of the Iwasaki family have
been appointed to leading administrative offices in Mitsubishi,
but this is exceptional and even in that concern does not repre-
sent a return to the former position. The significance of the
downfall of the families can, however, be overestimated. The
place of the *banto* in the determination of high policy has already

[1] Report of Japanese Government to United Nations on *Restrictive Business
Practices, passim*; and Fair Trade Institute, *Fair Trade*, September 1956, pp. 4–9.

been described, and with that in mind it is reasonable to regard the old structure of *Zaibatsu* ownership and administration as a convenient form through which centralized control was exercised rather than as an essential condition of the existence of the concerns themselves. Underlying circumstances still favour the concentration of economic power in Japan, and if this power is exerted through different means, this is not to argue that it will be any less real. Japanese big business has shed some of its traditional, so-called 'feudal' trappings; but this means simply that its organization has assumed a form familiar among its counterparts in the West, with control at the summit in the hands of a managerial group recruited by co-option. The fact that capital ownership is rather more widely diffused than before and that most of the securities are held by institutional investors rather than by families is likely to strengthen the power of the controlling group. The absence of a large class of private investor in Japan means that resources for new large-scale ventures must necessarily come from established businesses. In these circumstances the existence of great concerns with very wide-ranging interests may well be of marked advantage to an economy in process of diversification. The dissolution policy, which led immediately to the emergence of many independent specialized concerns, for a time weakened the capacity of Japan to develop quickly new fields of activity, because self-financing firms, if highly specialized, cannot easily branch into new types of production. In so far as the old *Zaibatsu* are recreated, this weakness will be remedied.

If the regrouping were to stop short at its present point, then specialized concerns would have a far more important part to play than before the war, for not all the *Zaibatsu* undertakings have yet come together. This applies particularly to the firms originally controlled by the lesser *Zaibatsu*. It applies also to Yasuda, which seems to have been content to concentrate on finance and to let slip its former industrial associates. Thus, up to the present only three of the four great *Zaibatsu* have emerged from the post-war disorganization, and there is now a considerably wider area of industry, trade, and finance occupied by firms specialized to one of those sectors and, indeed, to particular subdivisions of them. Whether this position will prove stable is impossible to predict. The recovery of the three great *Zaibatsu* is still in progress. In the past business concerns which lacked the buttress of banks and finance houses found themselves in times of stress drawn within the orbit of the great houses, and this may happen to the specialized successor firms of Nissan and Asano. It is tempting to argue that a new era marked by a structural separation of finance and industry is approaching, an era foreshadowed by the post-war career of Yasuda. But about this judgement must be suspended. New groupings are beginning to appear among companies that began their post-war career as independents. Recently the Fuji Bank [1] became deeply involved in the Marubeni combine.

Although an ample future now seems to be opening before the *Zaibatsu*, it is most unlikely that they will regain completely their former domination over the economy. Their empires will probably be less closely knit than in the past, and as agents of the State's economic policy they will have to share their activities with others. They are suspect in socialist and liberal circles, and if the forces of the Left were strengthened, any further extension of their economic power would provoke political opposition. On the other hand, the socialist solution to the problem of economic organization, which sought to transfer control over the great enterprises to the State, has so far been rejected in Japan. Indeed, direct State control over economic and especially over financial processes, after increasing during the early period of reconstruction, has lately diminished. Furthermore, many enterprises which had been brought under public corporations during the period of the *junsenji keizai* were returned after the war to private enterprise. In this respect the American decision to break up the 'national policy' companies proved to be inconsistent, as a means of liberalizing the economy, with the policy of dissolving the *Zaibatsu*, for in the end it helped to recreate the great centres of private economic power.

[1] I.e. the former Yasuda Bank.

CHAPTER X

Industrial Relations and the Rise of Trade Unions

ON several occasions in the course of their history the Japanese have been obliged to modify their institutions through pressure from without. They have long been accustomed to seek foreign models and deliberately to naturalize foreign techniques and institutions. Yet up to 1945 they were able to reserve for themselves freedom of choice and to discriminate in their borrowings from abroad. As a result of defeat and Occupation, however, the economic and social system was for some years exposed to reforms introduced by foreigners. Japan lay, almost helpless, before the policy, idealistic or vindictive, of the conquerors. We have already indicated that at the outset the chief aim of SCAP was to democratize Japanese institutions, with the object of destroying any seeds of militarism left behind after the plant itself had been uprooted, and that in the economic sphere this policy found its chief expression in the Land Reform, the dissolution of the *Zaibatsu*, and the encouragement of labour organization. By the ruin of the conservative landlords and the founding of a landowning peasantry, by the break-up of great aggregates of economic power and the wide diffusion of economic initiative, and by the overthrow of industrial paternalism and the creation of vigorous trade unions, it was hoped to bring into being an environment in which liberal political institutions could flourish.

The country was in a mood to welcome many of these changes, and there were Japanese who could be enlisted in the application of the policy. But Japanese society differed profoundly in its traditions and structure from that of the Western countries where those institutions had originated. More than this, although SCAP could enforce a revolution in certain social arrangements, it could not change the country's underlying economic conditions, particularly the relative factor supplies available to Japanese enterprise in the post-war world. Capital was even scarcer than before the war; large-scale entrepreneur-ship was still confined to a narrow range of undertakings; access to supplies of raw materials and foodstuffs was impeded by territorial changes and the loss of markets; and Japanese technology had fallen further behind that of the West. At the same time, the overpopulation of the countryside and the growth in the population as a whole meant that at a moment when economic opportunities had been reduced, a great mass of workers was seeking employment. It was evident, moreover, that during the next decade their numbers would increase at a formidable rate. In such circumstances the new institutions were unlikely to thrive unless they proved to be malleable to the pressure of economic necessity. It was fortunate, for the success of the innovations, that SCAP was soon compelled, by a turn in international affairs, to abandon its preoccupation with reform in favour of a realistic concern with economic rehabilita-tion. The change in policy made it possible for the Japanese the more easily to adapt the institutional innovations to the needs of their economy. Far from being a betrayal of liberal and democratic principles, this was in fact a condition of their sur-vival. By the middle 1950's the economy was operating in a fashion never anticipated by those responsible for the reforms. Yet several of the innovations, though much modified, had not only survived but had taken root. In certain branches of her life Japan will continue to bear the impress of the American re-forms. This is particularly true of industrial relations.

Before the war the system of industrial relations in Japan dif-fered greatly from that in Western countries. The wage system, when viewed from the standpoint of European or American practice, presented many peculiar features. Legislative and administrative measures for the protection of workers and the establishment of social security were a generation behind those of Great Britain. Western industrialists damaged by Japanese competition, and social reformers affronted by the relatively low standards of life of the Japanese workers, raised charges of 'social dumping' against Japan and justified discrimination against the Japanese export trade on those grounds. They usually neglected to notice that the Japanese workers were far better off than those of any other Asian country, and they failed to realize that many of the conditions which they deplored had been commonplaces in Europe fifty years earlier. The relative backwardness of Japan in this sphere should not have been surprising. Japanese industrialism made little advance before the beginning of the present century, and even in 1913 the number of workers in factories with five or more employees was less than a million. At that time, except in the cotton industry, Japan was only at the beginning of her career as a modern industrial country. Seventeen years later there were still less than 2 million factory operatives out of a total industrial labour force of $4\frac{3}{4}$ millions.[1] The rapid development of the 1930's raised the number of 'factory' workers to nearly 3 millions and the total industrial labour force (excluding building workers) to nearly $6\frac{1}{2}$ millions in 1937. Yet even then, as these figures suggest, most of the workers in manufacturing industry were employed in very small workplaces which provided an uncongenial environment for the rise of modern systems of industrial relations.

The bulk of the great increase in the working population after 1900 had been absorbed by manufactures, commerce, and the service trades, but in 1936 agriculture, forestry, and fishing still occupied some 14 millions out of a total working force of 32 millions. In these primary industries income per head compared very unfavourably with that of manufacturing industry. There was, therefore, a constant downward pressure, accentuated during the agricultural depression of the 1930's, upon the industrial labour market. A considerable proportion of the urban workers still regarded themselves as only temporarily engaged in industry. The young women who made up the greater part of the labour force in the textile mills were recruited from peasant families and returned to their homes after two or three years' service. Many of the urban male workers were seasonally employed, or moved between urban and rural work according to the state of trade. The permanent wage-earning class thus constituted a relatively small proportion of the total working population. This occupational structure might be unfamiliar to industrialized Britain of the twentieth century where the agricultural labour force had been reduced

[1] 'Factories' in this context are workplaces with 5 workers and over. In 1930 there were only 1,300,000 workers in manufacturing establishments with 50 or more employees.

to only 5 per cent. of the whole. But it was characteristic of every country during the period of early industrialization. As long as these conditions existed—and the most highly industrialized societies had passed through them—the growth of trade unions and the rise of modern systems of welfare and industrial relations were bound to encounter serious obstacles. Memories are short, but British critics of Japan at that time might well have recalled that although factory legislation in Great Britain had a long history, it was not until the end of the first decade of this century that a beginning was made with a system of public regulation of wages, that the State did not intervene to limit the hours of work of adult miners until 1908, and that a few years before the First World War the number of trade unionists in Great Britain was only $2\frac{1}{2}$ millions.

In Japan fundamental economic causes were reinforced by others of a social and political character. Japan had no tradition of political democracy or liberalism, and social relations were governed by concepts of mutual obligation and of loyalty to superiors derived from a so-called 'feudal' past. The very idea of individual rights was a Western importation, and the family group accepted far-reaching obligations for the welfare of its members in return for the deference which it received from them. This was not a soil where militant trade unionism could flourish. Western observers of Japanese industry were sometimes dismayed at the restrictions imposed even by the more beneficent employers over the lives of their workers, for example, the girls housed in the dormitories of the textile mills. They did not always realize that personal liberty was a luxury to which the Japanese seldom aspired. Again, the unsatisfactory workplaces and long hours that existed in many Japanese manufacturing industries were severely censured by observers who were not conscious that, bad as the conditions might be, they usually represented an improvement over those found in the depressed farming areas from which the workers came. It is significant that the worst conditions were (and are) to be found in the very small workplaces which bear the imprint of the pre-industrial society.

Workers' organizations first became of some importance during the years immediately after the First World War. The comparatively liberal attitude of the government during that period and the influence of foreign example helped to foster the growth of trade unions. The establishment of the International Labour Organization also lent some support, for the government was induced to nominate labour delegates from among union leaders. It was at this time that a central organization, the Japan Federation of Labour (*Sodomei*), was founded. But leadership was mainly in the hands of intellectuals who concerned themselves with rival political ideologies rather than with the immediate interests of their members. Consequently, although membership grew from 100,000 in 1923 to 370,000 in 1931, the movement did little to increase the bargaining power of the workers. After the Manchurian incident, it was split asunder by political disunity and declined further when, in the middle 1930's, the government abandoned its policy of toleration. With the outbreak of the Sino-Japanese War in 1937, the right-wing trade unions gave up the right to strike and the left-wing unions were suppressed. Membership declined steeply from the maximum of 420,000 reached in 1936. Finally, in July 1940 the government dissolved all independent labour organizations. This was the end of Japanese trade unionism as a wholly indigenous movement. Its achievement had been insignificant. Membership never attained more than 5 per cent. of the total industrial labour force. Only among the seamen and the transport workers had effective organizations existed. The right of collective bargaining had been conceded only in a very few instances, and standard rates of wages embodied in agreements were almost unknown. The unions had never sought to develop friendly society functions which had been so prominent in the activities of British trade unions.

In these circumstances the determination of wages was left largely to individual contracts between employer and worker, and a wide diversity of practice existed. For example, the female employees in the cotton mills were engaged according to the terms of contracts signed with their parents. These contracts provided that for the period of service part of the wages should be sent to the families, part should be paid to the girls as pocket money, and the balance settled when the girls left. The girls were housed and fed by the employers and a small deduction from wages was made for this accommodation. In all branches of industry the workers' remuneration was made up of wages, biannual bonuses, and payments in kind, but the practice of firms varied widely in regard to the share of each of these constituents in the total payment. Even the wage constituent itself was not to be considered as 'a rate for the job'. In every industry it was made up, in varying proportions, of a basic wage together with payments for length of service, age, personal character, and family responsibilities. These peculiarities of the wage structure will be discussed later in more detail, for they have been carried into the post-war world. Another characteristic of industrial employment in pre-war Japan was the allowance paid on retirement or on dismissal for other than disciplinary reasons. This was a symptom of the paternalism that mitigated the weakness of the wage-earners' bargaining position. It was associated with a reluctance to discharge workers (at any rate those regarded as 'established') in periods of bad trade, a reluctance that was often responsible for the overstaffing of firms, as judged by Western standards.

Government regulation played a very modest part in labour relations and working conditions. The first Factory Act, passed in 1911, was designed to protect women and young persons. Its chief provision, namely the abolition of all-night work for females, did not come into operation until 1929. Even so, many small workplaces (at first those with less than 15 workers and later those with less than 10) were outside its scope. Other measures of protection included limitations on the hours of underground mine workers, regulations concerning safety and hygiene in factories, certain safeguards for seamen, and workmen's compensation for accidents in building and civil engineering. Shortly after the First World War a National Health Insurance Scheme on the British model was introduced, and in 1936 a law was passed to make the payment of retirement allowances at a certain rate compulsory over a substantial part of industry. On the eve of the Second World War, Japan still lacked unemployment insurance, the public regulation of wages, and official conciliation or arbitration machinery for dealing with industrial disputes. To the large sector of industry composed of small and medium workplaces, the protective legislation either did not apply at all or was unenforceable.[1]

[1] Cf. I. Ayusawa, 'The Labour Problem in Japan', *Japan Quarterly*, vol. 1, no. 1, pp. 104–5.

With the outbreak of the war it fell into abeyance over the whole of industry.

When the Occupation began an official apparatus for social welfare and workers' organization for fostering the interests of labour scarcely existed. The authorities addressed themselves at once to filling these institutional gaps, and the measures which they caused to be introduced very soon transformed this part of Japan's economic life. The policy was embodied in three new laws, the Trade Union Act and the Labour Relations Adjustment Act of 1946 and the Labour Standards Act of 1947. The content of these Acts, and their subsequent amendments, must be briefly described.[1] The first of them, which was modelled on the American Wagner Act, gave workers the right to organize, to bargain collectively with their employers, and to take strike action. The only wage-earners to whom these rights were not accorded consisted of certain limited classes of public servants. Discriminatory acts by employers against workers who formed trade unions, and refusal by employers to bargain with union representatives, were prohibited under penalties. This law, and also the Labour Relations Adjustment Act, provided for the establishment of machinery for bargaining. A National Labour Relations Board and 46 Prefectural Boards were set up with powers to mediate and arbitrate in industrial disputes. These Boards were tripartite in membership, consisting of an equal number of workers', employers', and public representatives. Finally, the Labour Standards Law attempted to establish in Japan the employment standards embodied in the conventions and recommendations of the I.L.O. Among many detailed provisions, this legislation limited the hours of work of adult males as well as of women and young persons, and it prescribed conditions in regard to holidays with pay, employment in mines and dangerous occupations, factory hygiene and safety, apprenticeship and training, accommodation in factory dormitories, the procedure for dismissal and overtime pay, which was to be 25 per cent. above the basic wage. In places where 10 or more workers were employed, the employers were required to draw up 'employment regulations' by agreement with the trade unions, and these regulations were to constitute

[1] See Ministry of Labour, *Japan Labour Code* (Tokyo, 1953) and *Japan Labour Year Book* (various issues).

a legal standard with which the employers had to conform. Heavy penalties were imposed for breaches of this law, and a system of inspection was devised. Other enactments dealt with employment benefits, industrial health insurance, and compensation for accidents. A Ministry of Labour was set up in 1947. So, in two years, the Occupation authorities with the help of the native bureaucracy conferred on Japan, hitherto notoriously backward in labour relations, a labour code in accord with the most advanced standards of Western nations. It is important to consider whether these innovations were as revolutionary in practice as in law.

The immediate consequences were indeed remarkable. Between the end of the war and December 1946 the number of trade unionists rose from none to nearly 5 millions. By the end of 1948 there were nearly 34,000 trade unions with a total membership of 6,677,000.[1] The unions almost at once achieved considerable bargaining strength, for not only did they enjoy the favour of the Occupation authorities but they also found that managements, demoralized by war, Occupation, and inflation were in no shape to resist the most extravagant demands. The leaders, many of whom had been imprisoned during the war, were strongly influenced by socialist, syndicalist, or Communist ideas. In a number of instances they wrested management functions from the employers and actually seized control over the plants. Sometimes the breakdown of management left the unions to take charge of the employment, dismissal, and discipline of the workers. At the centre leadership was mostly in the hands of men preoccupied with political aims. The pre-war All-Japan General Federation of Labour (*Sodomei*) was revived and was dominated by the right-wing socialists. A rival organization, the All-Japan Congress of Industrial Labour Organizations (*Sanbetsu*), was formed and this passed under the control of Communists. The majority of the local unions were affiliated to one or other of these bodies, but there were some important independent organizations.

This period of extreme militancy was short-lived. SCAP soon took alarm at the monster to which its policies had given birth and in February 1947 it intervened to prohibit a general

---

[1] Ayusawa in *Japan Quarterly*, p. 113. For statistical data about Japanese labour see Ministry of Labour, *Year Book of Labour Statistics*.

strike. When the cold war began in 1948 enthusiasm for democratic reform noticeably cooled. Political idealism was an indulgence that could easily be afforded when the price had to be paid by the Japanese in economic inefficiency, but it was a luxury to be foregone when its consequences became incompatible with American strategic interests. The newly won privileges of the Japanese workers were, therefore, curtailed. Government employees had been prominent in the post-war labour movement. In July 1948 civil servants were deprived of the right of collective bargaining or of striking, and other government workers, while still allowed to bargain collectively on certain conditions, were prohibited from striking. Compulsory conciliation and arbitration were introduced to deal with disputes that involved these classes of workers. Later, employees of the local authorities were covered by the same regulations.

In 1949 and 1950 the labour movement received another setback as a result of the deflation that accompanied the application of the Dodge Plan. Small firms in particular suffered financially and many trade unions organized among their employees came to an end. In the large firms management began to regain its former bargaining power. At the same time the government tried to curtail political activities of the trade unions, and its emergency powers for dealing with general strikes were strengthened. Then, on the outbreak of the Korean War, Communists were purged from key positions in industry and government. The result was that the number of trade unionists fell steeply; in 1951 it was 5,690,000, about a million less than at the peak in 1948. The number of unions also declined, chiefly through the disappearance of very small organizations. Meanwhile, at the centre of the movement, considerable changes had taken place. The right-wing and left-wing federations (*Sodomei* and *Sanbetsu*), which had co-operated together in the late 1940's, dissolved their liaison council (*Zenroren*). The *Sanbetsu* suffered from internal disagreements, and a new organization, composed of *Sodomei* and certain dissident groups of *Sanbetsu*, combined to form the *Sohyo* (General Council of Trade Unions of Japan).

After 1951 a slight recovery in the number of trade unions and of trade unionists began. By 1954 there were over 31,000 trade unions with nearly 6 million members. Yet since the industrial labour force had increased during the previous five years, the proportion of industrial employees organized in trade unions was lower in 1954 than in 1948.[1] At the centre there was a succession of changes in organization which were related mainly to changes in political aims, and especially to the attitude taken by rival groups towards the Peace Treaty of 1952 and subsequently to the foreign policy pursued by the Japanese government. The *Sohyo* remained the largest body, but there were dissensions among its members as the political preoccupations of its leaders increased. In 1953 a split occurred, and some right-wing unions formed a new federation called *Zenro Kaigi* which wished to concentrate on industrial rather than political problems. During this period the attitude of the government towards the labour movement and industrial welfare also suffered a considerable change. When in 1952 Japan again became free to order her own affairs, the labour codes came under fire and a demand arose in certain business quarters for a drastic revision of the legislation of 1946 and 1947.[2]

The most interesting questions raised by the post-war development of Japanese labour organization relate, not to the activities of the central federations, but to the character of the constituent trade unions themselves and to the part they play in the wage contract. How does the typical Japanese trade union compare with its European counterpart? How far has the rise of the unions affected the structure of wages and the methods of wage determination? These are among the questions with which we shall now attempt to deal.

In Great Britain most of the trade unions fall into three categories, craft, industrial, or general workers' unions. In Japan none of these types is of major importance. There the characteristic union is the 'enterprise union'.[3] The national or regional bodies that exist in the several industries are loose associations of unions which are themselves limited to workers in particular firms. The 'enterprise union' is the real locus of power, and this is so even when the range of business undertaken is wide. For example, the national organization of the

---

[1] In June 1955 there were 18,000 unions with about 6¼ million workers.

[2] Cf. Japan Federation of Employers' Associations, *On Present Conditions of the Labour Movement in Japan* (Tokyo, 1953), p. 2 and *passim*.

[3] *Kigyo Betsu Kumiai*.

textile workers is divided into branches corresponding to the divisions of the textile industry itself (cotton, wool, rayon, and so on), but each 'enterprise union' has a scope equivalent to that of the firm in which its workers are employed even if the firm runs factories engaged in all types of textile production. Naturally these unions vary greatly in size and strength, but they are the bodies responsible for bargaining with the employers. The national unions to which they are affiliated are concerned mainly with giving mutual aid and with serving the political aims of the movement. They provide a means of co-ordinating the policies of the individual 'enterprise unions', but only rarely are they given authority for collective bargaining. While the larger 'enterprise unions' employ a considerable number of full-time paid officers, the national unions have small staffs and receive only a modest share of the dues collected from members.

The headquarters of the enterprise unions, and the premises of their local branches, are usually to be found at the plants themselves. In the early post-war period the firms often provided buildings and furniture for the use of the unions, and even in the middle 1950's it was common for union dues to be collected by the employers in the form of deductions from their workers' wages. In these circumstances it might have been expected that the union leaders would be amenable to pressure from the management, and it may be forgiven if Western observers sometimes found little difference between these unions and the 'company unions' of the United States. This, however, would be to misinterpret the facts. It has already been shown that in the early post-war period the unions, far from being subservient to management, often dominated it; indeed, members of the salaried staff and even of the higher management sometimes joined the unions. The financial assistance given by the firm was then deemed to be in accordance with the policy of the government and the Occupation authorities. By the middle 1950's management had regained its traditional functions, but the unions remained, in general, effective and independent bargaining bodies.

The explanation of this paradoxical situation is to be sought partly in the social traditions and the economic structure of Japan, and partly in the circumstances in which unions came to be formed. Paternalism was always a characteristic of

Japanese industrial relations, and the introduction of Western institutions has not destroyed, though it has weakened, older habits of loyalty to superiors and obligations to inferiors. It did not therefore seem extraordinary to the Japanese that when the government prescribed a policy of encouraging trade unionism, firms should readily follow this lead. The organizers of the new unions for their part were faced with the task of creating unions from among workers unfamiliar with any of the forms of labour organization which had grown up gradually in the West. These workers conceived their interests not as coincident with those of fellow workers in the same craft or industry but common only to those employed by the same firm. The structure of Japanese industry itself was congenial to this type of organization. In the large-scale industries production was concentrated in a relatively small number of great enterprises with a wide diversity of interests, while in the numerous small and medium-sized firms personal relationships between workers and employers were very close. Many of the workers in both classes of industry were immigrants from agriculture and had little conception of the common interests of industrial wage-earners as a whole.

These features of Japanese industrial relations exerted a strong influence over bargaining methods, and the structure of wages. At the outset SCAP urged the formation of joint councils of workers and managers, and the National Labour Relations Board, established by the Labour Relations Adjustment Law, recommended that councils of this kind should be set up as institutions for collective bargaining within each firm. These joint councils became very common, and they continued to play an important part in industrial relations. In this way negotiations between employers and workers, whether through these councils or through less formal machinery, became located at the level of the enterprise. In the large firms discussions are conducted between professional union negotiators and the personnel officers of the company. The decisions reached at the centre apply to the workers in all the establishments owned by the same firm. A corollary of this centralization is that there has been no growth of works committees nor of the shop-stewards movement. All disputes are handled at the headquarters of the enterprise. If organization at the shop level is undeveloped, so, as we have seen, is organization at the industrial level. It is true that in some fields where the boundaries of an enterprise are identical with those of an industry, as in the national railways, the distinction disappears. Industry-wide bargaining machinery has also been set up for shipping and coal mining. But these are still exceptions. Western observers are inclined to view the 'enterprise union' as a *pis aller*, a symptom of Japan's economic immaturity. This condescension is unjustified. When production takes place under such varying conditions as are found in many Japanese industries, the 'enterprise union' is the only obvious method of organization. Further, for a society that is intent upon rapid economic development rather than upon establishing uniform conditions of welfare among its working population, it has considerable positive advantages.

In many old-established British industries elaborate voluntary procedures for handling disputes were worked out long ago. These often involve agreements to refer outstanding questions to conciliation boards presided over by an impartial outsider, and even in the last resort to outside arbitration. In Japan such procedures are entirely lacking, except where the law has enforced their adoption, for the Japanese, both employers and employed, appear to be hostile to the intervention of outsiders. This is rather surprising in view of the important place that intermediaries occupy in other branches of social life. To some extent the nature of the issues that are the subject of negotiations may explain this reluctance. Collective bargaining, as introduced since the war, has not been concerned with the establishment of principles of employment, nor with the determination of the 'rate for the job'. Its main purpose has been to interpret, in the context of a particular enterprise, rights already conferred by law and to ensure that these are accorded. Under this head the formulation of rules of employment for the enterprise, as required by the Labour Standards Law, has been a leading activity of collective bargaining. A secondary purpose is to modify or enlarge benefits traditionally given by particular employers.[1]

---

[1] S. B. Levine, *Industrial Relations in Post-War Japan*, where these matters are more fully discussed. The present author was permitted to see this work in typescript and benefited greatly from his study of it.

Even before the war a distinction was drawn by Japanese firms between the permanent and the temporary labour force. The first group enjoyed the full benefits of a paternalistic system, including considerable security of employment and generous dismissal allowances if bad trade required a contraction of the labour force. The temporary workers, on the other hand, were not regarded as being members of the enterprise. This distinction has been preserved in the post-war period. Unions have been concerned almost exclusively with the welfare of the permanent or established labour force in each enterprise. In this way they hoped to secure benefits for their members (namely the established workers) which management would be reluctant to accord to every employee. The success of the unions in this aim has naturally induced the managements to increase the number of their temporary employees, and these have been the chief victims of post-war instability. It follows that while there are few 'closed shops' in Japanese industrial establishments, 'union shops', that is to say, shops in which all *permanent* workers are obliged to become union members, are common.

The complications of the traditional Japanese wage system have been maintained in the new era. Before the war, apart from the basic wage which was related to the nature of the job performed, the following ingredients in total monthly earnings were analysed: age allowance, education allowance, length-of-service allowance, attendance allowance, family allowance, housing allowance, transport allowance, cost-of-living allowance, incentives payments, and several others. In addition, workers normally received bonuses at *O-bon* [1] and New Year, and they were entitled to allowances on retirement or dismissal for reasons of bad trade. The proportion of each constituent in the total earning varied from firm to firm, from worker to worker, and from time to time. The rise of trade unions and the establishment of collective bargaining have not disturbed this system. If anything, the complications have increased. Post-war inflation led to a rise in cost-of-living allowances, and so to a decrease in the proportions of earnings provided by the basic wage. Some firms have recently introduced incentive-bonus schemes.

The trade unions have accepted this wage structure. In their

[1] The summer festival.

negotiations they have, of course, been intimately concerned with actual earnings. In particular, during the years of inflation they tried to ensure that wages kept in line with increases in the cost of living. They aimed at ensuring that the family needs of the workers should be given weight in wage determination. Yet while they might try to influence the relative importance of the several constituents in the wage, they have made no attempt to alter the system itself. In some firms they have bargained with the employers for increases in the aggregate sum paid in wages to the employees as a whole, and they have then shared out this sum among the several groups in their membership. The impact of 'enterprise' trade unionism on the traditional wage system is responsible for some of the peculiarities in the nature of the collective bargaining. Wage negotiations are not usually set going by periodical presentation of claims for increases in standard rates, as happens in the West, but they are directed in turn to each of the numerous constituents of the total wage and so form an almost continuous series.[1]

One of the consequences of this system of industrial relations and of wage-bargaining arrangements is that the wages of particular classes of workers differ from firm to firm, even when the establishments are broadly comparable in equipment and size. Over industry as a whole the contrasts are very sharp indeed, for the diversity of technical methods and the conditions of labour supply combine to produce wide disparities between the wages paid by firms in different size-groups. For instance, in manufacturing industry in 1954 average wages in establishments employing from 100 to 499 workers were only 70 per cent., and in establishments employing from 10 to 29 workers only 55 per cent., of those in establishments with over 1,000 workers.[2] These differences cannot be explained by disparities in the age and sex composition of the labour force in the several size-groups, for while the small businesses certainly employ a higher proportion of young persons, they also have a smaller proportion of women among their employees. It is true that large firms can select the best workers because of the

---

[1] Japan Federation of Employers' Associations, *Analysis of Personnel Practices in the Principal Industries of Japan* (Tokyo, 1953), *passim*; and All-Japan Cotton Spinners' Association, *Labour Situation of the Cotton Spinning Industry in Japan* (Osaka, 1955), pp. 10–22.

[2] *Economic Survey of Japan, 1955–6*, p. 193.

relatively high wages and good conditions that they can offer, but this merely emphasizes the existence of separate labour markets. Recruits to industry who fail to obtain the better-paid jobs in large firms are compelled to seek work in small firms which, because of the keen competition among the applicants, are able to secure their labour at low rates.

The wage disparities have fluctuated in recent decades. During the inter-war years the gap grew wider, for the industrial labour supply was then increasing rapidly and improvements in productivity were largely confined to the great factories. It narrowed during the war when all types of labour were very scarce and wages were subject to official control, and there was little change in the immediate post-war period on account of the slow recovery in the large-scale industries. After 1950 it widened again, and by the end of 1954 it was probably greater than before the war, partly because of the growth in productivity of the large firms, partly because the small firms were at that time suffering particularly from the deflationary policy, and partly because trade union activity was displayed mainly in large-scale industry. Since then industrial prosperity has lapped over into the small and medium-sized firms, and the wage gap has again tended to become narrower.[1] In retail distribution and in most of the service trades wages still compare very unfavourably with those in the factories, even if payments in kind are taken into account.

The Japanese have had their share of labour troubles in the post-war period. Most of the strikes, however, have been short, although there were exceptions in the long stoppages in the coal and electricity industries during 1952. The brevity of most of the strikes may be attributed to the readiness of both sides to compromise as well as to the lack of large strike funds. Significantly, one of the most serious strikes in recent years (that in the Omiya Silk Company in 1954) was directed against old-fashioned and paternalistic management practices which were uncongenial to the new race of post-war workers. It would be rash to speculate about the future. Institutionally the Japanese trade union movement is powerful, being upheld by strong and comprehensive laws; but its economic basis is still weak, for the conditions that frustrated development in pre-war days remain,

---

[1] At any rate, in some important industries. See p. 100 above.

namely the multiplicity of small establishments and the increasing supply of labour in search of employment. Trade unions gained successes in the spring of 1957, at the height of the industrial boom, but these favourable conditions are unlikely to persist. The legal foundations, moreover, could be undermined by any shift in political power, a danger that serves to emphasize the essential part that the State has played, and continues to play, in sustaining the new movement. As long as the trade unions remain dependent upon the favour of the central government, the original purposes of the Occupation authorities will be unfulfilled.

The policy of SCAP in this field rested on the proposition that the growth of a liberal democracy and the restraint of militant nationalism required the presence of institutions and group activities that derived their driving force from the mass of the people. By insisting upon the right of collective bargaining the authorities hoped that decisions about wages and working conditions could be reached in ways that did not require the active intervention of the State. As we have seen, however, the power of the State had to be invoked to bring these organizations into being, and the new trade union movement, in its central organization, was compelled to an active concern with politics so as to ensure that the central power continued to be exerted in a way that favoured its interests.

After the change in Occupation policy that followed the outbreak of the cold war State intervention was again necessary to protect the economy from the disruption caused by strikes. The result was that the original principle that informed the Occupation measures was drastically modified in its practical application. For example, after the right to strike had been withdrawn from civil servants in 1948, three Commissioners appointed by the Cabinet were authorized to fix terms and conditions of employment in the public service, while official bargaining machinery was also set up to deal with problems of industrial relations among other government employees, including those engaged on the railways and public utilities. The rules then imposed included an obligation to resort to arbitration in the case of disputes in the public sector. Even unions organized among employees of private industry were subjected in 1949 to stringent rules governing membership and strike action, and the Prime Minister was authorized to intervene in serious industrial disputes. Further, the tripartite Labour Relations Boards did not become, as had been expected, bodies for assisting in achieving settlements when negotiations between unions and employers had failed. On the contrary, disputes commonly came before these bodies at a very early stage and there have been few important disputes which have not required their intervention. These Boards, which were intended primarily for conciliation purposes, are not to be confused with wage-fixing bodies like the British Wages Councils. Under the Labour Standards Act, however, a central tripartite wage council was, in fact, established with the function of settling minimum rates of wages. But so far it has been ineffective. Indeed the complication of the existing wage system, and the fact that the concept of the 'rate for the job' is still alien to Japan, are likely to prevent rapid progress in that direction.

Nevertheless, much has been achieved in a very short time. It may be argued that a worsening of economic circumstances might well force the labour movement to withdraw from some of the positions which it has gained. The labour codes adopted immediately after the war may prove to be too far advanced for the absorptive capacity of the Japanese economy, and for many decades to come it is probable that considerable sections of Japanese industry will be little affected by them. The inspectorate has shown itself reluctant or unable to make use of its extensive legal powers in prosecuting offenders against the labour laws which have been disregarded in many of the smaller establishments, and the structure of Japanese industry will long present formidable obstacles to a general enforcement. Yet there can be little doubt that the reforms introduced during the Occupation period will leave a permanent impress. Nothing is less likely than a return to the system of industrial relations that existed before the war.

CHAPTER XI

The Problem of Foreign Trade

DURING the 1930's Japan became one of the great trading nations of the world. In 1938 her commodity exports to her colonies and to foreign countries represented 5·4 per cent. of world exports; they were exceeded only by those of the United States, the United Kingdom, and Germany. At the same time she had become a great sea carrier. Her mercantile marine was the third largest in the world, and her sales of shipping services to foreigners brought in receipts sufficient to pay for nearly one-tenth of her imports. Her exports had grown sharply during a period when international trade as a whole was stagnating. Between 1929 and 1937 the volume of her exports to foreign countries rose by 83 per cent. and the volume of her imports from them by 30 per cent.[1] The extreme dependence of her economy upon trade was a commonplace of economic discussion. In 1938 the ratio of imports to the national income was well over 20 per cent.[2]

Japan's trade was widely distributed, but two great regions predominated both as markets and as sources of supply. They were the Far East (the Japanese colonies and China) and the United States. In the period 1934–6 the former took 39 per cent. of her exports and provided 36 per cent. of her imports; the shares of the latter were 17 and 25 per cent. respectively. The other most important market and source of supply consisted of the countries of South East Asia. These took 19 per cent. of the exports and supplied 16 per cent. of the imports.[3] Japan's trade with these several regions fell into a clearly marked pattern. She sold raw silk, canned fish, tea, and pottery to the United States, machinery and other capital goods to Manchuria and North China, and manufactured textiles and cheap miscellaneous

---

[1] League of Nations, *Review of World Trade, 1937*, p. 41. Trade with Japanese colonies is excluded.

[2] S. Okita, *The Rehabilitation of Japan's Economy and Asia* (Tokyo, Ministry of Foreign Affairs, 1956), p. 8; see also *Economic Survey of Japan, 1955–6*, p. 37.

[3] Ibid. p. 11; and *Fuji Bank Bulletin*, September 1956, pp. 15–35.

consumption goods to a wide range of countries, especially to continental Asia and the South Seas.

Most of her imports consisted of primary products. She obtained her food imports (except for wheat) from regions under her own control, rice from Korea and Formosa, sugar from Formosa, and soya beans from Manchuria. Eastern and Southern Asia supplied cotton, rubber, vegetable oil, mineral oil and ores and metals, and North America raw cotton, mineral oil, wheat, steel scrap, and engineering goods, including motor vehicles and certain types of machinery. During the 1930's there had been significant changes in the importance of these regions. North America had declined relatively as a customer because of the fall in the value of the raw silk exports. The Far East had become much more important to Japan's trade as a result of her heavy investment in that area and of the privileges conferred on her traders in areas that had passed under her political control.

The export trade became more highly diversified during the 1930's and in this it reflected the changes which had taken place in Japanese industry. In 1929 nearly 70 per cent. of the trade of Japan Proper *with foreign countries* consisted of textiles, and her exports of metals and metal manufactures made up only 4 per cent. By 1936 the share of the latter group had risen to 14 per cent., and miscellaneous exports had also become more important. Yet textiles still provided well over half the total exports and Japan's specialization in this field, though diminished, had by no means disappeared.[1] Among the textiles themselves specialization on raw silk and cotton, though lessened by the expansion of wool, rayon, and knitted-goods exports, was still conspicuous. These two commodities were responsible for about two-thirds of the value of all textile exports.

Japan's achievement in foreign trade was a tribute to the resourcefulness of her merchants and manufacturers and to the resilience of her economy. The damaging restrictions imposed by foreign countries on imports of her manufactured goods and the chronic depression in her former chief export trade, raw silk, had failed to check her commercial progress. She had won

---

[1] In 1934–6 52 per cent. of the export trade of Japan Proper (*including* exports to her colonies) consisted of textiles and 15 per cent. of metals, metal goods and machinery. Cf. Allen, *Short Economic History*, p. 150.

trade from others in a period of general stagnation and she had created new demands by her ability to supply cheap manufactures to the impoverished Asian peoples. It is a curious commentary on the political sense of mankind that during this period Japan's commercial expansion and her territorial aggression were treated by many critics as moral equivalents, as though the sale to Asians of cheap goods that they were anxious to buy was as mischievous as the imposition on them of a political domination which they abhorred.

War and defeat completely destroyed this great commerce and recovery was very slow. Japan's trading organizations were dismembered, and her exporters were even deprived of offices and branches abroad from which to operate. From 1945 to 1949 the low level of industrial production excluded the possibility of exporting more than a meagre quantity of goods; the quantum index of exports (1934-6 = 100) was only 7·5 in 1948, 16·1 in 1949, and 29·6 in 1950. At the same time the destruction of the mercantile marine meant that Japan's enterprise in the carrying trade was suspended. Imports recovered hardly more rapidly than exports. In 1949 the quantum index of imports was only 28. Since Japan's terms of trade had worsened and since she now had a heavy deficit on her invisible trade, a high proportion of these imports had to be financed by United States aid. During the period from 1945 to 1950, the amount of aid was equivalent to 57 per cent. of the value of imports.[1] In the early post-war years most of these imports consisted of grain required to prevent starvation and raw materials for restarting industry.

At the beginning of the Occupation control over foreign trade was in the hands of SCAP which after December 1945 delegated certain administrative functions to a Board of Trade established by the Japanese government for the purpose. In April 1947 four official trade corporations were set up and until the end of 1949 these handled most of the overseas transactions, although after the summer of 1947 foreign trading concerns were permitted a limited operation. During these years transactions were conducted at rates of exchange that varied from commodity to commodity.

[1] Between 1945 and 1951, when aid ceased, the amount provided was $2,054 million. Data from Economic Planning Board and Ministry of Finance.

A tentative approach to normal methods of overseas commerce was made during 1949 with the institution of a single exchange rate and the transference of exchange dealings from SCAP to a Foreign Exchange Control Board appointed by the Japanese government. The Board of Trade was at the same time absorbed into the Ministry of International Trade and Industry. Early in 1950 controls over private trading were simplified and relaxed and the government's trade corporations were abolished. During that year also a number of bilateral trade agreements were signed with several countries; one of them, for example, provided for the exchange of Burmese rice for Japanese cotton goods.

The outbreak of the Korean War in June 1950 transformed the trading situation. In 1951 the dollar value of Japan's exports was 165 per cent. greater than in 1949. At the same time she began to earn large amounts of foreign exchange by her sales of goods and services to the United Nations forces in the Far East. In 1951 the ratio of procurement expenditure to exports was 44 per cent. and in 1952, when it reached its peak, 65 per cent.[1] Japan was fortunate that this procurement expenditure began just as American aid was coming to an end. The new orders called for an enlarged supply of raw materials and so imports also rose steeply.

The increased foreign demands led to a sharp rise in Japanese prices and, as already shown, the internal price level was maintained even after the war boom had collapsed and prices abroad had declined. The result was that the export expansion was checked, although special procurement remained high. In 1953 the dollar value of the exports was less than in 1951; in volume they were still not much more than a third of the 1934–6 quantity. On the other hand, the (dollar) value of imports continued to rise, for Japan proceeded to use the credits earned during the boom (and subsequently from procurement) to finance imports needed to re-equip industry and to raise levels of consumption. In 1953 the quantum index of imports reached 74.

The stagnation of the export trade and the disequilibrium in the balance of payments, however, called for drastic remedial

[1] Ministry of Finance, *General Survey of the Japanese Economy*, Attached Tables, p. 72.

measures. In addition to the deflationary policy introduced at the end of 1953, the Japanese government now began to make use of various devices to offset the disparity between the home price level and that of the outside world. Among these was the 'link system' which had for its model a method introduced in the early days of the Sino-Japanese War. Firms were granted import licences for particular commodities on condition that they exported specified manufactured goods. Since the import trade was controlled and the domestic prices of imported goods high, goods brought in under this system could be sold in Japan at prices well above those at which they were purchased. So an importer who obtained a licence could make a substantial profit on the deal, and this enabled him to subsidize the export which he had to undertake as a condition of acquiring it. Arrangements of this kind covered not only imports of raw cotton against exports of cotton textiles, but even imports of textile raw materials, sugar, petroleum, and bananas against exports of machinery, ships, and silk.[1]

Devices such as these, together with the narrowing of the gap between Japanese and international prices during 1954, brought about a steep rise in the dollar value of the exports in that year, a rise considerably greater than the fall in procurement expenditure. The value of imports declined. During the next year, while procurement suffered only a slight fall, the value of exports rose by nearly 24 per cent. This remarkable rate of increase continued throughout 1956, and in that year the value of exports was more than twice that of 1953. Thus after years of comparative stagnation, Japan's export trade in the middle 1950's achieved an impressively rapid advance. Meanwhile, imports grew at a lower rate. In 1955 the increase over 1954 was only 3 per cent., and although the boom in production caused them to rise even faster than exports in 1956 (by 31 per cent.), in that year they were only a third greater than in 1953. Yet although the recent recovery in foreign trade must be acknowledged as remarkable, comparisons both with pre-war days and with the growth in the economy as a whole are unfavourable. Industrial production in 1956 was more than double that of the middle 1930's, whereas the volume of foreign trade was still less than in the pre-war period. The quantum

[1] Cf. *Oriental Economist*, May 1954, p. 245.

index for exports (in 1956) was 73 and for imports 103.[1] The contrast with the 1930's is very striking. At that time Japanese exports were growing fast in spite of the depressed conditions in international trade as a whole. During the late 1940's and early 1950's her recovery in exports was hesitant although international trade was exceptionally buoyant. Even the recent recovery has left her with a much smaller proportion of world trade than before the war. In 1938 her exports accounted for 5·4 per cent. of world exports, in 1954 for 2·1 per cent., and in 1956 for 2·7 per cent.[2]

Both the delay in the recovery of trade and also its still comparatively modest amount call for an explanation. Up to 1950 the revival was retarded by the necessity for devoting resources to internal reconstruction. Then in the early 1950's the renewal of inflation was accompanied by a boom in domestic trade which checked exporting activities. The heavy procurement expenditure at this time was one of the chief factors in generating the boom, and the trade situation is liable to be seriously misunderstood if the effect of that expenditure is incorrectly evaluated. Further examination is therefore necessary. The ratio of foreign income earned by procurement to total foreign earnings for the period 1951–5 ranged from 21 per cent. (1955) to 38 per cent. (1952), and over that period as a whole income from procurement was sufficient to pay for about 30 per cent. of the commodity imports.[3] Before the export recovery of 1955, this degree of dependence gave rise to misgivings among the Japanese. They regarded procurement as a precarious source of income, while the financial dependence upon the United States which it involved meant that the pursuance of an autonomous foreign policy was out of the question. Yet, to abstract from politics and to consider only the economic aspects of the problem, the sale of goods and services to Americans in Japan is equivalent to a dollar export. Moreover, the commodity export trade and procurement expenditure are not independent variables. Despite the existence of under-employment, there are many scarce factors in the Japanese economy—capital equipment, man-

[1] *Economic Survey of Japan, 1955–6*, pp. 17, 25 ff. (1934–6 = 100).
[2] United Nations, *Monthly Bulletin of Statistics*; cf. also Okita, *Rehabilitation of Japan's Economy*, p. 6.
[3] Data from Economic Planning Board and Ministry of Finance.

agerial capacity, and certain kinds of technical skill. Consequently, exports have certainly been smaller, and imports larger, than they would have been if the Americans had spent less in Japan. In other words, in the absence of that expenditure which had its part in maintaining internal prices, Japanese goods during the years in which balance-of-payments difficulties were being encountered would have been far more competitive in world markets. The decrease in the expenditure after 1953 certainly enforced structural and price adjustments on the economy, and even now a sudden termination of it would produce a serious strain. Yet it may reasonably be held that in the political conditions of the 1950's income earned in this way is in fact no more precarious than that gained from the commodity export trade. In support of this argument one may point to the fact that procurement has fallen much less steeply during recent years than had been expected. Finally, it appears that the resilience of the post-war economy was underestimated and the difficulties of adjustment to a reduction in procurement expenditure much exaggerated. After 1953 Japan achieved an outstanding success in bringing her prices into line with world prices and in raising exports. The experience suggests, moreover, that the price elasticity of demand for Japanese exports is much greater than was supposed a few years ago.[1]

The above argument shows that the failure of Japan to rebuild an export trade on the pre-war scale is not so disquieting as the authorities have sometimes suggested. Yet if all allowance is made for the displacement of export by procurement, it remains true that the recovery in this sector of the economy has been only moderate. Even the most optimistic observer must admit to the presence of several new unfavourable factors. First, the dissolution of the great trading companies of the

[1] It is certainly significant that the fall of 4 per cent. in Japan's export prices between 1954 and 1955 was accompanied by a rise in the volume of her exports of 24 per cent. The expansion of world demand as a whole was, of course, partly responsible for the export boom; but the growth in Japan's trade was far greater than that of any other industrial country. In the United States exports rose by 10 per cent. and prices by 1 per cent., in the United Kingdom the increases were 8 per cent. and 2 per cent. respectively, and in Germany 15 per cent. and 2 per cent. Japan was the only country (except Switzerland) in which export prices went down, and it was her exports that made by far the greatest advance (International Monetary Fund, *Annual Report, 1956*, p. 15).

Zaibatsu struck a heavy blow at Japan's commercial efficiency, for those companies had been the most potent instruments of the export drive in the pre-war period. They are now being rebuilt, but as yet they have by no means regained their former effectiveness. A loss which is more damaging because more enduring is the shrinkage in the area in which Japanese traders formerly enjoyed special privileges. The break-up of Japan's empire and the loss of her special position in Manchuria and North China have had formidable consequences for her overseas trade. The restrictions imposed on dealings with Communist China have aggravated difficulties caused by the break-up of what was formerly a highly integrated economic unit centred upon Japan Proper. Throughout this great region (China and the former colonies), which, in 1934–6 took nearly two-fifths of Japan's exports and supplied more than a third of her imports, trade is now either restricted or occurs under far less favourable terms. In 1956 only 8 per cent. of the much diminished export trade and only 5 per cent. of the import trade was with those countries. In the early 1950's the proportions had been even lower.[1]

The disruption of trade with this region forced Japan to look for markets in places where her competitive advantages were fewer and for sources of raw-material and food supply which are necessarily more expensive. On the side of imports, rice, sugar, iron ore, coking coal, vegetable oils, and salt are among the commodities most affected by this diversion of trade. In the export trade, Japan, deprived of her former easy access to the markets of Eastern Asia, has become even more vulnerable than formerly to changes in commercial policy in the rest of the world. This was demonstrated in 1952 and 1953 when the countries of the British Commonwealth introduced import restrictions in order to safeguard sterling.

Other adverse influences on Japanese trade have come from technical change and industrial developments overseas. As already shown, the substitution of synthetic yarns for raw silk brought about the loss of one of her main exports, an export based, moreover, on indigenous materials. The rise of the cotton industry in former customer-countries, notably India, has likewise reduced export opportunities. Thus, political, terri-

[1] *Fuji Bank Bulletin*, September 1956, p. 15, December 1956, pp. 7–16.

torial, technical, and economic changes have all thrown obstacles in the path of Japan's trade recovery.

She has responded to the pressure of adversity in two ways, first by attempts to find new markets and sources of supply to replace those she has lost, and secondly by a resort to forms of production which reduce her dependence upon foreign trade. In both she has enjoyed some success, and for this the flourishing condition of international trade as a whole has been partly responsible. The strong demand for capital goods in the post-war world and the persistence of full employment in other industrial countries have enabled Japan to break into new markets, while technical innovations which she has borrowed from the West and adapted to her own needs have made it possible for her to dispense with certain raw-material imports without retarding her industrial progress.

As with other industrial countries the exports that have increased have consisted of goods in the metal and machinery groups which before the war were of minor importance. In 1934–6 only 15 per cent. of the total exports were in this class, and most of them went to privileged markets, especially to Manchuria. Between 1953 and 1956 the proportion has ranged between 28 and 33 per cent. and these goods have found markets in Europe and America as well as in South and South East Asia.[1] The causes of the advance are various. The inability of Western producers to supply all the steel for which the investment boom has furnished an urgent demand has brought orders for Japanese steel, in spite of its relatively high prices. The shortage of ships, especially of tankers, and the congestion in European yards have created a large demand from Western shipowners. Industrial developments in Asia have called for machinery, including textile machinery, locomotives, and rolling stock. New export trades in light engineering goods and instruments have been built up, such as sewing machines, cameras, and binoculars. Some of these goods have found important markets in North America. Finished manufactures with a high labour content are, of course, the type of product for which one would expect Japan to possess relative advantages as a supplier, but the exports of steel and heavy engineering

---

[1] S. Fujii, *Japan's Trade and Her Level of Living* (Tokyo, Science Council of Japan, 1955), p. 57; *Oriental Economist*, July 1956, pp. 328–30.

products are more surprising innovations. Whether Japan can hope to maintain a large trade in such goods when Western producing capacity has caught up with demand is a question which will be considered later.

The increase in the importance of the above classes of goods has been accompanied by a decline in textiles. Indeed, since the size of the export trade is still less than before the war, it is this decline rather than the absolute advance of the metal and machinery group that is responsible for the change of emphasis in the different branches of the trade. In the middle 1930's textiles supplied 52 per cent. of total exports; between 1953 and 1956 the proportion ranged between 35 per cent. and 40 per cent. This still represents a high degree of specialization on textiles in comparison with other industrial countries,[1] and Japan's difficulties in the export trade are in some measure related to this specialization. World trade in textiles has not shared the advances made in other classes of manufactures, and any specialist in that field is badly placed in its attempts to enlarge its exports. It is unfortunate for Japan that the industrial group in which her costs compare most favourably with those of her competitors should be the one in which there is little hope for a sustained expansion of foreign sales. Within the group, moreover, the two branches on which Japan formerly concentrated have been those most adversely affected. In 1954–5 the quantity of raw silk exported was only one-seventh of the pre-war amount, while cotton piece-goods exports (in square yards) had declined by one-half. The substantial growth of exports of rayon and staple-fibre goods have so far been insufficient to compensate for these heavy losses in the major branches of textiles.[2] In plans put forward by the government in 1955 for the development of the economy up to 1960, it was indicated that these trends were expected to persist. Although the volume of textile exports in 1960 is forecast as 38 per cent. greater than in 1954, most of the increase is to be provided by rayon-filament, staple-fibre, and synthetic-fibre goods. The cotton trade is expected to be stationary. The

---

[1] In 1954 textiles represented 13 per cent. of the export trade of the United Kingdom, 6 per cent. of that of West Germany, 13 per cent. of that of France, and 4 per cent. of that of the United States.

[2] Toyo Spinning Co., Institute for Economic Research, *Statistical Digest, passim.*

Japanese textile industries are no longer predominantly exporting industries as they were before the war when more than half the output was sent abroad. In the middle 1950's only two-fifths of the total production was exported, and according to the government's plan this proportion will decline further during the next four years.[1] In this respect Japan has been following a similar course to that of Great Britain.

The changes in the export trade have affected the composition of the import trade. The importance of textile materials has fallen while that of fuel (coal and oil) and ores has increased. The rise in the population has led to an increase in the relative importance of foodstuffs (especially wheat), which in 1955 represented over a quarter of the total imports.

The transformation in the structure of the foreign trade has been attended by changes in the importance of the different regions as customers and suppliers. The outstanding differences between the pre-war and the present position are the fall in the importance of Asia and the rise in the importance of the United States. The decline of Asia can be accounted for entirely by the loss of trade with North East Asia for, as we shall see, the importance of South and South East Asia has increased. The United States' position as a customer has much improved. In spite of the decline in the raw silk trade, the share in the total export taken by that country between 1954 and 1956 ranged between 17 and 22 per cent. The goods included not only traditional exports, such as silk, fish, tea, pottery, and textiles, but also a wide variety of finished manufactures from ships to sewing machines. As a supplier the United States has taken the lead over all others. Whereas in the middle 1930's it provided only 25 per cent. of Japan's imports, between 1954 and 1956 its share ranged between 31 and 35 per cent. The change occurred partly because America was for several years the only alternative source of supply of the raw materials and foodstuffs which Japan had formerly obtained from her near neighbours, and partly because of the special economic relations established between Japan and the United States during the last decade. It seems probable, however, that as Japan finds cheaper sources of supply the American contribution to her imports will fall, a tendency that can already be observed.

[1] *Survey of Japanese Finance and Industry*, March–April 1956, pp. 5–11.

South East Asia,[1] the other main area in which Japan's trading enterprise has been displayed, has also become more important. In pre-war days that area took about 19 per cent. of the exports; in the years 1952–6 the proportion ranged between 26 and 36 per cent. The exports consisted chiefly of textiles, machinery, and metal products. As a source of imports the area's importance has also grown. But the economic and political instability of the area has been a source of anxiety to the Japanese, and exports to the region as a whole and to its constituent countries have fluctuated violently from year to year.

The geographical redistribution of trade since the war has been influenced by exchange controls both in Japan and in the outside world. By reason of the procurement expenditure Japan has so far been well supplied with dollars. Dealings with the sterling area, however, have been covered by agreements between the United Kingdom and Japan regarding reciprocal trade and payments. At times Japan has been short of sterling, being unwilling to pay for sterling goods in dollars, although at other times she has accumulated sterling in excess of her needs, being precluded by the agreements from exchanging the balance into dollars. In the 'open account' countries Japan's trade has been governed by bilateral bargains and to some of these countries, notably Indonesia, she has in effect sold exports on long credits which recently have become frozen. This division of trade into distinct and separate currency areas has been a contributory cause of the violent fluctuations in dealings with certain markets, and only a complete return to multilateral trade can remove this source of instability.

Japan's capacity for adapting herself to changes in the outside world has not been demonstrated solely by the redistribution of her markets and sources of supply nor by the altered composition of her foreign trade. She has also become more self-sufficient. No doubt this has been at some cost to herself. Nevertheless, the rise in industrial production and the recovery of the standard of life to pre-war levels for her much enlarged population have been compatible with a reduced dependence upon imports. How this has been achieved requires examination.

[1] The Indian subcontinent, Ceylon, Burma, Malaya, Indonesia, British Borneo, Hong Kong, the Philippines, Thailand, and Indo-China.

It may surprise those who have accepted uncritically the proposition that Japan is exceptionally dependent upon international trade to learn that the ratio between her trade and her national income is now one of the lowest in the world. Whereas before the war (1934–6) the ratio was 23 per cent. for both imports and exports, by 1955 it had fallen to 11 per cent. for exports and 14 per cent. for imports.[1] Even if procurement sales are regarded as exports, the ratio is still relatively low. This condition had been brought about in part by the changes in the structure of production already described. The sector of industry in which the greatest expansion has occurred, namely the engineering industries, is one in which the ratio of imported raw-material costs to labour and capital costs is low. The other cause is the substitution of home-produced raw materials for imports in several of the leading branches of manufacture. Of this the changes in the textile industries provide an illuminating example. A steep reduction in the imports of raw materials required for this group of industries has been achieved through the rise in the importance of the rayon and synthetic-fibre trades and the absolute decline in cotton-goods production, and also through the substitution, in the manufacture of rayon pulp, of domestically-grown latifoliate trees for imported acerose trees. Similarly, in the manufacture of nitrate fertilizers, the former imports of soya-bean cake from Manchuria have been replaced by ammonium sulphate produced from domestic resources. In certain other branches of industry that have grown since the war, expansion has been possible without a proportionate increase in imports of raw materials. For example, in the manufacture of pig-iron, technical improvements have made it possible to use domestic supplies of iron sand and sulphuric-acid dross to a far greater extent than in pre-war days.[2] Finally, although Japan's sources of food imports have changed, her dependence upon overseas supplies as a whole has not increased in proportion to the rise in population because of a marked expansion in domestic food production.

Official plans have been framed with the object of securing additional economies in imports, but it may be doubted whether the post-war tendency can be carried much further. Food and

---

[1] *Economic Survey of Japan, 1955–6*, pp. 37–38.
[2] Ibid.; Okita, *Rehabilitation of Japan's Economy*, pp. 8–9.

raw-material imports on a large scale must remain indispensable for any considerable economic growth. Almost all the sugar, three-fifths of the vegetable oils and fats, two-thirds of the salt, and a fifth of the grain required must still be bought abroad. Imports are likely to be needed to supply most of the iron ore and high-grade coking coal which will be required as the steel industry expands. The same is true for nearly all the petroleum, wool, and cotton supplies. If industrial production and the standard of life continue to rise, more imports will be wanted in spite of economies in their use. If they cannot be obtained on good terms, Japan's prosperity will be threatened. Her export prospects must, therefore, be briefly considered.

It seems improbable that textile markets will offer more ample opportunities than in the recent past. So Japan must look to those goods in which international trade since the war has been buoyant, namely, metal and engineering goods. But here she will enter a field where she will encounter keen competition from the technically-advanced Western countries. The Japanese themselves are well aware that their recent success in the export of steel products and ships is attributable to the world-wide scarcity of these goods during an investment boom which cannot persist for ever. Japan's costs in metal manufacture and shipbuilding during 1955 and 1956 compared more favourably with those of foreign countries than they did a few years earlier. Nevertheless, for most classes of machinery they are still relatively high, especially for goods where Japan's technical inferiority to Western countries constitutes a serious handicap. Some markets have been obtained only by offering the goods at far lower prices than those charged at home. Thus it is not obvious that Japan is yet well placed for future competition in the engineering trades as a whole. The authors of a recent *Economic Survey* are inclined to the view that she is a marginal supplier of these products.[1] If this is so, then as productive capacity overtakes demand in the world's capital-goods industries, or if a slump occurs, she may be the first to suffer. Yet this judgement may be too pessimistic. Japan's technological advance has been rapid in recent years, and the remarkable improvement in the shipbuilding industry since

[1] *Economic Survey of Japan, 1955–6*, p. 21.

1953 suggests the need for caution in drawing conclusions. It may well be, for instance, that Japan will become increasingly important in furnishing Asian countries with certain types of plant needed for their industrial development, especially as she can offer the services of competent technicians at a much lower cost than Western countries.

It is not obvious that Japan possesses outstanding competitive advantages in the mass-producing industries, where efficiency depends upon capital-intensive production and highly advanced techniques, but in the manufacture of some kinds of finished metal goods she may find compensation for her lack of capital and her technical deficiencies in the adroit organization of her abundant supplies of assiduous and skilful workers. Her success in the export of such products as sewing machines, cameras, binoculars, and bicycles is an indication of where her chief relative advantages are to be found. There should also be scope in the export of miscellaneous wares, such as toys, pencils, and pottery, which are produced to a considerable extent by small and medium-sized firms. The rise in the export of clothing, especially hosiery, during the last few years points to another field that may become increasingly important. Much will depend, however, upon the condition of world trade as a whole. As we have seen, Japan has been one of the chief beneficiaries of its continued buoyancy. She would be vulnerable to any deterioration, especially as it might be accompanied by restricted measures imposed by foreign governments against her goods.

It might be expected that in most trades Japan's superiorities could most obviously be displayed in dealings with Asia, and she would certainly gain immensely from any acceleration in the rate of economic development in that continent. Yet she seems to have found more ample opportunities in the West (especially North America) during the post-war period than in those countries which are generally regarded as her natural markets. This result has come about, of course, for special reasons which may not persist. Her failure to re-establish satisfactory trading relations with her near neighbours is the cause on which the Japanese themselves are inclined to lay the greatest stress, and the delay in the recovery in the export trade and its future uncertainties have persuaded them to direct their attention increasingly to the future commercial prospects in those regions. They have had good cause. In 1955 Japan obtained only 3·2 per cent. of her imports from Communist China and sent there only 1·4 per cent. of her exports.[1] In the earlier post-war years the proportions were even smaller. Some critics of Japan's America-inspired foreign policy have held that the chief obstacle to trade expansion consists of the embargo placed since the Korean War on exports of many classes of goods to that country.

Many foreign observers have accepted the validity of this argument. No one can deny that Japan's economy has been seriously damaged by the loss of China as a market and source of supply, but it is easy to exaggerate the significance of this change. Before the war, even when Japanese traders enjoyed special privileges, especially in Manchuria and the North, China took only 18 per cent. of the total exports and supplied 10–12 per cent. of the total imports. Admittedly, the economic importance of China to Japan was greater than these figures suggest. The growth of certain industries in Japan was bound up with complementary developments in China. Japanese weaving sheds used cheap yarn produced in Japanese-controlled spinning mills in Shanghai. The Japanese steel industry drew coking coal, ores, and various semi-products from North China and Manchuria. Exports of Korean rice to Japan depended upon exports of Manchurian millet to Korea. Commercial dealings with China were obviously of very substantial value if not of such overwhelming importance as is sometimes suggested. Yet the part that China then played in Japan's economic life largely depended upon Japan's political domination of North East Asia. The post-war fragmentation of that area has destroyed the former system of economic relationships. Neither China nor Korea now looks for economic leadership to the Japanese. China is pursuing her own policy of development and turns to the Russians rather than to the Japanese or Westerners for expertise and capital. So it is most unlikely that the pre-war volume of trade could be restored merely by lifting the embargo. It is improbable that Chinese metal semi-products would then be abundantly available to the Japanese. It is even

---

[1] These figures may not be very accurate because of the trade that passes through Hong Kong; but the error is not sufficiently great to disturb the argument.

doubtful whether China would be able to supply large quantities of raw materials, such as iron ore, coal, raw cotton, and soya beans, at competitive prices, for unless she is able greatly to enlarge the output of these goods, her own manufacturing industries will absorb most of the supply. It would, of course, be rash to argue that in the long run Japan and China are unlikely to build up a large reciprocal trade. But the immediate prospects, even in the absence of the embargo, are of only moderate commercial expansion in that market.

In conclusion we must examine the position of the mercantile marine. During the 1930's the growth in Japan's shipping industry was as rapid as that of her foreign trade, and at the beginning of the Pacific War the mercantile fleet had a gross tonnage of over 6 millions. By the end of the war this great asset had been almost destroyed. In 1945 the tonnage left afloat was only 1,344,000, and most of it consisted either of obsolete ships or of ships built to an inferior wartime standard. Hardly any of them were capable of operating efficiently in the ocean-carrying trade. In the years that followed, recovery was impeded not only by the disorganization of the shipbuilding industry, but also by restrictions placed by SCAP on the operations both of the shipowners and of the shipbuilders. These restrictions were gradually relaxed, but it was not until 1950 that Japan was completely free to plan the reconstruction of her mercantile marine. At that time she still possessed only 1,700,000 gross tons and very few ocean-going ships.[1] Freedom from restrictions coincided with the recovery of industrial capacity. So, from then onwards, the shipping industry, assisted by low-interest loans from the government and the official banks, rapidly expanded. A considerable part of the new tonnage consisted of ocean-going vessels. By the end of 1955 the size of the fleet reached 3·5 million tons. A high proportion of these ships were new; in 1954 more than two-fifths of the tonnage was under five years old. The recovery still left the Japanese mercantile marine about 12 per cent. smaller than in the middle

[1] H. Yamamoto, 'The Recovery Method of the Japanese Shipping Industry in the Post-War World', in *Kobe Economic and Business Review*, pp. 89–97; Oriental Economist, *Japan Economic Year Book, 1954*, p. 89; Ministry of International Trade and Industry, *Foreign Trade of Japan, 1950*, pp. 31–34.

1930's and about two-thirds the maximum size which was attained in 1941.

In the middle 1950's foreign ships still carried a much higher proportion of Japan's imports and exports than before the war. Although by then Japan had restored most of her former liner services and was again carrying goods between foreign ports, she still had a net debit in her shipping account with the outside world. Whereas in 1936 she had earned $68 million (net) from shipping, in 1954 her net debit came to about $50 million and in 1955, when freight rates were higher, to $63 million.[1] Japan's mercantile marine has been deficient during a period when a given volume of her imports or exports made a higher demand on shipping services. This was because the reduction in the proportion of her trade with nearby countries lengthened the average voyage.

[1] Data from Ministry of Finance. In the fiscal year 1956–7 the net debit rose to $117 million.

CHAPTER XII

Achievements and Prospects

IN previous chapters we have described and explained the
processes by which Japan, in spite of her immense material
losses and the post-war collapse of the economy, at last over-
came her most pressing difficulties and once again emerged as
the leading industrial country in Asia. By 1955–6 she had
restored financial stability, rebuilt in large part her industrial
and commercial organization, increased manufacturing production to more than twice that of the middle 1930's, and raised
income a head well above the pre-war level. Her accomplishment was all the more remarkable since her traditionally inti-
mate economic relations with North East Asia were shattered
by territorial changes and political upheaval and since her
former specialization on textile production and exports proved
to be ill suited to the demands of post-war markets. In these
circumstances the rehabilitation of the economy called for
qualities of resilience and adaptability which, in her exhaustion
and despair at the end of the war, she seemed unlikely to command. Foreign opinion about her capacity to find a successful
issue from her troubles, though it fluctuated widely during the
last decade, by the early 1950's had turned pessimistic, largely
because in the outside world attention was directed primarily
towards the persistent weakness in the export trade. The
Japanese themselves long shared this opinion. If they have now
regained much of their former self-confidence, the prosperity of
the years since 1954 has not yet persuaded their leaders to
ignore, or to make light of, the real obstacles to future progress
that lie ahead.

The resilience of the economy has been particularly displayed
in the extension of the range of industries and products. This
tendency towards diversification, which was prominent during
the 1930's, has become more strongly marked since 1945.
Trades that first achieved significance during the pre-war decade have greatly expanded, while several entirely new
branches of manufacture have appeared. The result is that in

N

the middle 1950's Japan's industrial structure bore a much closer resemblance to that of the leading Western countries than it did twenty years ago. Her industrial activities are now centred upon the metal, engineering, and chemical industries, and she has joined the company of the few great countries that are responsible for the bulk of the output of the products of those industries.

In this development and in the recovery of the economy as a whole, it has been claimed that Japan owes a heavy debt to fortune. No one would deny that the Korean War and the sustained special procurement demand gave an immense stimulus to industry, especially to the heavy trades, and that they presented Japan with exceptionally favourable opportunities for acquiring foreign exchange essential for reconstruction. Indeed, the American demand for Japan's goods and services that was called into being by the political situation in the Far East may be said to have offset the damaging effects of the loss of trade with North East Asia, itself the consequence of the same train of events. Then in the middle 1950's, a further stimulus was administered by the world investment boom, and as this was accompanied by a large demand for ships, especially tankers, it brought expansion to a sector of industry in which Japan's competitive position had hitherto been undistinguished. Finally, at the end of 1956, the Suez crisis for a short period conferred considerable advantages on Japan in her competition with Western producers in Asian markets.

It has been frequently asserted that this succession of fortuitous events obscured deep-seated weaknesses in Japan's economy which, many observers believe, has sustained permanent and irreparable damage. Japanese economists themselves have been the first to insist upon their country's position as a marginal supplier of many classes of goods and upon its consequent vulnerability to any down-turn in world trade. These views cannot pass unchallenged. In the early 1950's they appeared to be well-founded, but the rise in industrial efficiency since then suggests that they were far too pessimistic. Japan owes her recent success to good management as well as to good luck. She will doubtless show herself sensitive to changes in world demand and she has still a long way to go before she restores her former position as an international trader. But it would be rash for her Western rivals to assume that her competitive strength is to be found, as in past times, solely in textiles and miscellaneous consumption goods and that in the capital-goods industries she is to be written off as a marginal supplier.

Responsibility for reconstruction has, of course, been shared with the Americans. For over six years after the end of the war the Occupation authorities were in control of policy, and even since 1952 the United States government has exerted a powerful influence upon it. In certain respects, the effect of the intervention, at any rate in the early post-war period, may have been to retard recovery; but on balance there can be no doubt that the American association with Japan's affairs during the Occupation period conferred signal benefits upon her. Without the aid so abundantly provided between 1945 and 1951, Japan would almost certainly have sunk deeper into economic chaos. The same conclusion applies to the subsequent period when, although her trading enterprise was handicapped by limitations imposed by the United States on her dealings with China, she nevertheless enjoyed the advantage of a vast dollar expenditure at this critical stage of her reconstruction.

Of the reforms introduced by the Americans, and of their continuing influence on the economy, it is more difficult to make a just appraisal. SCAP may be accused of impercipience in its effort to impose American ideals on a society where they were little esteemed, or of obtuse benevolence in trying by administrative measures to remove blemishes in social arrangements which were the manifestations of deep-rooted economic disabilities. Yet whatever may have been the immediate effect of the reforms in thwarting recovery and invoking social tensions, the enduring consequences were by no means deleterious. The reforms which were out of tune with Japan's purposes could not, and did not, long survive the end of the Occupation. This does not mean that any of the social and economic institutions or relationships have been restored to precisely their old form. The American impress was nowhere completely obliterated, nor did the Japanese themselves wish that it should be. But we have shown how in several spheres of national life (notably in economic and financial organization) the reforms soon yielded to the policy of the 'reverse course'. On the other hand, not all of

N 2

them were equally fragile. Some were acceptable to the Japanese and could readily be assimilated, even though they might not have been undertaken on native initiative. The Land Reform provides the outstanding example. This, besides serving the social and political aims of the Americans, may also have made some contribution to agricultural efficiency.[1] Again, innovations in labour relations, though now in process of adaptation, have survived intact. Here the result was to bring into existence, by edict, a code of industrial relations and a trade union movement which might otherwise have taken many years to evolve.

The initiative came from without, but even during the Occupation success in formulating and administering the reforms depended closely on the co-operation of the Japanese authorities and individuals. Where this co-operation was accorded, the reforms endured. Where there was opposition, they were fugitive. As in earlier times the Japanese showed themselves ready to tread new paths once they were convinced that the route led towards national well-being, as they conceived it. They certainly did not offer a sullen resistance to the zeal of the reformers merely because the latter were foreigners in occupation of Japanese territory.

Throughout the modern era responsibility for development and innovation had been shared between the State and the *Zaibatsu*. During the war economic authority became more highly centralized in the government, and the eclipse of the *Zaibatsu* after 1945 and the circumstances of the Occupation confirmed this concentration. For a time private entrepreneurial initiative seemed to have lost direction and purpose. Since 1952, however, the broad pattern of pre-war leadership in industry and commerce has been redrawn. The State has continued to play an important part in directing economic development and in discharging this task it has been able to call on a highly competent bureaucracy. But some of the great economic empires of the past have been reorganized, though as yet they have hardly achieved their former eminence, and other centres of private initiative have arisen. In this way the efficiency as well as the form of economic direction has been in large measure restored.

[1] A view shared by several Japanese agricultural economists.

Identities with the past can also be discovered in financial policy and organization. Traditionally Japan's monetary policy has been expansionist with the result that for long periods she found herself on the verge of inflation, with her balance of payments nearly always precarious. But the situation was never allowed to get out of hand, at any rate up to the outbreak of the Second World War. Short periods of ruthless deflation punctuated the general expansionist tendency. The post-war period reproduced these experiences. We have described how the violent inflation of the late 1940's was brought to an abrupt end by the Dodge deflation. This measure was, of course, imposed by the Occupation. But the Japanese authorities themselves were responsible for the successful deflation of 1954 which rescued the country from a serious financial crisis. Like the Inouye deflation of the inter-war period, this policy prepared the way for a forward surge in production and trade which in 1957 was still in flood. If the Japanese economy has shown itself responsive to the conventional 'aids' of monetary policy at a time when elsewhere their effectiveness has much diminished, this may be attributed to exceptionally favourable circumstances. In 1954 the monetary authorities were especially well placed to reduce bank liquidity. Difficulties of ensuring centralized control, which have been prominent in Japan's previous financial experiences, have returned with the rehabilitation of the great commercial banks, and in the near future her capacity to maintain financial stability may be severely tested. These are problems which Japan shares with others.

Although since the war Japan has made a rapid advance towards industrialism, there are still large sectors of her economy that retain the characteristics of earlier times. To the Asian she appears as a modern state masquerading as undeveloped; to the Westerner, and to many Japanese themselves, it is the vestigial remains of a pre-industrial society that are most prominent. Peasant agriculture, though far more efficient than elsewhere in Asia and yielding higher financial returns than before the war, is still over-stocked with labour. The same is true of the great mass of very small units in manufacturing industry and the service trades where (though by no means universally) productivity, incomes, and conditions of work compare unfavourably with those of large modern establishments.

Such contrasts are present in every branch of the economy. In transport the railway and shipping services are very efficient by present-day standards, whereas the still primitive roads hamper the growth of an adequate system of motor transport. In the cities premises occupied by large industrial and commercial firms are indistinguishable from their counterparts abroad, but throughout the country the standards of housing accommodation are exceedingly low and may even have deteriorated since pre-war days.

It is commonly asserted that the small-scale sector is characterized by 'disguised unemployment' or 'under-employment'. In this context, however, these terms may be misleading, for they imply that the condition can best be relieved by an increase in effective demand brought about by an appropriate monetary policy. In fact, short-run measures of that kind can hardly provide a complete and satisfactory remedy, for the dichotomy in the Japanese economy is derived from an insufficiency and a biased distribution of capital in a society in which the labour supply is rapidly increasing. Throughout the modern era a high proportion of new fixed investment has been directed into a relatively narrow range of industries, notably certain industries turning out capital and intermediate goods where for technical reasons factor proportions are rigid. The result is that agriculture and most of the consumption-goods industries and service trades, where the factor proportions are elastic, have attracted comparatively little investment and have been left to absorb in low-productivity occupations a large share of the increasing labour supply.[1] Such a distribution of capital is probably justified in a period when rapid development depends on the establishment of basic industries, especially those concerned with power and transport. But it may well be that during the early 1950's an excessively high proportion of new investment was orientated by the government and its financial agencies towards a few large-scale trades. The productivity of Japanese industry as a whole might have been more favourably affected if the smaller establishments had been able to obtain improved equipment and to gain readier access to new techniques. However this may be—and there are signs that the

---

[1] Cf. K. Okawa, 'Economic Growth and Agriculture', in the *Annals of the Hitotsubashi Academy*, October 1956, pp. 56–60.

government has accepted the criticism—it is clear that these contrasts in organization and productivity are likely to persist, for it is improbable that the demand for labour from large-scale industry will increase fast enough to lessen considerably the pressure for employment on the rest of the economy,[1] while the small-scale sector will find great difficulty in obtaining a sufficient share of the capital to permit it substantially to improve its techniques. At bottom the conditions described are probably an inevitable feature of a rapidly developing economy where the labour supply is growing fast and capital is relatively scarce.

In conclusion, we come to the fundamental question of whether future progress can be regarded as reasonably well assured. Present prosperity may tempt one to return a too facile and optimistic answer, just as the difficulties of the early post-war period led to errors of pessimism. To a large extent the answer must depend upon whether contemporary Japanese possess the energy and enterprise of their fathers and whether their social, economic, and political institutions are as favourable as in the past to material development. Here we enter a highly speculative field of inquiry. It may perhaps be rewarding to consider briefly the conditions that made possible the emergence of Japan as a modern state in Meiji times and underlay her subsequent achievements. Broadly, these conditions may be summarized as, first, a political and social system that presented opportunities for the exercise of leadership to persons (private individuals or bureaucrats) whose interests lay in promoting economic change; secondly, an inheritance of organizing capacity and skill; and finally, institutional arrangements conducive to the rapid accumulation of capital. The society that satisfied these conditions was hierarchical, drawing its leaders mainly from a privileged class constantly invigorated by the entry of men of talent from outside its ranks. When, by a conjunction of political and social changes, the leaders were enlisted on the side of modernization and economic development, they found in the mass of the people, long trained in obedience to authority, a ready instrument to their hand. There

---

[1] Except perhaps in periods of boom, when recruitment by the large-scale industries is likely to be limited by the shortage of men with the specific skills required.

was a fine legacy of skill in textiles and metal manufactures, and certain family businesses had a long experience of large-scale organization. The capital accumulation required for development was a function of the unequal distribution of income characteristic of that type of society and of the propensity of the wealthy to apply their savings to industrial and commercial development. The taxation system which succeeded the old feudal arrangements was very regressive, pressing lightly on high personal and corporate incomes and harshly on the peasants. These conditions persisted with comparatively little modification up to the Second World War.

The war, the inflation, and the post-war reforms destroyed powerful sections of the oligarchy, chiefly the military cliques and the rural landlords. These formed, however, the most conservative or reactionary element in Japanese society, elements which in Japanese opinion were largely responsible for the catastrophe of 1945. The dismissal of the chief 'architects of ruin' still left power highly concentrated and, in spite of the growth of parliamentary institutions, the leadership of the official and business oligarchies has not yet been seriously disturbed. Labour organizations have arisen, but since their economic foundations are weak, it may be doubted whether they will be capable for many years of wresting power from the established groups of leaders. On the other hand, the mood of the people has changed. They now breathe the air of freedom and are less docile than in the past. Some of the old concentrations of wealth have disappeared and the new fiscal system bears heavily on the rich and the middle classes. So incomes are more evenly distributed and certain groups of workers, namely the permanent employees of the large firms, are far better off than formerly. Even the peasants who up to the war derived the least benefit from Japan's expansion have achieved a new economic status. If these improved conditions were long maintained, the terms on which industrial labour could be recruited would be profoundly affected.

Yet the extent of the change must not be exaggerated. Japan is still far from possessing a society of the Western type, and in the most recent period she has even retraced some of the steps taken in the hey-day of reform. The fiscal system still permits a high rate of private capital accumulation; the labour market remains highly competitive; and welfare and labour legislation covers effectively only a part of the industrial community. Japan is moving along the path that Western industrial societies have travelled, but she is still some distance from the goal they have reached. Thus at present it seems that Japan has rallied her forces and renewed the impulse of ambition. Her people have remained vigorous and hard-working though they are less pliable than in the past and more concerned with enjoying the amenities of life. Her leaders have regained much of their self-confidence and authority, and her economic organization is being restored to its former cohesion and efficiency. She is striving to close the technical gap between herself and the West that was widened during the war. She has modified the American reforms that accorded ill with her purposes and has assimilated others.

How far the deeper springs of national life have been affected is a question which a foreigner can hardly consider without presumption. It has long been recognized that the progress that began in the Meiji era cannot be explained solely in terms of economic calculation. As in all great movements in human affairs, in the material no less than in other aspects of national life, an element of grandeur was present, a touch of the idealism which, as Alfred Marshall said, 'can generally be detected at the root of any great outburst of practical energy'. In Japan it was patriotic fervour that supplied the impulse to achievement and at the same time made it possible for her to undergo massive material changes without the disruption of social unity. In the end this sentiment was polluted and drove the country to a disastrous indulgence in military aggression. Present-day Japanese have been deeply affected by this experience and have displayed new powers of self-criticism. But they have not yet found an equally potent source of inspiration, and their writers, teachers, and politicians lament the absence of purpose among their countrymen. It is not surprising that those who were included among the victims of an age of faith should view with scepticism the various ideologies that distract the world. Yet without a strong unifying purpose it may be difficult for an emotional people such as the Japanese to resist corrosive influences from without and to maintain social unity unimpaired. The war interposed a screen between the old ways and the new, between the conventions of the middle-aged and the aspirations of the young. In academic circles Marxist ideas have a considerable vogue and the Communist party, though small, is vigorous and assertive. The history of modern Japan suggests that the ready acceptance of intellectual and political fashions does not necessarily have much effect on conduct among a people who are inclined to esteem administrative efficiency more highly than political principles. Nevertheless, it would be rash to predict that Communism would not enlist widespread support in the face of any deterioration in economic conditions, or that the unreasoned tradition of conduct upon which social stability ultimately depends can be preserved in spite of disintegrating influences from without.

These problems must be mentioned, since they are relevant to Japan's future as a progressive country, but they cannot be pursued further in this book. They are symptomatic of the stage of development to which she has come. Having moved forward to take her place among modern industrial societies, she now shares their perplexities. It is yet another question to ask how far the transformation in her economic life now proceeding will permit the survival of the more graceful qualities of the old Japan—the fine manners, the etiquette that relieves the acerbities of personal relations in a materialistic society, the aesthetic traditions, the strong sense of reciprocal obligation among individuals that corresponds to the recognition of public duty in the West. Such questions are posed in all countries during periods of rapid economic progress. In Japan's case, one need not dismiss the possibilities of reconciliation.

Statistical Appendix

TABLE 1

Population, 1930–56 *

	(’000)
1930	63,900
1935	68,700
1940	71,500 †
1945 ‡	72,400 §
1950 ‡	83,200 ‖
1955	89,400 ‖

* The figures are for October in each of the Census years. They cover the population, civilian and military, of the four main islands and the small outlying islands.

† Excludes overseas military personnel estimated at 1 million.

‡ Of the increase of 10,800,000 between 1945 and 1950, the repatriation of Japanese from overseas accounted for over 5 million (repatriates 6,250,000 less 1,190,000 emigrants—chiefly Koreans and Chinese—from Japan).

§ Excludes overseas military personnel estimated at 3 millions.

‖ Excludes Allied military and civilian personnel and their dependants.

TABLE 2

Industrial distribution of occupied population, April 1956

	(’000)
Agriculture & forestry	17,000
Manufacturing	7,640
Mining	420
Fishing	540
Building & construction	1,810
Transport, communications, public utilities . .	2,130
Wholesale & retail trade, finance, &c. . . .	7,060
Government	1,100
Other service industries	4,690
Other industries	30
	42,420

Source: Statistics Bureau of Prime Minister's Office. The classification is according to the main occupations and the figures cover persons above 14 years of age. The numbers in agriculture are subject to wide seasonal fluctuations.

TABLE 3

Agricultural employment

('000)

February	No. of farm households	Est. no. of persons engaged in farming
1935	5,511	13,720
1940	5,518	13,363
1946	5,697	15,914
1947	5,909	16,622
1950	6,176	17,770
1953	6,142	17,130
1954	6,105	16,670
1955	6,043	17,150

Source: *Statistical Abstracts* of Ministry of Agriculture and Forestry, and *Economic Survey of Japan, 1955–6*, Annex Tables, p. 34.

TABLE 4

Indices of agricultural and fishery production

1933–5 = 100

Year	Agriculture general	Rice	Vegetables	Livestock & products	Fruit	Cocoons	Fisheries
1936	105	112	109	81	96	92	111
1937	111	111	113	107	107	95	105
1938	107	110	108	113	109	84	105
1945	60	65	89	24	63	25	83
1946	77	102	104	30	48	20	53
1947	75	98	96	22	62	16	84
1948	86	104	87	62	89	19	104
1949	93	104	124	87	92	18	86
1950	99	107	131	119	109	24	109
1951	99	100	136	133	93	28	132
1952	111	110	139	154	176	31	171
1953	97	96	123	162	139	28	171
1954	107	101	123	181	173	30	171
1955	130	131	148	222	175	34	186
1956*	122	115	150	244	202	32	179

* Provisional.

Source: *Statistical Abstracts* of Ministry of Agriculture and Forestry.

TABLE 5

Indices of industrial production

1934–6 = 100

Year	Public utilities	Industrial production			Manufacturing production	
		Total	Mining	Manu-facturing	Durable	Non-durable
1937	119	130	118	131	138	124
1938	130	142	126	144	170	119
1939	137	148	131	1·49	178	122
1940	140	149	143	149	187	114
1945	88	60	73	59	98	22
1946	109	31	52	29	37	22
1947	124	37	67	35	45	27
1948	138	55	80	53	75	35
1949	155	71	92	69	100	47
1950	168	84	97	82	110	67
1951	185	114	111	115	164	89
1952	201	126	114	128	172	105
1953	221	155	123	160	210	132
1954	243	167	117	174	213	150
1955	263	181	118	189	222	168
1956	295	219	130	231	303	191

Source: Economic Counsel (Planning) Board, *Japanese Economic Statistics*, Section I, *Industrial Production*. Composite indices weighted by value added in base period.

TABLE 6

Indices of production of certain manufactured goods

1934–6 = 100

Year	Food & tobacco	Tex-tiles	Metals	Ma-chinery	Chemi-cals	Print-ing	Wooden products	Cera-mics	Rubber & leather goods
1937	117	114	131	148	144	115	113	120	104
1945	37	12	55	147	29	26	54	30	25
1947	37	18	23	60	34	30	91	40	23
1950	84	41	97	126	103	45	120	98	114
1951	105	58	144	197	141	55	157	137	129
1952	115	66	154	205	169	78	158	138	132
1953	162	77	184	267	217	107	170	156	172
1954	192	82	192	257	267	110	177	175	171
1955	207	86	219	250	318	125	185	175	178
1956	218	100	266	397	368	135	210	214	215

Source: As for Table 5.

TABLE 7

Output of certain industrial products

Year	Coal (m. metric tons)	Electricity ('000 m. kwh.)	Steel ingots & castings (m. metric tons)	Cement (m. metric tons)	Ships ('000 gross tons)	Ammonium sulphate (m. metric tons)
1937	45	30	5·8	6·1	499	0·9
1945	23	22	2·1	1·2	646	0·2
1949	38	41	3·1	3·3	140	1·2
1950	38	45	4·8	4·5	348	1·5
1951	43	48	6·5	6·5	434	1·6
1952	43	52	7·0	7·1	608	1·9
1953	47	56	7·7	8·8	557	1·9
1954	43	60	7·7	10·7	414	2·1
1955	42	64	9·4	10·6	829	2·1
1956	47	73	11·1	13·0	1,736	2·3

Source: Ministry of International Trade and Industry, and Lloyd's Register of Shipping. The figures for ships are for launchings of steel vessels of 100 gross tons and over.

TABLE 8

Textile yarn and fibre production

(million lb.)

Year	Pure cotton yarn	Rayon filament	Spun rayon yarn	Synthetic fibre & yarn	Wool yarn	Raw silk
1935	1,424	224	4	—	133	96
1937	1,586	336	81	—	148	97
1945	43	6	7	—	14	13
1947	266	16	14	—	26	15
1950	518	103	87	1	72	24
1951	712	138	150	7	113	24
1952	748	142	207	8	151	34
1953	861	163	250	13	187	33
1954	932	185	323	21	169	34
1955	827	195	411	35	185	38
1956	1,033	227	515	63	232	41

Source: Toyo Spinning Co., Institute for Economic Research, *Statistical Digest of Japanese Textile Industry.*

TABLE 9

Textile fabrics production

(million sq. yds.)

Year	Cotton	Rayon filament	Spun rayon	Wool	Silk and spun silk
1935	4,112	731	14	323	341
1937	4,826	1,034	263	280	439
1945	55	6	24	6	50
1947	662	46	32	21	38
1950	1,519	397	211	75	97
1951	2,179	487	323	115	118
1952	2,238	497	462	151	194
1953	2,810	595	504	168	170
1954	3,184	660	651	154	183
1955	3,018	774	896	186	209
1956	3,480	921	1,112	220	213

Source: As for Table 8.

TABLE 10

Textile equipment

(a) Operable spindles

End of year	Cotton (millions)	Spun rayon ('000)	Worsted ('000)	Woollen (set)	Spun silk ('000)
1937	12·2	—	1,128	684	462
1945	2·7	176 (1946)	235	425	151
1950	4·4	659	488	956	227
1954	7·9	1,888	1,175	1,272	84
1956	9·0	2,903	1,487	1,339	90

(b) Cotton power looms

('000)

End of year	Owned by spinners	Owned by independent weavers
1937	108	255
1945	24	112
1950	54	178
1954	81	252
1956	77	297

Source: All-Japan Cotton Spinners' Association.

TABLE 11

Changes in structure of manufacturing industry

(a) *Distribution of employment among various industries*
(as percentage of total)

	1930	1936	1955
Textiles	51·1	37·9	21·8
Metal & metal products . .	5·2	9·7	11·7
Machinery & vehicles . . .	10·8	18·3	18·5
Chemicals	7·6	11·1	12·5
Food	8·7	6·7	12·5
Wood products	3·6	3·7	9·4
Ceramics	3·7	3·9	5·3
Printing & publishing . . .	3·4	2·4	4·3
Others	5·9	6·4	4·0
	100·0	100·0	100·0

(b) *Distribution of output by value added*
(as percentage of total)

	1930	1955
Textiles	36·5	17·5
Metals & metal products . .	8·5	17·0
Machinery & vehicles . . .	11·6	14·6
Chemicals	15·2	19·1
Food	16·0	17·9
Wood products	2·7	5·1
Ceramics	2·7	3·4
Printing & publishing . . .	3·2	3·3
Others	3·6	2·1
	100·0	100·0

Source: Pre-war figures from the Ministry of Commerce and Industry, *Factory Statistics*; post-war figures from Ministry of International Trade and Industry. The two series are not precisely comparable.

TABLE 12

Size distribution of establishments in manufacturing industry in 1954

Size of unit	Percentage of workers in each size-group	
	1939	*1954*
3 workers or under 4–29	} 46·2	11·8 } 43·9 32·1
30–99 100–199	} 19·2	17·6 } 25·1 7·5
200–299 Over 300	} 34·6	4·5 } 31·0 26·5
	100·0	100·0

Source: Bureau of Statistics, *Establishment Census of 1954*; and E. P. Reubens, 'Small-Scale Industry in Japan', *Quarterly Journal of Economics*, August 1947.

TABLE 13

Foreign Trade

(a) *Index of volume of trade*

(1934–6 = 100)

	Exports	Imports
1948	8	18
1949	16	28
1950	30	33
1951	31	48
1952	31	54
1953	35	74
1954	46	77
1955	61	81
1956	73	103

Source: Economic Planning Board.

TABLE 13—*continued.*

(*b*) *Value of foreign trade*

(*$ million*)

	Exports (*f.o.b.*)	Imports (*c.i.f.*)
Sept. 1945–Dec. 1946	103	306
1947	174	526
1948	258	684
1949	510	905
1950	820	974
1951	1,355	1,995
1952	1,273	2,028
1953	1,275	2,410
1954	1,629	2,399
1955	2,011	2,471
1956	2,501	3,230

Source: Ministry of Finance.

TABLE 14

The structure of the export trade

(*in percentages of total value*)

	1934–6	1954	1955	1956
Textiles & products	52·0	40·3	37·3	34·8
Raw silk	11·1	2·9	2·5	1·7
Cotton fabrics	16·5	15·5	11·4	10·7
Clothing	—	3·4	5·3	4·9
Metals & metal products	8·2	15·3	19·2	13·6
Machinery & vehicles	7·2	12·4	12·3	19·3
Textile machinery	0·4	2·8	1·3	1·5
Sewing machines	—	1·9	1·7	1·4
Ships	—	3·5	3·9	10·4
Food & drink	9·5	8·3	6·8	7·2
Chemicals	4·3	4·8	4·7	4·3
Ceramics	2·9	3·9	4·2	4·1
Toys	0·9	1·9	2·1	2·2
Other goods	15·0	13·1	13·4	14·5
	100·0	100·0	100·0	100·0

Source: Oriental Economist, February 1957, and Ministry of International Trade and Industry.

TABLE 15
The structure of the import trade
(*in percentages of total value*)

	1934–6	1954	1955	1956
Food	23·3	27·3	25·3	17·3
Textile materials . .	31·8	26·6	24·4	24·7
Petroleum & coal . .	4·9	11·1	11·7	12·8
Iron ore & steel scrap . .	3·2	4·6	5·9	10·2
Machinery. . . .	4·7	7·4	5·4	5·0
Others	32·1	23·0	28·3	30·0
	100·0	100·0	100·0	100·0

Source: Mitsubishi Economic Research Institute. *Monthly Circular*, January 1957; and Ministry of Finance, *General Survey of Japanese Economy*, *1953*, p. 79.

TABLE 16
(*a*) *Changes in export markets*
(*in percentages of total exports*)

	1934–6	1954	1955	1956
United States . . .	17	17	22	22
China (mainland) . .	18	1	1	2
Korea & Formosa . .	21	8	5	6
South East Asia . . .	19	30	28	26
Europe (including USSR) .	8	9	10	10
Other countries . . .	17	34	34	34
	100	100	100	100

(*b*) *Changes in sources of imports*
(*in percentages of total imports*)

	1934–6	1954	1955	1956
United States . . .	25	35	31	33
China (mainland) . .	12	2	3	3
Korea & Formosa . .	24	3	4	2
South East Asia . . .	16	19	22	19
Europe (including USSR) .	10	8	7	7
Other countries . . .	15	33	33	36
	100	100	100	100

Source: Mitsubishi Economic Research Institute, *Monthly Circular*, January 1957; *Fuji Bank Bulletin*, September 1956, and *Oriental Economist* (various issues).

TABLE 17
Textile exports

	1934–6 (ann. av.)	1954	1955	1956
Raw silk (million lb.) . .	68·9	10·2	11·6	10·0
Cotton yarn (million lb.) .	52·9	29·5	26·2	27·3
Silk fabrics (million sq. yds.) .	84·8	25·9	30·0	47·9
Cotton fabrics (million sq. yds.)	2,944·5	1,278·1	1,138·9	1,262·0
Wool fabrics (million sq. yds.)	39·5	12·1	17·8	22·3
Rayon filament fabrics (million sq. yds.) . . .	502·5	264·0	342·5	438·1
Spun-rayon fabrics (million sq. yds.)	16·8 *	302·6	521·4	695·2

* 1937.

Source: Toyo Spinning Co., Institute for Economic Research *Statistical Digest of Japanese Cotton Industry*, and Ministry of Finance.

TABLE 18
Transport
(a) *Mercantile marine*
('000 gross tons)

1935 September	.	.	.	.	.	3,759
1939 ,,	.	.	.	.	.	5,729
1941 December	.	.	.	.	.	6,094
1945 ,,	.	.	.	.	.	1,344
1950 March	.	.	.	.	.	1,659
1951 ,,	.	.	.	.	.	2,290
1952 ,,	.	.	.	.	.	2,744
1953 ,,	.	.	.	.	.	2,984
1954 ,,	.	.	.	.	.	3,164
1955 ,,	.	.	.	.	.	3,303
1956 ,,	.	.	.	.	.	3,778

Source: Statistical Year-Books of Japanese Empire (for pre-war), and *Economic Survey of Japan, 1955–6*, Annex Tables, p. 38. Figures cover registrations of steel ships of 100 gross tons and over in Japan proper. In August 1945 it is estimated that only 557,000 gross tons were operable (see Cohen, *Japan's Economy*, p. 267).

TABLE 18—*continued.*

(*b*) *Motor vehicles in use*

('*000*)

Fiscal year ending March	Commercial vehicles & buses	Passenger vehicles
1936	123	70
1946	122	29
1950	298	56
1953	559	163
1954	644	188
1955	728	208
1956	849	242

Source: Economic Survey of Japan, 1955–6, Annex Tables, p. 39. Passenger vehicles exclusive of scooters.

TABLE 19

Wholesale price index

(*1934–6* = *1*)

Average for year		Average for year	
1946	16	1952	349
1947	48	1953	352
1948	128	1954	349
1949	209	1955	343
1950	247	1956	358
1951	343		

Source: Bank of Japan.

TABLE 20

Index of real wages in manufacturing industry

(*1934–6* = *100*)

1947	30	1952	102
1948	49	1953	107
1949	66	1954	108
1950	85	1955	115
1951	92	1956	126

Source: Ministry of Labour. The Index includes allowances and covers productive workers in establishments with 30 or more employees.

o

TABLE 21

Monthly wages according to size of factory in 1954

Size of factory	Index
1,000 workers & over	100
500–999 workers	83
100–499 ,, . . .	70
30–49 ,, ...	62
10–29 ,, ...	55

Source: *Economic Survey of Japan, 1955–6*, p. 193. Allowances are included with regular wages.

TABLE 22

Index of household consumption

(1934–6 = 100)

Average for year	Tokyo	Rural areas
1947	55	—
1950	70	94
1951	69	103
1952	84	122
1953	96	128
1954	101	129
1955	109	133
1956	110	137

Source: Economic Planning Board.

TABLE 23

Foreign income from American aid and special procurement

($ *million*)

	Aid	Procurement	Value of imports
Sept. 1945–Dec. 1946	193	—	306
1947	404	—	526
1948	461	—	684
1949	535	—	905
1950	361	149	974
1951	164	592	1,995
1952	—	824	2,028
1953	—	809	2,410
1954	—	596	2,399
1955	—	557	2,471
1956	—	595	3,230

Source: Ministry of Finance and Economic Planning Board. 'Procurement' includes Allied military expenditure in dollars and pounds, yen purchases for Joint Defence Account, expenditure of Allied soldiers and civilians in Japan, and payments in respect of certain off-shore procurement contracts.

TABLE 24

Foreign Currency Holdings

($ *million*)

End of calendar year		End of calendar year	
1949	. . . 207	1953	. . . 977
1950	. . . 561	1954	. . . 1,054
1951	. . . 916	1955	. . . 1,316
1952	. . . 1,139	1956	. . . 1,484

Source: Mitsubishi Economic Research Institute, *Monthly Circular*, January 1957, and International Monetary Fund, *International Financial Statistics*, March 1957. Holdings include dollar, sterling and 'open account' balances. In October 1956 the dollar balances were $1,054 million, and the sterling balances were worth $86 million. The deterioration in the balance of payments in the first half of 1957 reduced the reserves to $879 million in June 1957.

TABLE 25

(a) National income and tax revenue
(million yen)

Fiscal years beginning 1 April	National income distributed	National tax revenue	Local tax revenue	Total tax revenue	Percentage of total tax revenue to national income
1934–6 (ann. av.)	14,372	1,226	629	1,855	12·9
1949	2,737,253	636,406	142,441	778,847	28·5
1954	6,103,395	934,083	366,778	1,300,861	21·3
1956 *	6,971,000	961,236	397,684	1,358,920	19·5

* Budget. The estimated percentage for the 1957 fiscal year was 19·0.

(b) Public expenditure
Expenditure on each item in National Budget as percentage of total expenditure of Central Government (General Account only)

	1934 actual	1955 Budget
Administration, justice, police, &c. . . .	7·6	10·5
Grants to local authorities . ._ . .	0·2	15·8
Defence	43·7	13·3
Land development and conservation . .	9·1	12·9
Industry, agriculture, fisheries, communications, & trade	3·9	6·6
Education	7·2	12·3
Social security	1·8	14·0
Pensions	7·9	8·5
National debt	16·7	4·4
Others	2·0	1·7
	100·0	100·0

Source: Economic Survey of Japan, 1955–56, Annex Tables, pp. 46–47 and 50.

Table 26

Expenditure on gross domestic product

(*'000 million yen*)

Year	Total	Consumption		Gross fixed capital formation		Increase in stocks	Exports less imports of goods & services
		Private	Government	Government	Private		
1938	27	14	7	1	5	1	—
1950	3,973	2,443	435	189	438	360	107
1951	5,543	3,128	521	424	673	584	212
1952	6,193	3,763	682	471	802	385	90
1953	7,141	4,415	768	623	932	404	−1
1954	7,387	4,690	846	561	871	258	162
1955	7,924	4,913	872	713	872	396	158

Source: United Nations, *Economic Survey of Asia and the Far East, 1955*, p. 210. Time reference: calendar year for 1938; fiscal year beginning 1 April for post-war period.

Select Bibliography [1]

(a) Books [2]

Ackerman, E. A. *Japan's Natural Resources and Their Relation to Japan's Economic Future.* Chicago University Press, 1953.

Allen, G. C. *A Short Economic History of Modern Japan, 1867–1937.* London, Allen & Unwin, 1951.

—— *Japanese Industry: its Recent Development and Present Condition.* New York, Institute of Pacific Relations, 1940.

—— and A. G. Donnithorne. *Western Enterprise in Far Eastern Economic Development: China and Japan.* London, Allen & Unwin, 1954.

Bisson, T. A. *Zaibatsu Dissolution in Japan.* Berkeley, University of California Press, 1954.

Cohen, J. B. *Japan's Economy in War and Reconstruction.* Minneapolis, University of Minnesota Press, 1949.

Columbia University, American Assembly Graduate School of Business. *The United States and the Far East.* New York, 1956.

Farley, M. S. *Aspects of Japan's Labour Problems.* New York, Day, 1950.

Haring, D. G., ed. *Japan's Prospect.* Cambridge, Mass., Harvard University Press, 1946.

Ishii, R. *Population Pressure and Economic Life in Japan.* London, 1937.

Johnston, B. F. *Japanese Food Management in World War II.* California, Stanford University Press, 1953.

Jones, F. C. *Manchuria Since 1931.* London, Royal Institute of International Affairs, 1949.

Lockwood, W. W. *The Economic Development of Japan.* Princeton University Press, 1954.

Mitsubishi Economic Research Institute. *Mitsui, Mitsubishi, Sumitomo.* Tokyo, 1955.

Schumpeter, E. B., ed. *The Industrialization of Japan and Manchukuo, 1930–40.* New York, Macmillan, 1941.

Seki, K. *The Cotton Industry of Japan.* Tokyo, Japan Society for the Promotion of Science, 1956.

---

[1] Works in the English language or those with some English text.

[2] The books in this list are of use chiefly in giving information about Japan's prewar economic position and development.

United States Dept. of Commerce. *Japanese Banking*, by H. M. Bratter. Washington, 1931.

Uyeda, T., and associates. *The Small Industries of Japan.* New York, Institute of Pacific Relations, 1938.

(b) Japanese Official or Semi-Official Publications

Bank of Japan. *Economic Statistics Monthly.* Tokyo.

—— *Economic Statistics of Japan.* Tokyo, annual.

—— *Outline of Financial System in Japan.* Tokyo, 1953.

—— Foreign Capital Research Society. *Japanese Industry.* Tokyo, 1953 and 1954.

—— *Japanese Industry Today.* Tokyo, 1952.

—— *Statistical Data and Principal Cases of Foreign Capital Investment in Japan.* Tokyo, 1953–6.

Economic Planning Board.[1] *Economic Survey of Japan.* Tokyo, annual.

—— *Japanese Economic Statistics.* Section I: Industrial Production; Section II: Foreign and Domestic Commerce; Section III: Population, Labour, Food Supply and Prices. Tokyo, bi-monthly.

Economic Stabilization Board. *Annual Report for Japan to Food and Agriculture Organization.* Tokyo, 1951.

Holding Company Liquidation Commission. *Final Report on Zaibatsu Dissolution.* Tokyo, July 1951.

—— *Laws, Rules and Regulations Concerning the Reconstruction and Democratization of the Japanese Economy.* Tokyo, 1949.

—— *Report on Restrictive Practices to the United Nations.* Tokyo, n.d.

Ministry of Agriculture and Forestry. *International Comparisons of Productivity in Agriculture.* Paper by K. Okawa. Tokyo, 1949.

—— *The Land Reform in Japan.* Paper by Y. Kondo. Tokyo, 1952.

—— National Research Institute of Agriculture. *Summary Report of Researches, 1946–8.* Tokyo, 1951.

—— *Summary Report of Researches, 1949.* Tokyo, 1952.

Ministry of Finance. *General Survey of the Japanese Economy.* Tokyo, 1953.

—— *Monthly Return of Foreign Trade of Japan.* Tokyo, 1950– .

—— *Quarterly Bulletin of Financial Statistics.* Tokyo.

Ministry of International Trade and Industry. *Foreign Trade of Japan.* Tokyo, annual.

—— *A Guide Book on Agricultural Machinery and Implements in Japan.* Tokyo, 1954.

[1] The Economic Planning Board was known as the Economic Counsel Board before 1955 and as the Economic Stabilization Board before 1953.

Ministry of Labour. *Japan Labour Code.* Tokyo, 1953.
—— *Japan Labour Year Book.* Tokyo, annual.
—— *Labour Conditions in the Japanese Textile Industry.* Tokyo, 1952.
—— *Yearbook of Labour Statistics and Research.* Tokyo, 1948– .
Prime Minister's Office. *Japan Statistical Yearbook.* Tokyo, annual (post-war).
—— *Statistical Year-Book of the Japanese Empire.* Tokyo, annual (pre-war).

(c) Other Publications

All-Japan Cotton Spinners Association. *Labour Situation of the Cotton Spinning Industry in Japan.* Osaka, 1955.
—— *Monthly Report of Japanese Cotton Spinning Industry.* Osaka.
Asia Kyokai. *The Smaller Industry in Japan.* Tokyo, 1957.
Ayusawa, I. F. 'The Labour Problem in Japan', *Japan Quarterly* (Tokyo), October–December 1954.
Bank of Tokyo. *Semi-Annual Reports.* Tokyo (since 1954).
Beika, M. 'The Structure of Industrial Districts in Japan', *Kobe Economic and Business Review.* Kobe, 1956.
Central Raw Silk Association of Japan. *Raw Silk Statistical Monthly.* Tokyo.
Danno, N., *see* Japan Institute of Pacific Relations.
Ehrlich, E. E., and F. M. Tamagna, 'Japan', in B. H. Beckhart, ed., *Banking Systems.* New York, 1954.
Fair Trade Institute. *Fair Trade.* Tokyo, September 1956.
Fuji Bank Bulletin. Tokyo, quarterly.
Fujii, S. *Japan's Trade and Her Level of Living.* Tokyo, Science Council of Japan, 1955. (Economic series no. 6.)
Hadley, E. M. 'Trust-Busting in Japan', *Harvard Business Review*, July 1948.
Horie, S. *Banking System and Bank Liquidity in Japan*; report to International Credit Conference, Rome, October 1951. Tokyo, 1952, mimeo.
Hitotsubashi Academy. *Annals.* Tokyo, half-yearly.
Industrial Bank of Japan. *Industrial and Financial Statistics.* Tokyo, half-yearly.
—— *List of Principal Japanese Companies.* Tokyo, various dates.
—— *Survey of Japanese Finance and Industry.* Tokyo, bi-monthly.
Institute of World Economy. *Recent Trend of Japan's Economy.* Tokyo, 1951.
Inouye, T. 'Note on the Zaibatsu Combines', *Kobe Economic and Business Review.* Kobe, 1956.
International Labour Office. *Problems of Wage Policy in Asian Countries.* Geneva, 1953.

Japan Federation of Employers' Associations. *Analysis of Personnel Practices in Principal Industries of Japan*. Tokyo, April 1953.

—— *On the Present Conditions of the Labour Movement in Japan*. Tokyo, 1953.

—— *Outline of the Post-War Trade Union Movement in Japan*. Tokyo, 1951.

Japan FAO Association. *Agriculture in Japan*. Tokyo, 1953.

Japan Institute of Pacific Relations. Data Papers Presented to 12th Conference of Institute of Pacific Relations, Kyoto, 1954:

Arisawa, H. *Level of Living in Japan*.

Danno, N. *Japanese Agriculture Since the Post-War Agrarian Reform*.

Fujibayashi, K. *A Bird's Eye View of the Labour Movement in Post-War Japan*.

Miyashita, T. *Observations on Trade Relations between Japan and China*.

Morika, Y. *Changes in Standard of Living*.

Okawa, K. *Level and Standard of Living in Post-War Japan*.

Okazaki, A. *The Present and Future of Japan's Population*.

Japan Iron and Steel Federation. *The Iron and Steel Industry of Japan*. Tokyo, 1952.

—— *The Iron and Steel Industry—Recent Developments and Labour Conditions*. Tokyo, 1952.

—— *Statistical Year Book*. Tokyo.

Japan Silk Association. *The Raw Silk Industry of Japan*. Tokyo, 1953.

Kawata, F. *Japan's Iron and Steel Industry, 1953–4*. Tokyo, Tokyo Foreign Service, 1954.

—— 'Japan's Trade with South And South East Asian Countries', in *Kobe Economic and Business Review*. Kobe, 1953.

Kishimoto, E. 'A Short History of the Labour Movement in Japan', in *Kyoto University Economic Review*, April 1951.

Kondo, Y., *see* Ministry of Agriculture under section (*b*) above.

Kyoto University Economic Review. Kyoto, quarterly.

Meade, J. E. 'Japan and the General Agreement on Tariffs and Trade', *The Three Banks Review* (London), June 1957.

Mitsubishi Economic Research Institute. *Survey of Economic Conditions in Japan*. Tokyo, monthly.

Miyata, K. 'The Position of Japan in the Asian Economy', *Kobe University International Review*. Kobe, 1953.

Nose, N. 'A Research into Wage Income in Post-War Japan', in *Kobe Economic and Business Review*. Kobe, 1953.

Okawa, K. 'Economic Growth and Agriculture', in *Annals of the Hitotsubashi Academy*, October 1956.

—— *see under* Japan Institute of Pacific Relations, *above*.

Okazaki, A., *see under* Japan Institute of Pacific Relations, *above*.

Okita, S. *The Rehabilitation of Japan's Economy and Asia*. Tokyo, Ministry of Foreign Affairs, 1956.

—— *Japan's Trade with Asia*. Reprinted from *Contemporary Japan*, vol. 22, nos. 10–12. Tokyo, 1954.

Oriental Economist. Tokyo, monthly.

Oriental Economist. *Japan Economic Year Book*. Tokyo.

Pacific Affairs. New York, quarterly.

Reubens, E. P. 'Small Scale Industry in Japan', *Quarterly Journal of Economics* (Cambridge, Mass.), August 1947.

Shibata, G. 'The Present Status of Japan's Shipping', in *Kobe Economic and Business Review*. Kobe, 1956.

Society for Economic Cooperation in Asia. *The Major Industry and Its Technique in Japan*. Tokyo, 1954.

—— *The Smaller Industry in Japan*. Tokyo, 1954.

Sumitomo Bank Review. Osaka, quarterly.

Tokyo Foreign Service. *Japan's Iron and Steel Industry*. Tokyo, annual.

Toyo Spinning Company, Institute for Economic Research. *Cotton Industry Wages in Japan*. Osaka, 1955.

—— *Statistical Digest of Japanese Textile Industry*. Osaka, 1956.

Tsuru, S. 'Business Cycles in Post-War Japan', in International Economic Association, *The Business Cycle in the Post-War World*, ed. by E. Lundberg. London, Macmillan, 1955.

Uchida, K. 'Japan's Foreign Trade After the War', in *Bulletin of University of Osaka Prefecture*, vol. 1. Osaka, 1957.

United Nations. *Monthly Bulletin of Statistics*. New York.

—— Economic Commission for Asia and the Far East. *Economic Survey of Asia and the Far East*. Bangkok, annual.

Yamamoto, H. 'Can the Anti-Monopoly Legislation Preserve Competition?', *Bulletin of University of Osaka Prefecture*, vol. 1. Osaka, 1957.

—— 'The Recovery Method of the Japanese Shipping Industry in the Post-War World', in *Kobe Economic and Business Review*. Kobe, 1954.

Yawata Iron and Steel Company. *Guide to Japan's Iron and Steel Industry*. Tokyo, 1953.

Index

Reprinted by lithography in Great Britain
by Jarrold and Sons Ltd,
Norwich

Date Due